UNDERSTANDING
THE SPIRITUAL EXERCISES

In memory of
Paul Kennedy, S.J.,
and
James Walsh, S.J.,
with appreciation and gratitude

Inigo Texts Series: 4

UNDERSTANDING
THE SPIRITUAL EXERCISES

Text and Commentary
A HANDBOOK FOR RETREAT
DIRECTORS

Michael Ivens, S.J.

First published in 1998
Reprinted 2008

Gracewing
2 Southern Avenue
Leominster
Herefordshire HR6 0QF

and

Inigo Enterprises
Links View
Traps Lane, New Malden
Surrey KT3 4RY

*'The expense is reckoned; the enterprise is begun.
It is of God...'*

ISBN 978 0 85244 484 9

Typesetting by
Action Publishing Technology Ltd, Gloucester, GL1 1SP

Printed in Great Britain by the
MPG Books Group, Bodmin and King's Lynn

CONTENTS

TEXT WITH COMMENTARY

GENERAL INTRODUCTION

As a qualification for giving the Spiritual Exercises, book-knowledge is secondary to such qualities as empathy, intuition, insight and overall personal wisdom. But this does not mean that knowledge of the Exercises should be played down. To guide another person through the Exercises of St Ignatius a good knowledge of the Exercises themselves is also required, even given a director well endowed with the more personal and fundamental gifts.

The knowledge required of a director starts of course with the book itself. The director must study the book thoroughly, says the *1599 Directory*, 'have it at his fingertips, especially the Annotations and Rules ... and weigh every matter – indeed almost every word – with care.'[1] Four centuries later, despite all the changes of situation and thinking that separate a modern giver of the Exercises from the age of Ignatius, these injunctions retain their validity. But knowledge of the Exercises is more than literal familiarity with a text. The text itself does not, and never did, provide all the guidance that might help a director to present or adapt the Exercises in particular situations. Even for the sixteenth century the text had its own unclarities, and to the problems arising from these must be added today the difficulties caused by unfamiliar language and real or apparent shifts of culture. Therefore the Exercises have to be interpreted within an unfolding, living tradition, and hence the importance of the *Directories* in the sixteenth century, and of the specialised and popular studies of today. A modern director is certainly not called to become an academic specialist in the Exercises, but he or she does require familiarity with the book, and knowledge drawn both from the early sources (either directly or indirectly) and also from the insights and discoveries of contemporary Ignatian literature.

The aim of the present commentary is to help the ordinary director to attain this kind of knowledge. Though space is given to the practical questions of use and presentation, the main concern is simply to help the ordinary director to elucidate the meaning of the text itself, and to sense something of its spiritual doctrine.

---

[1] Palmer, Martin E., *On Giving the Spiritual Exercises: The Early Jesuit Manuscript Directories and the Official Directory of 1599*, The Institute of Jesuit Sources, St Louis (1996), p. 301.

Source material used in the commentary

Much of the material used in the commentary comes from modern books and articles. While some of this material will lie beyond the easy reach of the ordinary director, I have tried to select mainly from works written in English, or available in English translation, and likely to be found in the library or book shop of an Ignatian retreat house or spirituality centre.[2] In view of the scope of material available, any selection must necessarily be limited and there is no implication in the present selection that any writer or work not mentioned is of less significance than those included.

Among the primary sources, two especially call for a word of introduction: the texts of the Exercises themselves and the sixteenth-century *Directories*. With regard to the Exercises, a director should be aware that tradition has not handed down a single text, but rather three official versions:[3] the so-called 'Autograph' and two Latin versions (the Versio Prima and the Vulgate). The Autograph is a Spanish text corrected in Ignatius' own hand; it is the text on which the present translation is based. Of the two Latin versions, the Versio Prima is a fairly literal translation, made probably by Ignatius himself, while the Vulgate is a rendering into classical Latin by a French Jesuit of the Autograph text. All three texts were used by Ignatius himself, and both the Vulgate and the Versio Prima were approved by Paul III in 1548. Each can therefore be described as 'authoritative', and hence clarifications and even significant shifts of emphasis or tone found in the Latin versions can be taken as indications of Ignatius' own thought. The main differences between the three texts are noted in the commentary.

The term *'Directories'* applies to a series of practical and interpretative documents beginning with five emanating from Ignatius himself, and culminating in the *1599* or *Official Directory* commissioned and approved by the Jesuit General, Claudio Aquaviva. The latter is still a useful general resource, but the users of it should know that it contains, and has perpetuated, positions which seriously distort Ignatius' own views, especially in regard to the contemplative dimension of the Exercises. The *1599 Directory* has been available in English for many years;[4] but only since 1996, with the

---

[2]Two such centres in the United Kingdom are: Loyola Hall, Warrington Rd., Prescot, Merseyside L35 6NZ; and St Beuno's, St Asaph, Denbighshire LL17 0AS.

[3]There are also in existence other versions of the Exercises, complete or partial, dating from Ignatius' lifetime, notably: (i) the text taken down by the Englishman John Helyar, who made the Exercises in Paris, possibly under Favre, in or about 1535; (ii) a text left by Favre with the Carthusians of Cologne (1543–4); and (iii) a text attributed to Jean Codure (1539–41). See MHSI, vol. 100, pp. 418–590.

[4]W. H. Longridge, *The Spiritual Exercises of St. Ignatius of Loyola, with commentary and Directory*, London (1919). Also, *Directory of the Spiritual Exercises of St. Ignatius, Authorized translation*, Manresa Press, London (1925).

publication of the entire series,[5] has the English reader enjoyed access to the preceding twenty-nine documents, and to their wealth of evidence relating to the early history of the Exercises. All citations from the Directories in this commentary are taken from this translation.

Another translation of primary texts cited widely in the commentary is the Penguin Classics collection:[6] included here are the Autobiography (or *Reminiscences*), the Spiritual Diary, select Letters and the Spiritual Exercises. The present translation of the Exercises follows closely that contained in this edition, the main departures from it having been made to meet the purposes of the commentary. In addition to the Letters contained in this volume, others are available in the Inigo Texts volume,[7] and in the translation by William J. Young.[8]

The originals of all early source materials referred to in the commentary are published in the MHSI, the volumes mainly used being vol. 100 (*Exercitia Spiritualia*), vol. 76 (*Directoria*), and the 12-volume series of Ignatian Letters (*Epistolae et Instructiones*). Other volumes of the Monumenta Historica will be mentioned as appropriate, e.g. when a text is not available in translation.

The convention adopted in the commentary is to provide introductory material for each of the different sections, and then to comment on particular words or phrases in the text that are highlighted in *italics*. References to paragraphs of the text are in square brackets. Occasionally words are added in *angled* brackets; they are missing in the text, but clarify the meaning.

As a sequel to the present Commentary I hope to publish in the fairly near future a Dictionary of the Exercises, in which the Exercises will be approached on the basis not of sections but of the more important words. These can be explored in the context of a Dictionary at greater length than the overall sequence and limits of a Commentary permit.

---

[5]See note 1 above.

[6]*Saint Ignatius of Loyola: Personal Writings*, edited by Joseph A. Munitiz and Philip Endean, Penguin Books, London (1996).

[7]*Inigo: Letters Personal and Spiritual* (Inigo Texts Series: 3), ed. Joseph A. Munitiz, Hurstpierpoint (1995).

[8]Details given in the Bibliography.

ACKNOWLEDGEMENTS

The book owes its existence to William Hewett, director of Inigo Enterprises, who asked me many years ago to revise a draft translation of the Exercises made by the late William Yeomans and to write a short commentary. Throughout the lengthy process by which the commentary evolved to its present scale and format, I have become increasingly indebted to Joseph Munitiz, Master of Campion Hall Oxford, for reading the manuscript in its successive stages, advising me on layout, putting me in the way of recent Spanish books, and in the end easing me of much of the labour of final editing. I am grateful to James Crampsey Provincial of the British Province of the Society of Jesus and his predecessor Michael Campbell-Johnston for their unremitting encouragement. I wish also to thank David Brigstocke, Michael O'Halloran and John Marbaix, Superiors of the St Beuno's Jesuit community, and William Broderick, Damian Jackson, and Tom McGuinness, Directors of the St Beuno's Centre for giving me – and protecting – the time and space I needed to complete the work, especially in the protracted period of convalescence during which most of it was done. I have been helped at every stage by friendship and forbearance from all members of the St Beuno's team. A particular word of gratitude is due to Sister Mary Reidy D.J. for advice and practical help, and for the medical supervision that enabled me to sustain the physical and emotional energy without which the book could not have been completed. I wish especially to thank Philip Endean, Tom Shufflebotham and Joseph Veale for finding time to read the text in manuscript or proof and for valuable comments and suggestions. And finally a word of thanks to Br James Harkess for his essential secretarial help in the early stages of this work.

BIBLIOGRAPHY

ABBREVIATIONS

CIS = Centrum Ignatianum Spiritualitis (Rome)
Epp. Ig. = *Epistolae S. Ignatii*, MHSI Series prima, vols. I–XII, Madrid 1903–11
Inigo: Letters = see Munitiz, Joseph A. (1987)
MHSI = Monumenta Historica Societatis Iesu
PASE = see *Program to Adapt the Spiritual Exercises* (see Bibliography)
Personal Writings = see Munitiz, Joseph A. and Philip Endean, eds (1996)
Reminiscences = see ditto

Arzubialde, Santiago, *Ejercicios Espirituales de S. Ignacio. Historia y Análysis*, Mensajero and Sal Terrae, Bilbao-Santander (1991).

Aschenbrenner, George, 'Becoming Whom we Contemplate', *The Way, Supplement* 52 (1985), pp. 30–42.

Aschenbrenner, George, 'Consciousness Examen', *Review for Religious* 31 (1972), pp. 14–21 (reprinted in Fleming, David, ed., *Notes*).

Balthasar, Hans Urs von, *Dare We Hope 'That All Men are Saved'*? Ignatius Press, San Francisco (1988).

Best of the Review, see Fleming, David, ed., *Notes*.

Boyle, Marjorie O'Rourke, 'Angels Black and White; Loyola's Spiritual Discernment in Historical Perspective', *Theological Studies*, 44/2 (1983), pp. 241–54.

Buckley, Michael, 'The Contemplation to Attain Love', *The Way, Supplement* 24 (1975), pp. 92–104.

Buckley, Michael, 'Ecclesial Mysticism in the *Spiritual Exercises* of Ignatius', *Theological Studies* 56 (1995), pp. 441–63.

Chapelle, Albert, et al., *Exercises Spirituels d'Ignace de Loyola*, Éditions de l'Institut d'Études Théologiques, Bruxelles (1990).

Coathalem, Hervé, *Ignatian Insights: A Guide to the Complete Spiritual Exercises*, Kuangchi Press, Taichung, Taiwan (1961).

Connolly, William, 'Story of the Pilgrim King and the Dynamics of Prayer', *Review for Religious* 32 (1973), pp. 268–72, also available in Fleming, David L., ed., *Notes*.

Corella, Jesús, *Sentir la Iglesia*, Mensajero and Sal Terrae, Bilbao-Santander (1995).

Coventry, John, 'Sixteenth and Twentieth-Century Theologies of Sin', *The Way, Supplement* 48 (1983), pp. 50-9.

Cowan, Marian, and John Carroll Futrell, *The Spiritual Exercises of St. Ignatius of Loyola, A Handbook for the Director*, Le Jacq, Ministry Training Service, New York (1981).

Cowan, Marian, 'Moving into the Third Week', in Cowan and Futrell, *Handbook*, pp. 121-5.

Cusson, Gilles, *Biblical Theology and the Spiritual Exercises*, Institute of Jesuit Sources, St Louis (1988).

Cusson, Gilles, *The Spiritual Exercises Made in Everyday Life*, Institute of Jesuit Sources, St Louis (1989).

Dalmases, Cándido de, *Ejercicios espirituales. Introducción, texto, notas y vocabulario*, Sal Terrae, Santander (1987).

Decloux, Simon, 'Mary in the Spiritual Exercises', in *Mary in Ignatian Spirituality*, CIS 19, Nos. 58-59 (1988), pp. 2-3, 58-9, 100-44.

Dister, John E., ed., *A New Introduction to the Spiritual Exercises of St Ignatius*, Michael Glazier, Collegeville (1993).

Dulles, Avery, 'Finding God's Will', *Woodstock Letters* 94-2 (Spring 1965), pp. 139-52.

Dulles, Avery, 'The Ignatian *sentire cum ecclesia* today', CIS 25-2, No. 76 (1994), pp. 19-35.

Egan, Harvey D., *Ignatius Loyola the Mystic*, Michael Glazier, Wilmington (1987).

Egan, Harvey D., *The Spiritual Exercises and the Ignatian Mystical Horizon*, Institute of Jesuit Sources, St Louis (1976).

Endean, Philip, 'The Ignatian Prayer of the Senses', *Heythrop Journal* 31 (1990), pp. 391-418.

Endean, Philip, 'Ignatius and Church Authority', *The Way, Supplement* 70 (1991), pp. 76-90.

English, John, *Spiritual Freedom*, 2nd ed., Loyola University Press, Chicago (1995).

Fennessy, Peter J., 'Praying the Passion: The Dynamics of Dying with Christ' in *A New Introduction to the Spiritual Exercises of St Ignatius* (ed. John E. Dister): an earlier version of Fennessy's paper is published in *The Way, Supplement* 34 (1978), pp. 45-60.

Fessard, Gaston *La dialectique des Exercices Spirituels de Saint Ignace de Loyola*, Aubier, Paris (1956).

Fleming, David L., *The Spiritual Exercises, a Literal Translation and Contemporary Reading*, Institute of Jesuit Sources, St Louis (1978).

Fleming, David L., ed., *Notes on the Spiritual Exercises of St Ignatius of Loyola [The Best of the Review, Review for Religious]*, Review for

Religious, St Louis (1981).

Futrell, John Carroll, *Making an Apostolic Community of Love*, Institute of Jesuit Sources, St Louis (1970).

Futrell, John Carroll, 'Ignatian Discernment', *Studies in the Spirituality of Jesuits* 2/2 (1970).

Ganss, George E., *The Spiritual Exercises of St Ignatius, A Translation and Commentary*, Institute of Jesuit Sources, St Louis (1992).

Ganss, George E., *The Constitutions of the Society of Jesus. Translated with an Introduction and Commentary*, Institute of Jesuit Sources, St Louis (1970).

Gouvernaire, Jean, *Quand Dieu entre à l'improviste*, Collection Christus, Desclée de Brouwer, Paris (1980).

Green, Thomas H., *Wheat among the Weeds*, Ave Maria Press, Notre Dame, Indiana (1984).

Grogan, Brian, 'To make the Exercises Better: The Additional Directions', *The Way, Supplement* 27 (1976), pp. 15–26.

Grogan, Brian, 'Giving the Exercise on Hell: Theological and Pastoral Considerations', *The Way, Supplement* 48 (1983), pp. 66–84.

Gueydan, Édouard, et al., *Exercises spirituels*, Collection Christus, Desclée de Brouwer, Paris (1985).

Guibert, Joseph de, *The Jesuits. Their Spiritual Doctrine and Practice*, Institute of Jesuit Sources, St Louis (1986).

Guillet, Jacques, et al., 'Discernement des esprits', *Dictionnaire de Spiritualité* (III, 1222–91), Beauchesne, Paris (1967) translated by Innocentia Richards as *Discernment of Spirits*, Liturgical Press, Collegeville (1970).

Hughes, Gerard J., 'Ignatian Discernment: A Philosophical Analysis', *Heythrop Journal* 31 (1990), pp. 419–38.

Iparraguirre, Ignacio, *A Key to the Study of the Spiritual Exercises*, The Little Flower Press, Calcutta (1955) (translation of *Líneas Directivas de los Ejercicios Ignacianos*, Bilbao (1949).

Kolvenbach, Peter-Hans, 'Do not hide the Hidden Life of Christ', CIS 24–3, No. 74 (1993), pp. 11–25.

Kolvenbach, Peter-Hans, 'The Easter Experience of our Lady', in *Our Lady in Ignatian Spirituality*, CIS 19, No. 58–9 (1988), pp. 145–63.

Kolvenbach, Peter-Hans, 'The Spiritual Exercises and Preferential Love for the Poor', *Review for Religious* 43 (1984), pp. 801–11.

Lefrank, Alex, and Maurice Giuliani, *Freedom for Service: Dynamics of the Ignatian Exercises as Currently Understood and Practised* (1989). Gujarat Sahitya Prakash, Anand; World Federation of Christian Life Communities, Rome.

Longridge, W. H., *The Spiritual Exercises of St. Ignatius of Loyola, with commentary and Directory*, London (1919, 2nd. edn 1922).

Lonsdale, David, *Eyes to See, Ears to Hear*, Darton, Longman and Todd, London (1990).

Lonsdale, David, *Dance to the Music of the Spirit*, Darton, Longman and Todd, London (1992).

Lonsdale, David, '"The Serpent's tail": Rules for Discernment', in Philip Sheldrake, ed., *The Way of Ignatius Loyola*, pp. 172–4.

Martini, Carlo-Maria, *Letting God Free Us. Meditations on the Ignatian Spiritual Exercises*, St Paul's Publications, Slough (1993).

Munitiz, Joseph A., *Inigo: Discernment Log-Book; The Spiritual Diary of Saint Ignatius Loyola* [Inigo Texts Series, 2], Inigo Enterprises, London (1987).

Munitiz, Joseph A., *Ignatius Loyola: Letters Personal and Spiritual* [Inigo Texts Series, 3], Inigo Enterprises, Hurstpierpoint (1995).

Munitiz, Joseph A., and Philip Endean, eds, *Saint Ignatius of Loyola: Personal Writings*, Penguin Books, London (1996).

Murphy, Laurence, 'Consolation', *The Way, Supplement* 27 (1976), pp. 46–7.

Nonell, Jaime, *Ejercicios, Estudio sobre el texto de los Ejercicios*, Manresa, San José (1916), (also available in French: *Analyse des Exercices de S. Ignace de Loyola* (Collection de la Bibliothèque des Exercices; Museum Lessianum, Section Ascétique et Mystique, 17), Bruges (1924)).

O'Leary, Brian, 'What the Directories Say', *The Way, Supplement* 58 (1987), pp. 13–19.

O'Malley, John, *The First Jesuits*, Harvard University Press, Cambridge, Mass. (1993).

O'Reilly, Terence, 'Erasmus, Ignatius Loyola and Orthodoxy', *Journal of Theological Studies* 30 (1979), pp. 115–27.

O'Reilly, Terence, 'The Spiritual Exercises and the Crisis of Mediaeval Piety', *The Way, Supplement* 70 (1991), pp. 101–13.

Örsy, Ladislas, 'On being one with the Church today', *Studies of the Spirituality of Jesuits* 7, 1 (1975), pp. 31–41.

Palmer, Martin E., *On Giving the Spiritual Exercises: The Early Jesuit Manuscript Directories and the Official Directory of 1599*, The Institute of Jesuit Sources, St Louis (1996).

Peters, William A. M., *The Spiritual Exercises of St Ignatius. Exposition and Interpretation*, Jersey City, PASE (1967) (also published by CIS, Rome (1980)).

Place Me With Your Son. The Spiritual Exercises in Everyday Life, The Maryland Province of the Society of Jesus, Baltimore (1985).

Pousset, Édouard, *Life in Faith and Freedom*, Institute of Jesuit Sources, St Louis (1980) (translation of *La vie dans la foi et la liberté*, Paris (1971)).

Program to Adapt the Spiritual Exercises (PASE), or *Program to Promote the Spiritual Exercises*, books and brochures, Jersey City, New Jersey.

Puhl, Louis, *The Preparatory Prayer: A Summary of the Fruit of the Exercises*, PASE (n.d.).

Rahner, Hugo, *Ignatius the Theologian*, Geoffrey Chapman, London (1968).

Rahner, Karl, 'A Spiritual Dialogue at Evening: on Sleep, Prayer and Other Subjects', *Theological Investigations*, vol. III, Helicon Press and Darton, Longman & Todd, Baltimore and London (1967), pp. 220–36.

Rahner, Karl, 'The logic of concrete individual knowledge in Ignatius Loyola', in *The Dynamic Element in the Church*, Herder and Herder, New York (1964), pp. 84–170.

Rickaby, Joseph, *The Spiritual Exercises of St Ignatius Loyola, Spanish and English with a continuous commentary*, Burns & Oates, London (1915).

Schmitt, Robert L., 'Presenting the Call of the King', *The Way, Supplement* 52 (1985).

Sheldrake, Philip, ed., *The Way of Ignatius Loyola*, S.P.C.K., London (1991).

Stanley, David, *I Encountered God*, Institute of Jesuit Sources, St Louis (1986).

St Louis, Donald, 'The Ignatian Examen', in Philip Sheldrake, ed., *The Way of Ignatius Loyola*, pp. 154–64.

Tetlow, Joseph A., 'The Fundamentum: Creation in the Principle and Foundation', *Studies in the Spirituality of Jesuits* 21/4 (1989).

Thomas, Joseph, *Le Christ de Dieu pour Ignace de Loyola*, Desclée de Brouwer, Paris (1981).

Toner, Jules J. A., *A Commentary on Saint Ignatius' Rules for the Discernment of Spirits*, Institute of Jesuit Sources, St Louis (1982).

Toner, Jules J. A., *Discerning God's Will*, Institute of Jesuit Sources, St Louis (1991).

Toner, Jules J. A., 'Discernment in the Spiritual Exercises', in E. Dister, ed., *A New Introduction*, pp. 63–72.

Townsend, David, 'The examen and the Exercises – a re-appraisal', *The Way, Supplement* 52 (1985), pp. 53–63.

Townsend, David, 'The examen re-examined', *Drawing from the Spiritual Exercises*, CIS 55 (1987).

Veale, Joseph, 'The First Week: Practical Questions', *The Way, Supplement* 48 (1983), pp. 15–27.

Veltri, John, *Orientations, vol. 1 A Collection of Helps for Prayer*, Loyola House, Guelph (1993 2nd edn).

Veltri, John, *Orientations, vol. 2 For those who Accompany Others on their Inward Journey*, Part A and Part B, Guelph Centre of Spirituality, Guelph (1998).

Walsh, James, 'Application of the Senses', *The Way, Supplement* 27 (1976), pp. 49–68.

Wolter, Hans, 'Elements of Crusade Spirituality', in Friedrich Wulf, ed., *St Ignatius of Loyola, his Personality and Spiritual Heritage*, Institute of Jesuit Sources, St Louis (1977), pp. 97–134.

Young, William J., *Letters of St Ignatius of Loyola*, Loyola University Press, Chicago (1959).

ANNOTATIONS

J H S

[1] [1] ANNOTATIONS (NOTES) TO PROVIDE SOME EXPLANATION OF THE
SPIRITUAL EXERCISES WHICH FOLLOW. THEY ARE INTENDED TO PROVIDE
ASSISTANCE BOTH TO THE PERSON GIVING THE EXERCISES AND TO THE
PERSON WHO IS TO RECEIVE THEM.

The Exercises begin with twenty wide-ranging explanatory notes (in effect,
they are the first of the 'directories'). Of these annotations, some are intended directly for the exercitant, while others deal with the general use of the
Exercises and with certain principles for giving them. It was Ignatius' own
practice to give the exercitant Annotations 1, 20, 5 and 4 at the beginning,
and 3, 11, 12 and 13 after the 'Foundation'.[1]

Annotation 1: The method and purpose of the Exercises and their characteristic dynamic

[2] *First* annotation. The term *'spiritual exercises'* denotes **every way
of examining one's conscience, of meditating, contemplating, of
praying vocally and mentally, and other spiritual activities as will
be explained later.** [3] **For just as strolling, walking and running are
exercises for the body, so 'spiritual exercises' is the name given to
every way of** *preparing and making ourselves ready* **to get rid of all
disordered affections** [4] **so that, once rid of them, one might seek
and find** *the divine will* **in regard to** *the disposition of one's life* **for
the salvation of the soul.**

First The purpose of the Exercises is explained as being a conversion of heart
resulting in a new quality or a new direction of life. Conversion is both a
'turning to' and a 'turning from'. 'Turning to' in the language of the

---

[1]*Directory dictated to Fr de Vitoria* also known as the *Dictated Directory*
(MHSI 76, pp. 100, 103 [trans., Palmer, pp. 21–2]). All English quotations are taken
from the translation of the *Directories* by Martin E. Palmer, see General
Introduction.

1

Exercises consists in seeking and finding the will of God, while the correlative 'turning from' is the process of getting free from the influence of 'disordered' drives and attachments that stifle love and impede integrity of intention.

spiritual exercises Once an ordinary term serving to designate any kind of personal religious practice. Ignatius' comparison with bodily exercises slightly highlights the elements of deliberation and purpose. It is important, however, that inappropriate gymnastic associations should not be read into the word.

prepare and make ourselves ready Liberation and redirection of heart is the work of the Spirit, in which our own action is a graced collaboration; it is not achieved simply by performing 'exercises'.

disordered affections 'Affection', a key term in the language of the Exercises, refers to the many variants of love and desire, together with their antitheses, hate and fear. The affections operate on many levels, from that of quite transient feelings to the level where they affect a person's ways of perceiving reality, making judgements, choosing and acting. The Exercises have to do with the *conversion* of affectivity, with letting the Spirit enter into our affectivity, change it and act through it. Only when this is clear, is it possible to understand Ignatius' insistence on freedom from 'disordered affections' – our affectivity in so far as it moves us in directions not 'ordered', or conducive, to the transcendent 'end' of the human person (cf. [23]).

In English, this sense of the noun 'affection' has been lost, and substitutes such as 'tendency', 'inclination', 'propensity', 'attachment' only partly convey it. The earlier sense survives, however, in 'well affected', 'disaffected', 'disaffection'.

the divine will In the course of the Exercises, a variety of expressions are employed to denote the relationship to God which is the object of human life and the norm of human choice. In addition to 'seeking and finding God's will', we find availability to be 'used by God' [5], 'honour' [16], 'glory' [16], 'service' [16], 'praise' [23], the 'pleasure' of God [151], and, of course, the triad 'praise, reverence and service' [23]. Expressing fundamentally the same idea, each of these expressions carries its own emphasis. In the Exercises, 'will of God' is used in connection with choices made in situations where objective criteria are not determinative.

the disposition of one's life Not necessarily the choice of a 'state in life'. Though the text envisages especially an exercitant needing to choose a state in life, 'life' has a wider sense in the Exercises than 'state'. What is stressed here is that one makes the Exercises in order to find a direction in one's life.

for the salvation of the soul In the Exercises, ultimate motivation always includes the good (or the salvation) of the soul, which Ignatius presumes the exercitant to desire, just as today an exercitant can be presumed to wish to 'choose life'. At the outset of the Exercises the whole programme (finding God's will in the disposition of one's life) is presented as meeting this fundamental personal concern. Later, personal salvation will normally be found in formulas which include it in the glory (or praise, or service) of God see [20] and [23] with comments).

Annotations 2 and 3: Prayer in the Exercises

Prayer in the Exercises is a particular form of the process traditionally described as reading, meditation, affective prayer, and contemplation (*lectio, meditatio, oratio, contemplatio*). The process is based on the 'solid foundation' of a given piece of material; and in order to assimilate this material it is usually necessary to start with some degree of discursive reasoning. But from this beginning, the process moves from the level of reason to that of the affections, from the 'given' to the personal, from the complex to the simple.

The danger, especially at the start of the Exercises, is that the process gets blocked at the first stages. The second and third annotations, one addressed to the director, the other to the exercitant, forewarn against this tendency and establish from the outset the contemplative character of the Exercises. The Exercises are ordered 'not so much to knowledge and speculation as to the affections and to the activity of the will'. Indeed, 'pure speculation is not prayer at all, but study'.[2]

[2] [1] Second annotation. *Someone who gives* to *another* a way and a plan for meditating or contemplating must provide a faithful account of the history to be meditated or contemplated, but in such a way as to run over the salient points with only brief or summary explanations. [2] For if the other begins contemplating with a true historical foundation, and then goes over this history and reflects on it personally, he or she may by themselves come upon things which throw further light on it or which more fully bring home its meaning.
[3] Whether this arises out of the person's own reasoning or from the enlightenment of divine grace, more gratification and spiritual fruit is

[2]*Breve Directorium* (MHSI 76, p. 446 [trans., Palmer, p. 207]).

to be found than if the giver of the Exercises had explained and developed the meaning of the history at length. [4] For *it is not much knowledge but the inner feeling and relish of things that fills and satisfies the soul.*

Someone who gives Directors must be aware that they themselves can impede the contemplative process by saying too much, leaving nothing for the exercitant to discover for him or her self. The director's job, says the *Official Directory*, is to 'point out a vein which the exercitant can then mine for himself', though a slightly fuller explanation might need to be given to those of less capacity.[3]

another In the original texts the 'other' is designated as 'the one who makes' or 'receives' the Exercises. Like 'director', 'exercitant' is a post-Ignatian term.

it is not much knowledge but the inner feeling and relish of things that fills and satisfies the soul This is a key phrase for understanding the spirituality of the Exercises. It should be read not as distinguishing between knowledge in an objective sense and the subjective experiences of feeling and relish, but between different levels of knowledge: the knowledge that exists solely or largely on the level of intellect, and the felt knowledge which involves the affections. The latter will be referred to in the Exercises as inner knowledge (see [63, 104, 333]). It can be called 'inner' in two senses: it belongs to the 'interior' (or heart) of the person knowing; and it penetrates beyond the immediately obvious to the 'inner' mystery of meaning of the person or truth known.

[3] [1] Third annotation. Throughout the following spiritual exercises we make use of the *understanding* in order to think things over, and of the *will* in order to rouse the affections. [2] We should therefore note that in the activity of *the will* when we speak *vocally or mentally* with God our Lord or with his saints, [3] greater *reverence* is required on our part than when we use the intellect to understand.

[3] *1599 Directory* (MHSI 76, p. 607 [trans., Palmer, p. 303]). The proviso about giving a fuller account to those with less capacity is explained by Polanco as follows: 'It is important that while allowing for differences in the intelligence, learning or experience of his exercitants, the director should, on the one hand, avoid explaining the points too fully – both so that the exercitant may have greater relish in what he himself discovers and so that more room may be left for lights and movements from above; on the other hand, he should avoid being overly brief and schematic, but should give enough to ensure that the exercitant understands the points correctly and is able to see his way into the meditation.' (MHSI 76, p. 287 [trans., Palmer, p. 124]).

understanding ... will For the exercitant the prayer of the Exercises is reduced to two simple functions; that of the understanding (the faculty of reasoning) and that of the will (the affective faculty).

the will Here, as frequently in the Spiritual Exercises and in classical spiritual literature in general, the word 'heart' can be substituted for will.

vocally or mentally 'vocally', with words (but from the heart); 'mentally', any kind of non-verbal prayer.

reverence 'showing God the honour and respect due to him' [38] This is primarily an attitude of heart, but has bodily implications [75, 76]. For Ignatius, loving reverence is the essential stance of the creature before God. Prayer is therefore particularly a moment of reverence, and the closer one comes to God in prayer the more will prayer be reverential. But more specifically, the directories read this annotation as a statement about the primacy of affective prayer.

Ignatius and the authors of the early *Directories* considered it important to stress this point, especially in connection with the First Week meditations, in which 'it often happens that at first the understanding alone is nourished by the novelty and interest of the topics, and there is only very slight interior relish in the will'.[4]

Annotation 4: Parts of the Exercises and duration

[4] [1] *Fourth annotation*. The following Exercises take four weeks. These correspond to the four parts into which the Exercises are divided: [2] first, the consideration and contemplation of sins; second, the life of Christ our Lord up to and including Palm Sunday; [3] third, the Passion of Christ our Lord; fourth, the Resurrection and Ascension, together with three ways of praying.

[4] This however does not mean that each week necessarily lasts seven or eight days. [5] In the first week, some people happen to be slower in finding what they are looking for (namely, contrition, sorrow, tears over their sins), [6] while some make more rapid progress than others or find themselves more agitated and tried by various spirits. [7] This being the case, it may be necessary sometimes to shorten the week and at other times to extend it. The same also holds of the other weeks, for in them, too, one must always be looking for the *fruits appropriate to the proposed material*. [8] Nevertheless, the Exercises should be completed in about thirty days.

[4]*Directory of Dávila* (MHSI 76, p. 504 [trans., Palmer, p. 247]).

Fourth annotation This annotation outlines the material covered in the Exercises, including, under the fourth week, the three ways of prayer. See commentary on [238–260].

But the Exercises are not just a programme; they are a personal faith-journey of 'seeking and finding'. As such, they involve an interplay between the prescribed and the personal, between the programme on the one hand, and on the other the unpredictable needs, rate of progress and varieties of experience of the individual. The individual must, therefore, be given the space he or she needs to seek and find the graces anticipated in the various stages of the journey. For this reason the weeks may be lengthened or shortened. It should be noted that the sole requirement made here is that the *pace* of the Exercises be accommodated to the pace of the retreatant. On fidelity to the content and order of the Exercises, see notes on [20] below.

fruits (lit 'the things') are here the various graces of the Exercises. As in the first week the exercitant seeks the graces here specified (contrition, etc.), so in subsequent weeks, he or she continues to seek the graces that correspond to the particular stage reached. On the search for specific graces as a feature of the Exercises, see notes below on [48, 106].

appropriate to the proposed material 'Proposed material' translates a Latin phrase in the Autograph *materia subjecta*. Taken literally, it refers to the given content of the Exercises. But this must be understood in relation to the Exercises as a personal process. In the course of this process, graces are asked for not only according to the given 'matter', but according to the exercitant's own reactions and to his or her developing personal needs. The point is made explicitly by the Versio Prima which translates: 'According to what both the persons and the proposed materials require' – thus adding to the Autograph text a subjective dimension. In this sense the expression 'according to the proposed matter' should be understood throughout the Exercises (cf. [48, 49, 74, 105, 204, 225, 226, 243]). On its use in [199] see below.

Annotation 5: The fundamental disposition

[5] [1] *Fifth annotation*. It is *highly profitable* for the exercitant to begin the Exercises in a *magnanimous spirit and with great liberality* towards their Creator and Lord, and to offer him all their powers of desire and all their liberty, [2] so that the Divine Majesty may avail himself of their person and of all they possess, according to his most holy will.

This *Fifth annotation* contains the quintessential spirit of the Exercises,[5] and anticipates in specific detail the language of the prayer of the Contemplation to Attain Love, in which one offers one's liberty and all one possesses to be disposed of according to God's will [234]. At this stage, even before the Principle and Foundation, Ignatius does not, however, expect of the exercitant the full dispositions of the Contemplation to Attain Love. At the end the exercitant may be graced with a transformed vision of reality and a quality of élan and spontaneity in his or her self-giving which are not presupposed at the outset. But a person can be possessed of generosity at various levels, and at the very beginning Ignatius asks the exercitant to bring to God all the resources of generosity they have – and in a candidate for the Exercises he presumes these to be already considerable. This incipient self-offering is to be made with trust in the generosity of God.[6]

highly profitable Even on a perfunctory reading of the Exercises, it will be striking how frequently the terms 'profit' and 'profitable' occur. Essentially the terms are to be understood in relation to the exercitant's desires. What 'profits' is what helps me get 'what I want' – here the fundamental graces of the Exercises, spiritual freedom and finding the will of God (cf. [1, 21]).

magnanimous spirit and with great liberality Words suggestive of a kind of benevolence. While our own magnanimity and liberality towards God are a response to his generosity and liberality to us, it is characteristic of Ignatius' spirituality to insist that on our side we can approach God with magnanimity and liberality, as well as service, praise, reverence, affection, humility, etc.

Annotation 6: When nothing seems to happen

[6] **[1]** *Sixth annotation.* **When the giver of the Exercises becomes aware that the exercitant is not being affected by any spiritual movements, such as consolations and desolations, and is not agitated by various spirits, [2] the exercitant should be questioned closely about the exercises, as to whether they are being made at their**

[5]The importance of the Fifth Annotation can be gauged from its initial appearance in the history of the Exercises as the first of three preliminary 'precepts', the other two being the present Foundation and the Presupposition: cf. text taken down by John Helyar, the Englishman who made the Exercises in Paris, c. 1535 (MHSI 100, p. 429)

[6]*1599 Directory* (MHSI 76, p. 583 [trans., Palmer, p. 295]).

appointed times, and in what way, [3] and similarly as to whether the additions are being carefully followed. The giver should inquire in detail about each of these points.

[4] There are remarks below on consolation and desolation [316–324], and on the additions [73–90].

The *Sixth annotation* does not imply that the absence of spiritual stirrings is necessarily a sign of half-heartedness. In the Exercises it may occur, without such an implication, in the form of the Third Time of Election. Nevertheless, in the Exercises Ignatius attaches considerable importance to the experience of various 'spiritual movements'. There are elements in the Exercises which will ordinarily arouse resistance, particularly in cases where the choice of a state of life is involved,[7] and if nothing seems to be happening, it may be a sign that something is amiss in the way the Exercises are being made. The director must be prepared to question the exercitant not only on points of observance and method, but also about consolation and desolation.[8]

The directories link this prescription with two others:

(1) If things are going well, the director need not spend much time with the exercitant but should 'allow God to deal with his creature and the creature in turn with God' (see [15]).

(2) The director must take care not to give the impression of having a poor opinion of the exercitant, 'even when he has not done as well as he might'.[9]

Annotation 7: The approach to an exercitant observed to be in desolation

[7] [1] *Seventh annotation. If the giver of the Exercises sees that the exercitant is desolate and tempted, it is important not to be hard or curt with such a person but gentle and kind,* [2] *to give courage and strength for the future, to lay bare the tricks of the enemy of human nature, and to encourage the exercitant to prepare and make ready for the consolation which is to come.*

The *Seventh annotation* points out that those in desolation need to be

---

[7]Ignatius considered the Exercises 'better for someone who has not yet decided on a state of life, because then there is a greater diversity of spirits' (MHSI 76, p. 114 [trans., Palmer, p. 29]).

[8]*Directories* (MHSI 76, pp. 378, 438, 442 [trans., Palmer, pp. 166, 202, 204]).

[9]As above (pp. 378, 495, 605 [trans., Palmer, pp. 166, 241, 303]).

treated 'gently and kindly'; yet there is more than a hint in this annotation that many directors' instinctive reaction to desolation might indeed
be one of harshness (arising perhaps from their own difficulties in handling
desolation). The point is underlined in the *Official Directory* in the chapter
on the qualities of a director: 'The director should be kindly rather than
austere, especially toward persons suffering from temptations, desolation,
aridity or weariness'.[10] As well as being gentle, the director will encourage the exercitant in desolation by means of the first set of discernment
rules (especially [7, 8, 11–14]).

The *Official Directory* makes the further observation that 'despondency
and bitterness' often come 'from the ambition to excel', and that it is 'important that when a person has done his best, he should leave everything else to
the will and charity of God, trusting that the very aridity from which he
suffers is permitted by God for his best. This affection of humility and
subjection of oneself to God is often the surest way to win the grace of
praying well.'[11]

Annotations 8 to 10: The employment of the two sets of discernment rules

[8] [1] **Eighth annotation. As the giver of the Exercises becomes aware
of the exercitant's particular needs in the matter of desolations and
the tricks of the enemy, as well as in the matter of consolations, [2]
instructions can be given about the *rules* of the First and Second
Weeks for recognizing various spirits [313–327, 328–336].**

These *rules* are not a body of knowledge which the exercitant acquires at a
set point of the programme. They are intended to speak directly to experience, and explanations are therefore given to the exercitant when and as
required. Note the word 'explain': the early directors did not give exercitants
the rules to study for themselves; they 'explained' them. Indeed, with reference to the first set, Polanco specifies that it may not be necessary to deal
with all the rules, but that explanations should be given of those which meet
the exercitant's perceived needs.[12]

[9] [1] ***Ninth annotation.* The following should be noted when the exercitant is making the exercises of the First Week. If the exercitant is a
person unversed in matters of the spirit, and experiences *gross and***

[10]*1599 Directory* (MHSI 76, p. 597 [trans., Palmer, p. 300]).
[11]*1599 Directory* (MHSI 76, p. 605 [trans., Palmer, p. 303]).
[12]*Polanco Directory* (MHSI 76, p. 297 [trans., Palmer, p. 130]).

manifest temptations – [2] such as those in which hardships, human respect, or fear inspired by worldly honour are suggested as obstacles to progress in the service of God our Lord – [3] the giver should not talk about the Second Week rules for various spirits. [4] For just as the First Week rules will be very profitable to such a person, so will those of the Second Week do harm, as the matters they deal with will be too subtle and too elevated to be understood.

The principle formulated in the *Ninth annotation* governs the decision when to give the second set of rules. To explain these to a person who is not in the situation to which they are addressed would be positively detrimental. They deal with deceptions within consolation itself; only the person subject to temptation under the appearance of positive good is amenable to being helped by their subtle and more advanced distinctions.

gross and manifest temptations – 'gross', i.e. 'labours, shame, fear for good name' are not just exerting an influence but massively dominate the person's outlook: 'manifest' as opposed to 'hidden' (under the appearance of good).

[10] [1] Tenth annotation. When the giver of the Exercises becomes aware that the exercitant is being assailed and tempted under the appearance of good, that is the time to speak about the Second Week rules mentioned above. [2] For normally the enemy of human nature tempts more under the appearance of good when persons are exercising themselves in the *illuminative life*, which corresponds to the exercises of the Second Week. [3] Such temptations are less common in the *purgative life*, which corresponds to the exercises of the First Week.

The *purgative* and *illuminative life* The classic three ways, the purgative, the illuminative and the unitive, are not so much three discontinuous stages, as three aspects of Christian life, one or the other of which may predominate in the situation of an individual at a particular time, the 'higher' stages becoming increasingly habitual with spiritual growth. The purgative way, characterized by conversion from sin, is never completely transcended, and in the First Week the exercitant chooses to give full attention and commitment to its demands – one 'exercises oneself' in it. With this preparation, the illuminative aspects of Christian life – lucidity of spirit, and a certain spontaneity of response – will be enhanced as one goes through the Second Week. Ignatius here refers only to the first two stages of the triad (which he calls the purgative and illuminative life). As providing an interpretative key to the Exercises, many leading commentators have attached importance to the classic triad, placing the Fourth Week (and sometimes the Third) under the 'unitive way'. Ignatius on the other hand makes no other reference to the three ways.[13] Both the Versio Prima and the Vulgate replace the word *life* by 'ways'.

Annotations 11 to 13: Two ways of evading the process

[11] [1] *Eleventh* **annotation. While the exercitant is in the First Week, it will be an advantage that nothing should be known of what has to be done in the Second Week.** [2] **Rather, the exercitant should strive to obtain what is being sought in the First Week as though nothing good were to be hoped for in the Second.**

The *Eleventh* annotation points out that the grace of the Exercises at any particular moment is in the present, even if the present may be laborious. Hence Ignatius warns against the temptation to escape from the present into a future stage of the Exercises. During the First Week, the exercitant will be less tempted, knowing nothing about the turn the Exercises will take in the Second Week (though Annotation 4 shows that Ignatius did not intend the exercitant to be completely in the dark about the overall programme).

[12] [1] **Twelfth annotation. The giver of the Exercises should be insistent in drawing the exercitant's attention to the following: since an hour has to be spent in each of the five exercises or contemplations to be made each day,** [2] **the exercitant should always try to find contentment in the thought that a** *full hour* **has indeed been spent in that exercise – and more, if anything, rather than less;** [3] **for as a rule the enemy leaves nothing undone in his efforts to get the hour of contemplation, meditation or prayer shortened.**

[13] [1] **Thirteenth annotation. It should also be noted that whereas in time of consolation it is easy and undemanding to remain in contemplation for the full hour, in time of desolation it is very difficult to last out.** [2] **Consequently,** *in order to act against desolation* **and to overcome temptation, the exercitant must always stay on a little more than the full hour, so as to get into the way not only of** *resisting* **the enemy, but even of** *defeating* **him completely.**

[13]Ignacio Iparraguirre writes in criticism of the inclusion of a chapter on the three ways in the *Official Directory* that 'instead of making more universal the doctrinal base of the Exercises, it restricted it, curtailing it within a particular current, which is doubtless magnificent in itself, but is the product of the tastes of one epoch. One can produce a genuinely Ignatian commentary enclosing the Exercises within this system. But one can also understand the Exercises while prescinding from this tendency.' *Historia de los Ejercicios de San Ignacio*, vol. II, p. 446. Cited by O'Leary in 'What the Directories Say'. O'Leary's article will be referred to below in reference to the Third Week.

full hour The other evasion consists in curtailing the time for prayer. Two texts in particular are recommended in the Directories for the encouragement of exercitants suffering from tedium in prayer: Luke 11:9–10 and Habbakuk 2:3 ('if the vision tarry, wait for it, for it will surely come').

in order to act against desolation This is an application of the principle of 'going against' (*agendo contra*): a disordered tendency should be dealt with by a deliberate emphasis on its opposite, in order eventually to find the mean. The principle appears in the Exercises frequently (e.g. [16, 325, 350, 351]). It operates against excess in both rigour and indulgence (e.g. too much or too little sensitivity of conscience [350]).

resisting/defeating To 'resist' and to 'defeat' are not synonymous. The two terms appear again [33, 34, 324].

Annotations 14 to 16: Election. Dispositions of director and exercitant. The dynamics of finding God's will

On the central importance of the theme of election in the Exercises, even for those with no major choice to make within the Exercises themselves, see [21] and [169–189], with commentaries. In the following three annotations Ignatius summarizes his doctrine of choice-making as a function of the Creator/creature relationship [16 [3,4,6], 17]. Annotations 14 and 15 also draw attention to two principles regarding the director's role in relation to a retreatant's election.

[14] [1] **Fourteenth annotation. If the giver sees that the exercitant is going ahead in consolation and full of fervour, the latter ought to be forewarned against making any *unthinking or precipitate* promise or vow.** [2] **The more unstable in temperament the exercitant is known to be, the greater the need for warning and admonition.** [3] **It is true that one can legitimately encourage another to enter a religious order, with the intention of taking vows of obedience, poverty and chastity;** [4] **and it is also true that a good work done under vow is more meritorious than one done without a vow.** [5] **Nevertheless careful consideration must be given to the *individual temperament and capabilities* of the exercitant, as well as to the helps or hindrances that may be met with in fulfilling promises that such a person might want to make.**

unthinking or precipitate In the Exercises life-decisions are frequently, and reliably, made on the basis of tested consolation [176]. But tested consolation is one thing and impetuosity another. The present annotation alerts the director to the possibility that in immature or volatile personalities psychological factors might produce effects that the exercitant, and indeed an impressionable director, might fail to distinguish from true movements of the Spirit. The section on election in the body of the Exercises makes no mention of these cautions, but taking them as read puts the emphasis on generous availability. The director needs, however, to be aware of this annotation, which recalls an incident in Ignatius' own early experience as a director.[14]

vow On making a vow during the Exercises the *1599 Directory*, taking up the position of Polanco and others, admits that a vow might be made, but at the same time it insists on the need for caution. 'In moments of ardour or consolation vows are often made which are regretted later. This precaution needs to be taken especially with persons of ardent, hasty, or unstable character.'[15] In any case the director should in no way urge such a vow.

individual temperament and capabilities Caution is particularly called for when three factors coincide: (1) strong emotion, (2) an unstable personality, (3) a choice which seems unlikely to succeed either because of the exercitant's previous psychological, physical or moral quality or because of serious obstacles in the way of implementing the decision.

Implicit in Ignatius' position on election is the principle that grace creates new capacities. In an authentic experience of consolation a person may be called (and therefore empowered) to make a choice with consequences which they could not sustain without that call and empowerment. But precisely for this reason, the director should not endorse a decision, especially one involving a way of life, which a person may not in fact be asked to make.[16]

[15] [1] **Fifteenth annotation. The one giving the Exercises *must not encourage* the exercitant *more towards poverty* or to the promise of it rather than to the contrary, nor to one state or way of life than to another.** [2] **Outside the Exercises it can indeed be lawful and meritorious for us to encourage all who seem suitable, to choose continence, virginity, religious life and every form of evangelical perfection;** [3] **but**

---

[14]*Reminiscences* §77 (*Personal Writings*, p. 50).

[15]*1599 Directory* (MHSI 76, p. 721 [trans., Palmer, p. 338]).

[16]In the matter of religious life the early directors were especially alive to the dangers of embarking on this out of unreflective fervour: 'A person who appears altogether unfit for religious life because of natural infirmity or other apparently insuperable impediments should by no means be urged to the religious state. Experience shows how their fervour later cools and the natural impediments and difficulties create problems for the persons. The result is that they eventually abandon religious life or remain in it to their own or others' harm.' *Directory of Fr Dávila* (MHSI 76, p. 490 [trans., Palmer, p. 238]). On 'election' and religious life see also below on [21].

during these Spiritual Exercises, it is more opportune and much better that *in the search for the divine will* the Creator and Lord communicate himself to the faithful soul, [4] *inflaming*[17] *that soul in his love and praise*, and disposing her towards the way in which she will be better able to serve him in the future. [5] Hence the giver of the Exercises should not be swayed or show a preference for one side of a choice rather than the other, but remaining in the centre *like the pointer of a balance* [6] should *leave the Creator to deal with the creature*, and the creature with the Creator and Lord.

must not encourage While a director may discourage an unsuitable person from choosing religious life, he or she must never, during the Exercises, positively influence a person to choose it, however suitable a candidate he or she might seem to be.

more towards poverty The language of this annotation recalls that of the Contemplation to Attain Love, and the definitions of consolation in the discernment rules. It establishes from the outset the contemplative climate of the Exercises as a whole, and particularly the expectation in which Ignatius would have the exercitant enter upon the election.

in the search for the divine will I.e. the context is election.

inflaming that soul in his love and praise A person approaching election should wish (but cannot presume) to find God's will in a disposition of love which transforms the affectivity and takes up the whole person in the desire to do God's will. Though the connection between this text and the definitions of consolation in [316] and [330] is not absolutely clear, the expectation here described would of course find complete realization in 'consolation without cause'.

like the pointer of a balance The image used later of the exercitant [179] is here applied to the director. In the approach to election, it is for the director to help the exercitant identify factors in the latter's attitudes or desires which might not arise from the desire for God's will. But essentially the role of the director is to accompany the exercitant towards a relationship between God and creature into which another person must not intrude.

leave the Creator to deal with the creature Cf. Ignatius' use of the imagery of

---

[17]The word here translated as 'inflaming' can also be understood in the sense of 'embracing': cf. *Personal Writings*, p. 80 (Spiritual Diary), 'I was on fire', with note 18.

intimate friendship in [231]. In Ignatius' lifetime, when the main charge made against the Exercises was that of illuminism, the contention that Creator and creature deal with one another directly was a prime target for criticism.[18]

[16] [1] **Sixteenth annotation.** *For this*, **namely, that the Creator and Lord may** *work more surely in his creature,* [2] **if the soul in question happens to be** *attached or inclined to something in an ill-ordered way*, **it is very useful for her to** *do all in her power to bring herself round* **to** *the contrary* **of that wrong attachment.** [3] **This would be the case, for example, if a person were bent on seeking to obtain an appointment or benefice, not for the honour and glory of God our Lord, nor for the spiritual good of others, but for one's own advancement and temporal interests.** [4] **One must then set one's heart on what is contrary to this. One should be** *instant in prayers* **and other spiritual exercises, and ask God our Lord for the contrary,** [5] **namely, not to want the appointment or benefice or anything else,** *unless the Divine Majesty gives a right direction* **to one's desires and changes the first attachment,** [6] **so that the motive for desiring or keeping this thing or that be** *solely the service, honour and glory of the Divine Majesty.*

for this This annotation can only be properly appreciated when read as a continuation of the preceding one.

work more surely in his creature The annotation gives a summary of the way in which Creator and creature work together in a decision situation. The key to the whole process is desire. The action of God consists primarily in giving the grace of desire for the service and glory of God, not just in a general way but as the criterion for choice precisely in one's present situation. The part of the creature is to pray for this desire, to yield to it, to remove obstacles which stand in its way. To the extent to which 'disordered' attachment to one of the alternatives (e.g. a benefice) constitutes such an obstacle, Ignatius commends the 'going-against' explained in the present annotation.

attached or inclined ... in an ill-ordered way It is not the attachment as such that creates an obstacle, but the egocentricity of it – 'personal interests and secular advancement'.

do all in her power to bring herself round The language, implying an element

<hr />

[18]In a report on the Exercises commissioned by the Archbishop of Toledo in 1553 this statement was censured as 'clearly made by an illuminist'. Cf. *Polanco Chronicon* (MHSI, vol. 3, pp. 503–24). For the historical context see O'Malley, *The First Jesuits*, pp. 43, 294.

of (graced) striving, emphasizes the seriousness of the demand made of the person and the fact that freedom from the power of egocentric desire does not come casually. The context of this 'striving', however, is the growing love and knowledge of Jesus and the growing commitment to discipleship which are the graces of the Second Week.

the contrary The contrary to wanting something in a disordered way is not to hate the thing, but simply to cease to want it – unless and until one is moved to want it for the glory and service of God. What immediate counter-actions may be needed before one can come to this point are specified in [155 and 157] which the present annotation anticipates.

instant in prayers The primary initiative on our part is prayer – earnest petition that God himself act in our hearts.

unless the Divine Majesty gives a right direction, etc. Conversion is not only a matter of going against 'disorder' in our affections, or even eliminating this – it consists in allowing God to enter into our affections and direct them; *right direction*, i.e. the desire for personal advantage is changed to a desire for the praise and service of God. The distinction between the negative step (the opposing of disordered desire) and the positive action of God should not be over-simplified. Even in the initial attempt to 'bring ourselves to the contrary', the desire for God's service and glory is already, even if obscurely, at work.

solely the service, etc. (cf. [46] – the preparatory prayer of every exercise; also [155]). Those who yield to the influence of the Spirit will come increasingly to desire this ideal and to tend towards it, and it is the desiring and the tending which are important. *Solely* does not imply that this transcendent motivation excludes immediate motivation (e.g. the interest or satisfaction in doing a job) but rather that all other motives are integrated into it. What is excluded is the motivation of the 'second class' ([154], cf. also [169]) which subordinates the service of God to a primary motive consisting of immediate self-interest.

service, honour and glory of the divine Majesty A variant of the 'praise, reverence and service' of the Principle and Foundation. *Service*, significantly, comes first; *honour* – the honour of God, as opposed to the honour accruing to self (e.g. from high office); *glory* – for Ignatius has the nuance of the fulfilment of the purposes of God in the world.

The matter of the Sixteenth Annotation is dealt with in more detail in the Foundation [23] and in the Third Class [155, 157] and further discussion will be found in the commentary notes on these sections.

Annotation 17: Openness with the director

[17] [1] **Seventeenth annotation. There is much profit to be gained if the giver of the Exercises, without wishing to inquire about or know the exercitant's personal thoughts or sins,** [2] **is given a** *faithful account* **of the various** *agitations and thoughts brought about by the different spirits*; [3] **for then depending on the greater or less profit to be gained, the giver can provide some spiritual exercises appropriate and suited to the needs of a soul agitated in this way.**

faithful account The exercitant will 'profit greatly' by being open with the director about whatever the latter needs to know in order to help him or her here and now in the Exercises. What the director needs to know consists mainly in the movements of the spirits; the Exercises are about present discernment. But though the annotation places certain restrictions on directors – who should not inquire into or wish to know the exercitant's personal thoughts or sins – its main purpose is to encourage exercitants on their side to let themselves be known. Moreover both from the text of the Exercises and from the Directories it is clear that the director is expected to have a good knowledge of the exercitant – their personality, temperament, tendencies, strengths and weaknesses, etc.[19]

agitations and thoughts brought about by the different spirits 'Thoughts' in the Exercises are not abstract ideas, but rather what Ignatius calls 'movements of the spirits' (cf. note on [313]); they involve imagination and feeling, and they tend towards actions, either interior or exterior. *Personal thoughts* are those we either initiate or choose to entertain. *Thoughts brought about by the spirits* are thoughts, good or bad, in so far as they come unbidden and, as it were, from 'outside' ourselves (cf [32, 347]). Thoughts of the latter kind are the material of discernment, and helping the exercitant discern the spirits is the main role of the director.

In the early days of the Exercises, the director and confessor were ordinarily not the same person (cf. note on confession [44]).

---

[19]The essential relationship of exercitant to director is filled out in the *Directory of Polanco*: 'The exercitant should disclose to the director how he is making the Exercises and should give him an account of them. In this way, if he has failed to understand anything fully, he can be instructed. His insights and illuminations can be subjected to scrutiny. His desolations and consolations can be discerned. And he can be helped with advice on any penances he does or temptations that beset him.' (MHSI 76, p. 289 [trans., Palmer, p. 125]).

Annotations 18 and 19: Adaptations of the Exercises

Annotations 18 to 20, contain the principles of all adaptation of the Exercises, i.e. the Exercises are an organic whole, and to make them in their entirety, whether in seclusion or in daily life, requires essential fidelity to the whole programme and to its order; but they are also a resource which can be used in many ways to meet a wide variety of situations and personal needs. Even in Ignatius' lifetime and in the period of the *Directories*, the actual forms of adaptation developed beyond the strict limits of these three annotations. The process of adaptation continues into modern times, and so long as the general principles of adaptation are preserved, there is no need to try to fit every form of adaptation of the Exercises into one of these three annotations.[20]

[18] [1] **Eighteenth annotation. The Exercises are to be *adapted to the capabilities* of those who wish to engage in them; that is to say, age, education or intelligence are to be taken into consideration.** [2] **Thus, those lacking in education or in poor health should not be given things that they cannot undertake without fatigue and from which no profit is to be derived.** [3] **Similarly, so that each might derive the more help and profit, what is given to exercitants should be accommodated to their dispositions.**

[4] **Hence people hoping to get some instruction and to reach a certain level of peace of soul, can be given the particular examen [24–31], then the general examen [32–43];** [5] **and together with this, for half an hour in the morning, the way of praying about the commandments, the deadly sins, etc. [238–248].** [6] **Such people can also be recommended to make a confession of sins each week, if possible to receive communion every fortnight, and better still every week, if they are so inclined.**

[7] **This arrangement is more suited to simple and uneducated people, to whom explanations can also be given of each commandment, each of the deadly sins, the precepts of the Church, the five senses and the works of mercy.**

[8] **Likewise, should the giver of the Exercises see that the exercitant is a person of weak constitution or having little natural capacity, and from whom not much fruit is to be expected,** [9] **it is more suitable to give some lighter exercises until the person has been to confession.** [10] **Afterwards some forms of the examen of conscience can be given and**

[20]Maurice Giuliani suggests that 'the three annotations 18, 19, 20 surely cannot encompass the social and cultural reality that is ours today' and that the wisest move is simply to give up regarding the Nineteenth and Twentieth Annotations as the authorities which justify our setting up the 'retreat in daily life' and the 'enclosed retreat'. See Lefrank and Giuliani, *Freedom for Service*, p. 255.

the instruction to confess more frequently, so that the progress made may be maintained. [11] The giver should not go onto the materials dealing with election or to other exercises outside the First Week, [12] especially when the exercitant can gain greater profit from other exercises and there is not time for everything.

adapted to the capabilities The annotation outlines ways of adapting the Exercises to those for whom the full Exercises would be either unprofitable or burdensome. The latter include people in poor health but Ignatius offers no specific advice for these. The categories explicitly dealt with in this annotation fall under three heads:

First, those of limited aspiration: people who want something, but are not ready for the radical conversion which is the object of the full Exercises. For comments on the materials proposed to such people, see notes on Examen and the First Way of Prayer.

Second, those of limited mental ability or education, many of whom in Ignatius' day would have been illiterate (while emphatically not an intellectual undertaking, the Exercises require a certain culture and mental discipline). The programme here is similar to that provided for the preceding situation, but with more emphasis on instruction. In fact we have here a programme of basic catechesis; but catechesis taking the form precisely of 'spiritual exercises' not only of instruction.

The third category consists of people who can be given the First Week, but lack the capacity to go beyond it – an incapacity which may be 'perceived' as things go along. The meaning of the term 'lighter exercises' is not altogether clear. The interpretation that seems best to fit the distinctions drawn in this annotation, as well as Ignatius' practice, is to equate the 'lighter exercises' with all the meditations of the First Week; these being 'light' not in content, but in the sense that the ordinary person can cope with them. Ignatius himself approved of the First Week exercises being given without limitation of persons.

[19] [1] **Nineteenth annotation A** *person taken up with* **public affairs or necessary business,** [2] **and who is educated or intelligent, can set aside for the Exercises an hour and a half a day. One can explain to such an exercitant about the end for which the human person is created,** [3] **as well as giving for half an hour the particular examen, then the general examen and the way of confessing and of receiving communion.** [4] **On three days the exercitant can devote one hour each morning to the meditation on the first, second and third sins [43–53];** [5] **then for three days at the same hour the meditation on the record of sins [55–61];** [6] **and for another three days the meditation on the punishments which correspond to sins [65–72].** [7] **During these three sets of**

meditations the ten additions [73–90] should be given. [8] For the mysteries of the life of Christ our Lord the same procedure should be followed, as is explained in detail further on in these same Exercises.

person taken up with This annotation turns to ways of adapting the Exercises to people capable of making them in their entirety, but prevented by circumstances from making them in seclusion. Though the text details the contents of the First Week, the Nineteenth Annotation (known in the sixteenth century as the 'open' Exercises) covers in fact the full course. For those who make them in this mode the Directories allow considerable liberty in the matter of times of prayer and the distribution of material.[21]

Today, after falling virtually into oblivion, the Nineteenth Annotation Exercises have developed into the concept of 'the exercises made in the stream of life'.[22]

Annotation 20: The full and integral Exercises

[20] [1] Twentieth annotation. A person who is more at liberty and who desires to profit as much as possible, should be given *all the Spiritual Exercises* in the *exact order in which they are set down*. [2] In general, there will be the more profit, the more one takes appropriate steps to *withdraw* from all friends and acquaintances, and from all secular preoccupations. [3] For example, one can change residence and go to another house or room so as live there in the most complete privacy possible, [4] but with the opportunity to attend Mass and Vespers daily without the fear of acquaintances getting in the way.

[5] Three principal advantages, among many others, will be gained by this seclusion.

[6] The first is that in drawing apart from numerous friends and acquaintances, as well as from distracting business, in order to serve and praise God our Lord, one gains no small merit before the Divine Majesty.

[7] The second is that in this state of seclusion, with a mind not divided amongst many things but entirely taken up with one alone, namely, *the service of one's Creator and the good of one's soul*, [8] one's natural powers can be devoted all the more freely to the wholehearted search for what one's heart desires.

[21] *1599 Directory* (MHSI 76, pp. 615–17 [trans., Palmer, p. 306–7]).

[22] On this development, cf. Cusson, *The Spiritual Exercises made in Everyday Life*, in which as well as drawing on his own extensive experience to suggest a method, the author provides an outline history of the Nineteenth Annotation Exercises. The reader is also referred to Lefrank and Giuliani, *Freedom for Service*.

⁹ **The third: the more we are alone and in seclusion the fitter we
become to approach and attain to our Creator and Lord; ¹⁰ and the
more nearly we approach him, the more we become disposed to
receive graces and gifts from his Divine and Supreme Goodness.**

all the Spiritual Exercises The Twentieth Annotation Exercises, the form to
which Ignatius admitted only those of 'outstanding' suitability,[23] is characterized by fidelity to the 'order' of the text, and by a situation of seclusion.

exact order in which they are set down This should not be understood with
rigid literalism; a degree of adjustability to the individual is of the essence
of the Exercises and even in this, the 'purest' form of the Exercises, adjust-
ments should not be regarded as a 'concession' (cf. [4, 17, 72, 129, 162,
209], and also the note in the Versio Prima and the Vulgate following [71]).
Nevertheless the Exercises are an entity and any way of giving them that fails
to respect this does not come under the category of the 'Twentieth
Annotation'. In particular, it is important to respect the 'order' (or dynamic)
of the Exercises.[24]

withdraw The Exercises should be made as far as possible in conditions of
physical and even psychological separation from the exercitant's everyday
world. Separation from the world does not, however, mean unconcern for it;
indeed in the Exercises the opposite is true. In the Exercises one turns away
from the immediately distracting and invasive aspects of the world not so as
to forget the world but to 'order' one's relationship to it and to find one's
personal way of serving the Kingdom within it.

the service of one's Creator and the good of one's soul For other statements
in which the good of the soul is set explicitly in relation to the service of
God, see [152], [166], [169], [179], [189], [339]. See also comments on [1]
and [23].

[23]To some extent Ignatius' restrictive attitude was influenced by practical
considerations – the small numbers of available directors and the heavy claims made
on their time. But practical considerations apart, he saw the full Exercises as demanding more than ordinary spiritual and psychological quality.

[24]While adaptation finds its fullest scope in the situations of the Eighteenth and
Nineteenth Annotation Exercises, in every form of the Exercises the director must be
able to hold the balance between two principles. 'On the one hand he is supposed to
keep exactly to the order, method and detailed instructions found in the book, and the
more strictly he does this the more God will work together with him. On the other
hand, he is allowed considerable discretion, in view of the differences among persons
who make the Exercises or of the spirits by which they are moved, to alter the exercises or prescribe others appropriate for individual needs.' *1599 Directory* (MHSI 76,
p. 609 [trans., Palmer, p. 304]).

FIRST WEEK[1]

PURPOSE AND PRESUPPOSITION

[21] SPIRITUAL EXERCISES HAVING AS THEIR PURPOSE THE *OVERCOMING OF SELF* AND THE *ORDERING OF ONE'S LIFE* ON THE BASIS OF A *DECISION* MADE IN FREEDOM FROM ANY DISORDERED ATTACHMENT

This paragraph is not so much a *title* as a *summary* of the Exercises in terms of ends and means. The statement thus corresponds to the last part of Annotation 1, but in two respects it is more specific: it associates the Exercises with making a decision; and secondly, it emphasizes the ascetical/psychological implications of making a decision in freedom from disordered affection.

With regard to election, Ignatius preferred, other things being equal, to give the Exercises to persons having to choose a state in life, but the early generation of directors, following the example of Ignatius himself, also gave them to people with no such choice to make.[2] Indeed, both Ignatius and the authors of the *Directories* were cautious about whom they allowed to make major decisions in the Exercises.[3] In the matter of election, then, flexibility of usage is to be found from the beginning.

Nevertheless, a director of the Exercises should be aware that while the *use* of the Exercises admits of flexibility, the *text* of the Exercises is centred around the election of a life-situation, and specifically the election

---

[1]In the Autograph the title 'First Week' appears at this stage at the head of the page. The first week material properly so-called consists in the Exercises on sin [45ff.] (see [4.2]).

[2]The early directors, as well as excluding from the election any exercitant lacking in the right qualities or dispositions, did not give the election material to those such as religious or the married already in stable life-situations. Neither was a Jesuit exercitant ordinarily given the election material, unless he wished to deliberate about 'some matter which the superior leaves in his hands', *Directory (Miró)* (MHSI 76, pp. 395–6 [trans., Palmer, p. 175]; cf. also pp. 171, 177, 252 [trans. pp. 66, 69, 102]).

[3]Where choice of the way of the counsels was concerned, one reason for caution was the danger of people failing after the Exercises to maintain their resolve and spreading it around that the Jesuits had 'made them poor, moving them to poverty and the religious life', *Directives and Instructions of Ignatius* (MHSI 76, p. 112 [trans., Palmer, p. 27]). On election and religious life, see also above on [14].

of one of the two Christian 'states' – the way of the counsels and the way of the commandments.[4] Indeed, the text can only be properly understood in relation to election in this sense. But this does not mean that to give the Exercises to people not having to make a life-choice is to give them in an attenuated mode; a choice of some kind will always arise in the Exercises.[5]

Lacking even a mention of God or his will, the title hardly does full justice to the nature of the Exercises. Its purpose is immediate and practical: to make clear to the person embarking on the Exercises what on their side is the objective (to make a decision in affective freedom) and the condition for reaching it (overcoming the blocks to freedom in themselves). That the decision is an assent in love to the wishes of God, and that the end is achieved and the means pursued in the Spirit and in the context of a growing relationship with Christ, is for the moment left implicit.

overcoming of self See note on [87].

ordering of one's life To 'order' is to bring into line with the 'end' to be proposed in the Principle and Foundation.[6]

decision The connection between this 'ordering' and a decision or 'election' is made more explicit in the Vulgate: 'Some spiritual exercises, by which a person is directed in order that he or she might overcome the self and establish a way of life by a decision free from harmful affections.' For 'election' see below, Introduction to Week 2 and commentary [169–189].

[22] PRESUPPOSITION

[1] So that the giver of the Exercises and the exercitant may the better *help and benefit each other*, [2] it must be presupposed that every good Christian should be readier to *justify* than to condemn a neighbour's statement. [3] If no justification can be found, one should ask the other in what sense the statement is to be taken, and *if that sense is wrong* the other should be corrected with love. [4] Should this not be sufficient, let every appropriate means be sought whereby to have the statement interpreted in a good sense *and so to justify it.*

---

[4]This distinction is made and developed by Joseph de Guibert, *The Jesuits*, pp. 126ff. in connection with the controversy about the 'end' of the Exercises, between the 'election' and the 'perfection' schools. On this controversy, associated particularly with the names of Léonce de Grandmaison, and Louis Peeters, see Ganss, *The Spiritual Exercises*, p. 147.

[5]See below, Introduction to Election.

[6]Cf. Annotation 1, commentary on 'disordered affections'.

In a final preliminary to the Exercises proper, Ignatius enunciates principles relevant to all Christian communication and applies them particularly to the communication between the director and exercitant. Features of the text as it stands reflect the situation in which the Exercises were first given: the charge of illuminism often made against them and the fact that Ignatius and the companions lacked the authority their successors were later to enjoy.[7] But the Presupposition also refers to the qualities of mutual respect and trust which must characterize the director/exercitant relationship as such. In the director, these qualities establish a climate favourable to the candid disclosure of personal thoughts and feelings.[8] In the exercitant, the spirit of the Presupposition shows itself in a trust in the director, but also in the Exercises themselves, a trust extending to specific proposals and statements.[9]

The positive attitude commended by the Presupposition will often prevent misunderstandings from arising at all, but even with good will uncertainty as to the other's meanings, or a sense of not being heard or understood might persist; and Ignatius does not ask for the suppression of real doubts or difficulties that could impede the progress of the retreat. But these too must be dealt with in the same spirit of love that prompts the initial instinct to prefer where possible the favourable interpretation of another's statement.

Not only for their bearing on the Exercises themselves, but for their broader implications for Christian communication across differences of theology or outlook, the principles of the Presupposition are as pertinent today as they were in the sixteenth century. But in presenting these principles within the Exercises the modern director needs to discern the ways best suited to an individual or situation. A presentation that might be highly appropriate for one exercitant could leave another in a state of puzzlement or anxiety.[10]

[7]Cf. *Directory (Dávila)* (MHSI 76, p. 500 [trans., Palmer, p. 244]). The problem is well illustrated by the story of Diego Hoces (later to join the companions) who arrived to make the Exercises under Ignatius armed with books in case 'by chance his director might be wanting to lead him astray' (*Reminiscences* §92 [trans., *Personal Writings*, p. 58]). For allegations of illuminism, see *Directories* (MHSI 76, p. 482 [trans., Palmer, p. 232]) and also note on [15] above.

[8]For the link between the Presupposition and the exercitant's openness on these points, see *Directory (Dávila)* (MHSI 76, p. 500 [trans., Palmer, p. 244]), and also *Directories* (MHSI 76, pp. 445, 482 [trans., Palmer, pp. 207, 232]) where the Presupposition is explicitly linked with Annotation 17 and First Week Rules for Discernment, No. 13 [326].

[9]In the *Directory* dictated to de Vitoria, Ignatius insists that the exercitant interpret 'whatever is done or said in his regard in good part' (*Directories* (MHSI 76, p. 96 [trans., Palmer, p. 19]). For Miró one of the purposes of the Presupposition is that 'the exercitant may be admonished where necessary to put a good construction upon whatever is done or said' (*Directory (Miró)* (MHSI 76, p. 378 [trans., Palmer, p. 166]). See also *Directories* (MHSI 76, p. 445 [trans., Palmer, p. 207]).

[10]In the view of both Dávila and the *Official Directory (1599)* the Presupposition should no longer be proposed as a matter of course. Dávila indeed suggests that presented as it stands, the text might only arouse 'suspicion and fear',

help and benefit each other Though often referred to in the Directories in master–disciple terms, the relationship is here described as one of co-operation. Director and exercitant have a common project: that the exercitant find God through the Spiritual Exercises. In working together towards this, the one who gives and the one who receives are required to 'help' each other. The help is two-way.

justify Literally, to 'save', i.e. to interpret in an acceptable way.

statement Literally, 'proposition': in connection with the Exercises the term is to be understood not only of statements but also of the various proposals put to the exercitant in the annotations, additions and other suggestions and directives. The statements referred to include everything said by the exercitant in recounting his or her thoughts and experience, and everything said by the director in response.

if that sense is wrong As they stand, the words refer to situations where the issue is one of truth. Ultimately a proposition can be 'saved' or judged 'false' in relation to the given boundaries of orthodoxy, assumed in the Presupposition, no less than in the Rules for Thinking with the Church (cf. [365]). Since, however, the sense of orthodoxy often produces suspicion and defensive condemnation, Ignatius' own strict sense of orthodoxy could be said to make the fair and open attitude of the Presupposition all the more striking.

and so to justify it As well as the reading given here the Spanish allows the final sentence to be translated in the sense that it is the 'person' who is saved from error, but the context seems to indicate that the concern is to save the 'statement'.[11] In connection with the Exercises any statement in them that might at first cause a difficulty can be shown to a well-disposed questioner to admit of an orthodox interpretation.

FOUNDATION

The Principle and Foundation (or the 'Foundation', as regularly referred to in the *Directories*) is described in the *1599 Directory* as 'the groundwork of the whole moral and spiritual edifice'[12] of the Exercises.

Directory (Dávila) (MHSI 76, pp. 500, 643 [trans., Palmer, pp. 244, 311]). In many cases Dávila's misgivings about a literal presentation might be highly relevant today, but this does not justify neglect of its spirit and essential content. For an example of a presentation adapted to the situation of the Exercises today, cf. Fleming, *Spiritual Exercises*, p. 21.

[11]Cf. Dalmases, ed., *Ejercicios Espirituales*, p. 53.

[12]*1599 Directory* (MHSI 76, p. 643 [trans., Palmer, p. 311]).

As the Exercises go on, its axioms will be specified or complemented in various ways, especially by the missionary vision and the love-inspired preferences arising out of the Second Week contemplations, and by the emphases of the 'Contemplation to Attain Love'.[13] But the Foundation is never superseded. It remains a basic point of reference throughout the Exercises – and throughout life.

While not the first of the named exercises (cf. the title of [45]) but a preliminary to the programme as a whole, the Foundation is itself an 'exercise' in the sense that the exercitant devotes a certain period of time to 'making' it. As an exercise, how is it to be understood? For many reasons (e.g. the absence of any mention of preludes, colloquy, or repetition, the explicitly logical structure, and at first sight the academic tone) the Foundation is plainly an exercise other in kind from the meditations and contemplations of the four Weeks; and the description best suited to it is that of a 'consideration', or meditative rumination. It is important, however, not to misread the implications of this description. The Foundation is not a philosophical text, as distinct from a properly Christian one,[14] and it calls not only for intellectual assent, but for the engagement of the whole person. To appreciate the nature and purpose of the Foundation, we must remember that Ignatius himself gave it to persons recently presented with the Fifth Annotation.[15] It is made therefore in the affective climate of large-hearted liberality towards one's Creator and Lord evoked by that Annotation.

Since the text is a unity, not a series of disparate points, one has only

[13]The main differences between the Foundation (F) and the Contemplation to Attain Love (C) can be briefly summarized: F emphasizes more our dependency on God, while C puts greater stress on God's gift of himself to us; in F we use creatures to relate to God, in C God 'uses' his creation to give himself to us; F calls forth primarily the response of service, C that of gratitude; in F the concrete conditions of service (right use and indifference) are presented as a task or as objectives to be achieved, while the self-offering of C is presented as lovingly spontaneous. In brief it could be said that the emphases of F are preparatory to those of C, and essential to the authenticity of the latter. The two texts however are mutually complementary, each dealing with the themes of God's creative purpose and of the place of humankind within that purpose, and it is too simple to see the difference as between the 'rational' and 'affective' or the 'purely ascetical' and the 'contemplative'.

[14]This interpretation is explicitly rejected in the *Directory* of G. González Dávila, who says that it should be made clear to 'learned' exercitants that the indifference of the Foundation is not that of Greek philosophy, but corresponds to the doctrine of St Thomas (MHSI, vol. 76, p. 501 [trans., Palmer, p. 245]. It is now universally accepted that the God of the Foundation is the Trinitarian God of Christian revelation and that the Foundation is directly ordered to the following of Christ.

[15]The association of the Fifth Annotation and the Foundation is clear in an earlier version of the Exercises which begins with three preliminaries, corresponding to the present Fifth Annotation, the Foundation and the Presupposition; cf. text of John Helyar, the Englishman who made the Exercises in Paris probably under Peter Favre c. 1535 (MHSI 100, p. 429).

properly 'made' the Foundation when each of the parts has been duly considered and its significance perceived in relation to the whole. But this does not mean that every element in the text will have equal weight for the exercitant approaching the text for the first time. In this situation what must be paramount is the opening declaration about the 'end' for which human beings and their universe exist. This might be called the 'foundation of the Foundation', and the effectiveness of the entire exercise depends on how the exercitant assimilates it.[16]

In this matter there are two ways in which a director can sell a retreatant short: by passing too quickly to the 'practical' themes, or else while encouraging the exercitant to spend time on the opening propositions, treating these only as abstractions. Both approaches deprive the Foundation of vision. For Ignatius himself, behind these concise and somewhat academic propositions there lay the faith-vision, contained in his personal experience at Manresa.[17] If the Foundation is to be made effectively, for the exercitant too these propositions need to open up his or her own vision of self and all created reality in relation to God. In this way the 'end for which I am created' and the relationship of all things to God's creative and salvific purpose are perceived not as abstractions or as bases of obligation, but as objects of longing and sources of inspiration. It need hardly be added that to find this vision one must break open the 'textbook' concision of Ignatius' language, and here the assistance of the director may be essential, e.g. in providing Scripture materials.[18]

It is in the context of this fundamental vision that the practical themes of the 'ordered use of creatures' and 'indifference' should be considered. The exercitant's reactions to these themes will depend partly on his or her general dispositions and partly on the extent to which sensitive personal issues are raised by them. Sometimes, even at this early stage, an exercitant will be stirred by a desire to serve and live for God, such that for the moment indifference is simply 'there', a grace 'given', a fact of experience. On the other hand, the immediate grace of the Foundation may consist not so much in 'having' indifference as in wanting it, difficult as it might be.[19] But in any

[16]A position endorsed by Annotation 19 where 'the end for which human beings are created' designates the whole text.

[17]For the importance of vision as the basis of the Foundation, the reader is referred particularly to Cusson, *Biblical Theology*, pp. 47–51; *Everyday Life*, pp. 31–40; Tetlow, 'The Fundamentum'.

[18]Note that the director should 'explain' the Foundation, not just 'give' it (cf. [19]).

[19]In the *Directory* dictated to de Vitoria Ignatius himself says that one of the fruits of the Foundation is precisely to bring the exercitant to sense that it is difficult to 'make an indifferent use of the means God our Lord has given us', and grasping this, to place oneself unreservedly into God's hands, *Directories* (MHSI 76, p. 100 [trans., Palmer, p. 21]).

event, what is crucial at the beginning is the vision, and the exercitant should not be left contending with the practical demands of the Foundation without having been opened in mind and heart to the vision of reality of which the practical demands are the implications.[20]

Two practical questions

Two related questions are frequently raised in connection with giving the Foundation. The first concerns the length of time an exercitant might be expected to devote to it in the Twentieth Annotation Exercises. On this subject the director with a sense of the objective of the Foundation – a vision of reality in relation to God's creative and salvific plan, and the desire to lead a life grounded in God – will follow the principle of the Fourth Annotation that some are more prompt and others slower in finding what they want. The director will also recognize that for all its importance, the Foundation is preparatory to the process to come, rather than a moment of conversion or breakthrough in its own right. Further guidance is to be found in the Ignatian *Directories*, from which it appears that Ignatius himself used the Foundation in two ways, corresponding to the exercitant's dispositions at the outset of the retreat. To those already 'making great progress' he would propose the Foundation on the first day together with the two examens, before coming on in the evening to the meditation on sin. Those less well disposed, on the other hand, might stay with the Foundation for two or three days.[21]

The second question has to do with the practice common today of preceding the Foundation with prayer of a more general kind, sometimes referred to as 'disposition days'. Such a practice seems to assume that one could be unready for the Foundation on starting the Exercises, yet become ready for it after a few 'disposition days'. Is this a reasonable assumption to make? As noted above, the Foundation is for the large-hearted; its characteristic attitude is that of liberality towards God. Hence it is not necessarily the best starting point for the person of immature faith or pusillanimous spirit. However the fact that an exercitant may need to be 'unblocked' in relation to this radically theocentric text does not of itself indicate a pusillanimous spirit. Latent generosity can be inhibited by distorted images of God which may have impeded the development of trust or a sense of God's

---

[20]'It is more important to encourage the contemplation of the content of the vision evoked by the first part of the text – God, man, all created things – than to speculate on the virtues which would spontaneously flow from it, and which are dealt with in the second part of the text. Time must be allowed for contemplation to bear its fruit.' Cusson, *Biblical Theology*, p. 39.

[21]*Directories* (MHSI 76, p. 100 [trans., Palmer, p. 20]).

love and goodness, and experience has shown that for people affected in this way, a few days of prayer on precisely these themes can have the effect of releasing the dispositions in which the Foundation can be fruitfully considered. It should be noted, too, that when the first sentences of the Foundation are interpreted as opening up a whole God-centred vision of reality, the distinction between 'disposition texts' and entering on the Foundation is less hard-and-fast than it has sometimes been made out to be.

[23] [1] PRINCIPLE AND FOUNDATION

[2] *The human person* **is** *created* **to** *praise, reverence and serve God our Lord*, **and by so doing** *save his or her soul*; [3] **and it is for the human person that the** *other things on the face of the earth are created*, **as** *helps to the pursuit of this end.*

[4] **It follows from this that the person has** *to use* **these things in so far as they help towards this end, and to be free of them in so far as they stand in the way of it.**

[5] *To attain this, we need to make ourselves indifferent* **towards all created things, provided the matter is** *subject to our free choice* **and there is** *no prohibition*. [6] **Thus** *for our part we should not want health more than sickness*, **wealth more than poverty, fame more than disgrace, a long life more than a short one – and so with everything else;** [7] *desiring and choosing* **only what conduces more to the end for which we are created.**

The human person To be understood in both its individual and collective reference. The import of the Foundation is weakened considerably if the sense of the individual ('God created me ...', 'All things are there for me ...') is allowed to obscure the sense of human society as a whole, of which 'I' am a member, and in whose corporate responsibilities I share. The Foundation is the norm of every exercise of collective and individual power.

created In the Ignatian vocabulary, 'create', 'creator', 'creation' are highly charged words, evoking not only an act in the past but a present process (cf. [236]).

praise, reverence and serve These and similar terms – 'honour', 'respect', 'obedience' and above all 'giving glory' – echo the 'hallowed be thy name, thy will be done' of the Lord's Prayer, and express an attitude of radical God-centredness, a desire simply that God be God and that his purposes be realized. The meaning of the words is not exclusively cultic. God is praised not only by formal worship, but when we so live that in our heart and behaviour God is acknowledged to be God and his will is done in all things. Again, we give praise, reverence and service in becoming involved in God's

29

'project', which is simultaneously the ongoing conversion of our own lives and the establishment of his reign in the world.

God our Lord The God of the Exercises – i.e. the Trinity, whom we praise, revere, and serve in and through Christ, the Incarnate Word.[22]

save his or her soul Later, the emphasis here placed on personal salvation shifts to the praise, glory and service of God, in which the salvation of the soul is included (see [1.4], [20.7] and comments).

other things on the face of the earth are created 'Things' are to be understood of physical nature, of the world as 'humanized', of the components of our personal make-up (body, mind, emotion, imagination, talents, qualities of personality, etc.). But 'things' in this context must also cover every kind of event and situation, and in the case of these the concept of creation must be expanded to include that of Providence, a concept admitting of various interpretations, but without which the Foundation would hardly be applicable to large areas of human reality.

helps to the pursuit of this end The idea of creatures as 'helps to an end' serves to pinpoint a basic principle of Ignatius' 'theology of the world'. In God's creative project, there is a unity of purpose, and the key to that purpose is God's project for humankind. In relation to the transcendent end of the human person, the world is not a neutral backdrop, still less in itself an obstacle or embarrassment. Immediate reality in a sense is the raw material of our relationship with God; it is for the most part precisely in and through our commerce with this reality that our praise, reverence and service of God come about. The idea of creatures as 'helps to an end' can however convey a misleadingly utilitarian impression, and it must not be understood as denying the value of things in themselves.

to use (and avoid) To be human is to make constant choices of use and avoidance in regard to reality (not to make such choices is to be a victim of circumstances). The potential of reality to help towards the praise, reverence and service of God is realized to the extent to which that 'end' is the criterion of our particular choices to use or avoid.[23] The word 'use', like the word 'things', does not refer only to physical use, but to the entire gamut of human

[22]Cf. Hugo Rahner, *Ignatius the Theologian*, p. 63. In the Exercises 'God our Lord', though in some passages (e.g. [39], [135], [155], [343]) probably referring to Christ, is ordinarily a Trinitarian title: cf. Egan, *Ignatius Loyola the Mystic*, p. 77.

[23]The theme of the 'use of creatures' recurs frequently in Ignatius' letters, e.g. 'May the Lord give us the light of holy discernment so that we may use created things by the light of the Creator' (from a letter to a superior on the topics of food and drink, and the preservation of health), MHSI, *Epp. Ig.*, vol. 9, pp. 374–5 [trans., *Personal Writings*, p. 277].

responses to reality – interest, love, every kind of creativity, enjoyment,[24] together with inner responses such as the acceptance or not of situations, and the meanings we are free to confer on these, etc.

To attain this Indifference is proposed not as an end in itself but as a means to God-directed choices regarding the use of or abstention from creatures – choices made, it should be remembered, within the positive and ungrudging view of reality set out at the beginning of the text.

we need to make ourselves indifferent[25] Note the introduction of the personal pronoun as the text moves from the plane of general principles to that of personal implications. In the immediately obvious sense, 'indifference' consists in an attitude of equipoise, and such an attitude, neutralizing as it does the effects of disordered affections, may obviously in some situations be a prerequisite for making a right choice. But indifference should also be thought of in a positive way; and regarded positively it is an affective space within which the movements of the Spirit can be sensed and things seen in relation to the signs of God's will, an affective silence making possible an unconditional listening. The indifference of the Exercises is a stance before God, and what makes it possible – and also something quite other than either apathy or stoicism – is a positive desire for God and his will.

The dynamic of the Exercises does not require that indifference, at least in regard to a specific issue (e.g. whether to keep or get rid of a fortune, cf. [150ff.]), be yet the fully attained disposition that Ignatius will later consider a necessary condition for election (cf. [179]). At this stage it may be a felt need, a project, still to be fully realized as the exercitant proceeds step by step through the subsequent Exercises. In this case the exercitant will 'make' him or her self 'indifferent' by working with the Spirit through the process of the Exercises.

subject to our free choice ... no prohibition We are not asked to be – and indeed we should not be – indifferent all the time or in regard to everything. The grace of indifference is a potential, to be activated when appropriate; and explicit indifference is appropriate in times when we are seeking the will of God. When we judge that we have found it, the appropriate attitude towards the course indicated is one of commitment, controlled by integrity of intention.

[24]Cf. [229.4] where 'making use of' the pleasure of the seasons obviously means choosing to enjoy these pleasures in so far as they might help towards finding 'joy in the Lord'.

[25]The Vulgate avoids the technical terms 'indifference' and 'indifferent', substituting for them, both here and in [157] the phrase *'absque differentia nos habere'* ('we should hold ourselves without difference, i.e. partiality').

for our part I.e. in the circumstances designated, it is for us to approach choice in a spirit of indifference, in order that God, on his side, may move us towards a particular course and rouse in us a desire for that course (cf. [5], [155]).

we should not want The essence of indifference is freedom to choose in accord with the praise, reverence and service of God; though this requires freedom from the influence of present wants and disinclinations it does not require the total cessation of these.

health more than sickness, etc. The particular eventualities mentioned can enter our lives unavoidably; but they may be specifically entailed in the exercitant's 'election'. Thus one might, as many who make the Exercises do, choose a situation of poverty and low esteem as being in itself a more literal imitation of Christ. Sickness would not ordinarily be chosen in this way;[26] but one might choose a course of action or way of life in the recognition that sickness or early death would be the likely or inevitable consequence (such would be the case in the sixteenth century of the choice of a missionary life). But for some people the immediate implications of indifference may lie in other and more specific directions, and Ignatius' reference to 'everything else' should not be overlooked.

desiring and choosing Isolated from desire, indifference would have a meaning quite different from that of the Exercises, where indifference must be understood in relation to the deeper desires, given by the Spirit, to do whatever conduces more to the praise, reverence and service of God, and more specifically to follow Christ and to live by the values of the gospel. It has a double relationship to these deeper desires: it is the *condition* for experiencing them, yet only where to some degree the desire is already effective can indifference itself be possible.[27]

---

[26]Unless in response to a special movement of the Spirit requiring, of its nature careful discernment. The Foundation makes us aware however that the preservation of health, though always a high priority, is not an absolute.

[27]The Foundation itself nowhere suggests that 'poverty' or 'dishonour' might in fact be objects of preference. Right choices are those which in one's own case conduce more to the praise, reverence and service of God; and in approaching any choice one must be not only ready for the harder or more challenging way, but also aware that in a particular situation what makes more for God's praise, reverence and service might be any use of creatures not in itself sinful. Hence in the *Directory* dictated to de Vitoria, Ignatius suggests that the director explain to an exercitant making the Foundation that every state of life can in itself be a way either of salvation or of perdition: 'Some who possessed riches have earned heaven, and others who possessed riches have earned hell', *Directories* (MHSI 76, p. 101 [trans., Palmer, p. 21]).

EXAMINATION OF CONSCIENCE ('EXAMEN')[28]

Ignatius and the early directors introduced the exercitant to all the material on the examen at the point assigned to it in the text, namely between the Foundation and the opening meditation of the First Week.[29] The Ignatian examen was of course unfamiliar to the first generation of exercitants, and it was proposed in the Exercises both for use during them, and as a general resource. Within the Exercises, the particular examen served to sustain fidelity to the method and to 'uproot any weeds or thorns that might impede the good seed of the Exercises'.[30] The section on the General Examen could prepare the way for the meditations of the First Week by 'opening the exercitant's eyes to know the sins of his or her past life'.[31]

It is as a resource for the whole of life, however, that the examen comes fully into its own.[32] As such a resource, it helps keep the person open to the action of the Spirit. It facilitates the process of liberation, which must continue through life, from the things that obstruct this action. In general, it helps us to work the graces of the Exercises into the events and relationships and personal growth-situations of daily life. For these reasons Ignatius held the examen in the highest esteem; he was never willing to dispense from it, and in his own life the practice formed a central motif.[33]

The love-inspired inclination towards the more literal imitation of Christ that becomes one of the predominant themes of the Second Week, in a sense takes the exercitant beyond indifference as expounded here, but it is essential to realize that such an attitude in fact includes indifference (cf. [157], [167]); for the final criterion of choice is *always* the glory of God. So whatever one's own preference (inspired by love for Christ and the desire for imitation) the glory of God cannot be pinned down prior to discernment to one side or the other of the poverty/riches, honour/dishonour spectrum.

[28]The examination of conscience is ordinarily designated by Ignatius by the single word 'examen', a word absent from the English dictionary but retained in the present translation as part of the received vocabulary of Ignatian spirituality. Note that the procedures explained in this section do not exhaust the theme of examination in the Exercises. The First Method of Prayer [238–47] has affinities to the examination of conscience. The reflection after prayer [77] is a kind of examen, and the theme of examination appears again in the Rules for Discernment [319, 333, 334].

[29]*Directory, de Vitoria* (MHSI 76, pp. 102–3 [trans., Palmer, p. 22]).

[30]Ibid.

[31]*1599 Directory* (MHSI 76, p. 649 [trans., Palmer, p. 313]).

[32]'At the end of the Exercises, the exercitant should be strongly urged to commit themselves to the examen as an aid to perseverance', ibid.

[33]'He has always kept this habit of examining his conscience every hour and of asking himself with careful attention how he had passed the hour. If at the end of it he happened upon some more important matter, or a task which prevented this pious practice, he postponed the examen, but at the first free moment or the following hour, he made up for this delay' (Ribadeneira). Cf. de Guibert, *The Jesuits*, p. 66.

But if the examen is to be fruitful in this way, it must be made with discernment and be integrated into the entire process of ongoing conversion; and more specifically, it should always be ordered to the motivations, and practised within the overall spiritual consciousness, promoted by the Exercises. Certain implications of this, easily overlooked if this section is read hastily, or without reference to the Exercises as a whole, call especially for attention. (1) The examen, especially the 'particular examen' must be seen as part of a positive growth-programme, characterized by the development of positive qualities, not just the eradication of negative ones. (2) The examen does not preclude, but rather presupposes, recourse to whatever is a help to inner freedom at every level. (3) While an element of 'practicality' is a defining characteristic of the examen, it must never be made solely with a view to controlling or changing behaviour but always out of the desire to cooperate in the work God wishes to do in oneself, and through oneself for the service of others. (4) The content of the examen will shift as the individual grows in the Spirit, so that with maturity one's examen becomes increasingly a presence to oneself at the levels where one senses the movements of the spirits.

Particular

[24] [1] DAILY PARTICULAR EXAMEN
The daily particular examen contains *three times, and two examens.*
[2] The first time is in the morning immediately on rising; the exercitant should make a firm resolve to take great care to avoid the particular sin or defect that he or she desires to correct and amend.

[25] [1] *The second time comes after the midday meal,* when one should ask God our Lord for what one desires, namely: the grace to remember how many times one has fallen into that *particular sin or defect,* and to amend for the future. [2] Then the first examen is made. It consists in demanding of oneself an account of the particular point proposed for correction and amendment, [3] running over each hour or each period of time, beginning from the moment of rising up to the hour and moment of the present examen. [4] On the first line of *the diagram* below as many marks should be made as there have been lapses into the particular sin or defect. [5] Then I should resolve again to amend before the next examen to be made.

[26] [1] The third time is after supper, when the second examen should be made in the same way, going from hour to hour from the first examen to this second one. [2] On the second line of the same diagram

as many marks should be entered as there have been lapses into the particular sin or defect.

[27] ¹ *Four additions* through which to get rid of the particular sin or defect more quickly.
² The first addition. Each time one falls into the particular sin or defect, one should put a hand to one's breast in sorrow for having fallen. ³ This can be done even in the presence of many people without any one noticing.

[28] Second addition. As the first line of the diagram represents the first examen, and the second line the second, one should see at night if there is an improvement from the first line to the second, that is, from the first to the second examen.

[29] Third addition. The second day should be compared with the first, that is today's two examens with yesterday's two examens, to see if there is an improvement from one day to another.

[30] Fourth addition. One week should be compared with another to see if there is an improvement between the present week and the preceding one.

[31] ¹ Note. The large g at the top of the following diagram stands for Sunday, the second, smaller, letter stands for Monday, the third for Tuesday, and so on.
²

three times and two examens The essential of the method, though it will be amplified by the 'additions' immediately following, is the programme set out here, consisting of three moments of recall and resolution.

N.B. Since the overall tone of this section is practical and ascetical, it is especially desirable to be aware of the Ignatian assumptions, and to realize that without these the particular examen could be employed in questionable ways.

The second time comes after the midday meal The second and third times correspond to the two daily examen-times that are integral components of the Ignatian prayer day. Hence the particular examen has its place within the general examen outlined below [43], but without loss of its own specific character.

particular sin or defect The basic principle of the particular examen is summarized in the observation of Polanco that 'in every person there is generally one or other sin or defect which is the source of many others'.[34] Ignatius however applied the practice to a wide range of faults, from neglect of the additions by an exercitant,[35] to behaviour contrary to good relationships on the part of a temperamentally 'choleric' apostle.[36]

the diagram The letter g is explained in various ways: as standing for the Basque word *gaur* (= 'today'), the Spanish word *gula* ([=] 'gluttony'), the Italian word *giorno* (= 'day'). In the Vulgate the lines become progressively shorter as the week goes on.

Four additions These additions represent an intensification of the essentials set out in [24]. Reflective awareness is now taken beyond three 'times' to become a methodically cultivated thread of awareness running through the day [27] and over longer sequences [29, 30]. The directions proposed here are, nevertheless, 'additions' to the three-times' programme, and in the case of some individuals the way they are put into practice may require discernment and guidance.

General

[32] ¹ GENERAL EXAMEN OF CONSCIENCE IN ORDER TO PURIFY THE SOUL AND *TO MAKE A BETTER CONFESSION*
² **I presuppose that there are *three kinds of thought processes* in me, one sort which are properly mine and arise simply from liberty and will, ³ and two other sorts which come from outside, one from the good *spirit* and the other from the bad.**

to make a better confession While the General Examen, like the Particular, is an aid to continual integration of life, it is also proposed as a means of preparing for confession (reconciliation). Though not every examen explicitly

---

[34]*Directories* (MHSI 76, p. 292 [trans., Palmer, p. 127]); *1599 Directory* (MHSI 76, p. 647 [trans., Palmer, p. 313].
[35]See below [90, 160, 207].
[36]Cf. MHSI, *Epp. Ig., No. 32*, vol. 1, p. 179 (trans., *Inigo: Letters*, p. 53).

envisages the sacrament, Ignatius understands the practice of examen in relation to his view of spiritual progress as fed by the related streams of prayer and
the two sacraments of reconciliation and eucharist (cf. [44]).

three kinds of thought processes Some thoughts proceed from our own
freedom. They are properly 'ours'; we are responsible for them. These are
distinguished from non-voluntary thoughts, which are the material of
discernment. The latter thoughts come from 'outside ourselves' in that their
source is not in our own volition (cf. [17, 337]).

spirit For the sense of 'spirits', cf. [313.4] with commentary.

[33] [1] THOUGHTS
[2] There are two ways of gaining merit when a bad thought comes from
outside. [3] First, the thought comes to my mind of committing a mortal
sin, I resist it promptly and it is permanently overcome. [34] [1] Second,
the same bad thought comes to me and I resist it; but it returns again
and again and I keep on resisting until the thought goes away defeat-
ed. [2] This second way is more meritorious than the first.

[35] [1] One sins venially when the same thought of committing a mortal
sin comes to mind and one gives ear to it, delaying over it a little, [2] or
taking some sense of enjoyment from it; or when there is some negli-
gence in rejecting the thought.

[36] There are two ways of sinning mortally. The first is when one
consents to a sinful thought in order to put one's consent into immediate effect, or to act on it if one could. [37] [1] The second way of
sinning mortally is when the sin is actually committed. This is a more
serious sin for three reasons: [2] first, the time spent is longer; second,
the intensity is greater; third, more harm is done to both persons.

[38] [1] WORDS
[2] One should not swear either by the Creator or by the creature except
with truth, necessity and reverence. [3] By 'necessity' I do not mean any
situation in which a truth of some kind is affirmed by oath, but one in
which the matter is of some importance with relation to spiritual or
bodily welfare or temporal interests. [4] By 'reverence' I mean that
when invoking the name of one's Creator and Lord one is mindful of
the honour and reverence which are his due.

[39] [1] It is to be noted that although a vain oath is a greater sin when
we swear by the Creator than when we swear by the creature, [2] it is

more difficult to swear as we ought – with truth, necessity and reverence – by the creature than by the Creator for the following reasons:

[3] First. When we want to swear by some creature, the choice of invoking the creature does not make us careful and alert to tell the truth or to affirm it only with necessity, as would the choice of invoking the name of the Lord and Creator of all things.

[4] Second. In swearing by the creature it is not as easy to pay reverence and respect to the Creator as when swearing by and invoking the name of the Creator and Lord himself. For the choice of invoking God our Lord brings with it more submission and reverence than is aroused by the choice to invoke the created thing. [5] Therefore, it is more permissible for the perfect to swear by the creature than it is for the imperfect; [6] for *the perfect, owing to constant contemplation* and to the enlightenment of the mind, are more in the habit of considering, meditating and contemplating how God our Lord is in every creature according to his essence, presence and power. [7] Thus when swearing by the creature they are better prepared and predisposed to pay homage and reverence to their Creator than are the imperfect.

[8] Third. With persistent swearing by the creature, the imperfect are in more danger than the perfect of falling into idolatry.

[40] [1] 'Speak no idle word.' By this I understand words of no profit either to myself or to others, and those not directed to that end. [2] Consequently, to speak about anything that benefits or seeks to benefit my own soul or my neighbour's, or that is for the good of the body or for temporal welfare, is never idle. [3] Nor is it idle to speak of things which do not belong to one's state of life, for example, if a religious speaks about wars or trade. [4] Rather, in all these cases there is merit in speaking to a well-ordered purpose, and sin in ill-directed or aimless talk.

[41] [1] One should say nothing to defame another or to spread gossip, for if I make known a mortal sin which is not public knowledge, I sin mortally, and if the sin is venial, I sin venially, while in making known a defect, I show my own defect. [2] But given the right intention, there are two possible ways of speaking of the sin or fault of another:

[3] The first way. When the sin is public, as in the case of a public prostitute, a sentence passed in court, or when a public error contaminates the minds of those with whom we deal.

[4] The second way. When a hidden sin is revealed to someone so that such a person can help the sinner to rise from sin. In this case, however, there should be some expectation or probable likelihood that help can be given.

[42] **¹** Deeds
² One should take as subject-matter the Ten Commandments, the precepts of the Church and *the recommendations of superiors*; any action done against any of these three is a greater or smaller sin depending on the greater or less importance of the matter. **³** By 'recommendations of superiors' I mean, for example, the *Crusade Bulls* and other indulgences, such as those granted for peace treaties, which can be obtained by confession and reception of the Blessed Sacrament. **⁴** There can be no little sin in inciting others to act or acting oneself against this kind of pious exhortation and recommendation of those in authority.

This material, without claiming to be comprehensive,[37] might serve as an instruction preparatory to the First Week, and also as preparation for confession. The approach owes something to the confession manuals of the time, but while the latter were based on the Decalogue or the capital sins, Ignatius here adopts the simpler division of the *Confiteor*, thoughts, words, deeds. In connection with words, both the Versio Prima and the Vulgate specify that the sins mentioned can be supplemented by further examples, 'as the director judges necessary'.

the perfect, owing to constant contemplation In the unexpected context of a catechesis on oath-taking, we find a statement about the way in which the effects of spiritual maturity extend to a person's total outlook and to the significance of everything he or she says or does. The vision of God in all reality, identified here as characteristic of the 'perfect', is that in fact of the Contemplation to Attain Love [230–7].

the recommendations of superiors The Versio Prima and the Vulgate specify that it is sinful not only to act against these, but also to despise them.

Crusade Bulls These were dispensations from fasting and abstinence in return for alms (originally a dispensation to those taking part in the Crusades). The subject is taken up again in the Rules for Thinking with the Church (cf. [358] with comment).

Method

[43] **¹** Way of making the general examen containing *five points*
² The *first point* is to give thanks to God for the benefits I have received.

[37]*1599 Directory* (MHSI 76, p. 649 [trans., Palmer, p. 313]).

³ The *second point* is to ask for grace to know my sins and reject them.

⁴ The *third point* is to ask an account of my soul from the hour of rising to the present examen, hour by hour or from one period to another, ⁵ first with regard to thoughts, then words, and finally deeds, following the order given in the particular examen [25].

⁶ The fourth point is to ask God our Lord for pardon for my sins.

⁷ The fifth point is to resolve to amend with his grace, ending with an Our Father.

The *five points* are a 'method of prayer' properly so-called; their simple and open structure is suited to any situation and to every level of spiritual maturity.

first point ... second point To appreciate the General Examen as a method of prayer, full weight – and time – must be given to the first two points. A common distortion of the Ignatian General Examen comes from a tendency to regard these opening points as perfunctory preliminaries. The method begins with thanksgiving for blessings, the attitude epitomized in the Contemplation to Attain Love, and which belongs to the very heart of the Ignatian spirituality of finding God in all things. With regard to the prayer for 'light' (point 2), while of course we need 'light' to appreciate blessings, the placing of this petition immediately before the recall of one's sins accentuates the fact that sin can be known only in the light of Christ (and not in any other 'light').

third point Exponents of the examen today emphasize the need to ask where one has responded or failed to respond to God, rather than to look simply for right or wrong actions. Approached in this way, the examen brings the discernment of spirits into daily life. Through it one is helped to recognize the often subtle drawing of the 'good' spirit, and the (again, often subtle) influences of the 'bad' spirit within everyday experience; to become familiar with the processes through which these operate (cf. especially [333, 334]). While this interpretation might seem at first sight to exceed the *thoughts, words and deeds* of Ignatius' text, it must be remembered that 'thoughts' include the 'movements of the spirits'.[38]

---

[38]For further reading on the Ignatian examen, the following articles are especially recommended: Aschenbrenner, 'Consciousness Examen'; St Louis, 'The Ignatian examen', (reprinted in (ed.) Sheldrake, *The Way of Ignatius Loyola*); Townsend, 'The examen and the Exercises – a re-appraisal'; 'The examen re-examined', *Drawing from the Spiritual Exercises*.

General Confession and Communion

In an age of normally infrequent recourse to the Sacrament of Reconciliation, Ignatius, as we have seen, recommended regular, even weekly, use of it (cf. [18, 19]). In addition to their regular confession, a person might also on occasion make a 'General Confession', reaching back over the entire past or at least over a significant part of it. Such a confession might include material not previously brought to the sacrament. But essentially its matter is sin already absolved. It must always be regarded as an exceptional procedure, suited to threshold moments, 'when one is especially moved by God to a desire to inaugurate a new life'.[39] But given this situation and the background of the First Week, the graces of a General Confession will be those of a deepening insight into what God has forgiven; a sense of reconciliation not only as a present event, but as the history of God's constancy and fidelity; and a commitment of one's whole future to Christ made purer and more steadfast by a new level of repudiation in regard to past sin.

[44] **[1]** GENERAL CONFESSION AND COMMUNION
[2] **Anybody wanting *of their own accord* to make a General Confession will find in it three particular *benefits* among many others.**

[3] *First.* **While granting that a person who goes to confession every year is not obliged to make a general confession, [4] yet if such a person does make one, there will be greater profit and merit because of the greater present sorrow for all the sins and wrongs of one's whole life.**

[5] *Second.* **During the Spiritual Exercises one gains greater interior knowledge of sins and their malice than when one is not engaged in the same way with matters of the inner life. [6] Having now this greater knowledge and sorrow, one will have greater profit and merit than before.**

[7] *Third.* **As a consequence of making a better confession and of being better disposed, one is fitter and more prepared to receive *the Blessed Sacrament* [8] (the reception of which helps us not only to avoid falling into sin, but also to keep on increasing in grace).**

[9] **This General Confession is better made *immediately after the exercises of the First Week*.**

General confession was to be made *of one's own accord*. In this connection note should be taken of the pitfalls the practice might incur for the scrupulous, as González Dávila and *The Official Directory* recognize, while at the

---

[39] *1599 Directory* (MHSI 76, p. 629 [trans., Palmer, p. 309]).

same time insisting on the value of the General Confession precisely as a protection against anxiety.[40]

First and Second benefits The relationship between regular confession and the regular prayer of the examen has been already noted. Here the special practice of General Confession is linked with the special prayer of the First Week, in which the exercitant will take stock of the sins of his or her life, gain increasing 'interior knowledge' of these, and experience a renewal of gratitude for God's mercy.

Third benefit In this context, reception of the *Blessed Sacrament* refers immediately to the exercitant's communion at the end of the First Week; but the statement expresses Ignatius' general understanding of the relationship between sacramental practice and the process of conversion and growth.

    With regard to communion, someone in the sixteenth century would not ordinarily receive this daily. Going against common practice, Ignatius commended weekly reception, but as a man of his time he would have regarded a more frequent reception as exceptional.

immediately after the exercises of the First Week The case for deferring the General Confession until the completion of the First Week exercises will be clear from the above mentioned *benefits*. But there is the further practical consideration that in the sixteenth century preparation for a General Confession was time-consuming, and detailed, and often done with help from a manual.

The appropriate confessor?

Where the director is a priest, will he ordinarily be the exercitant's confessor? In the *Autograph Directory* Ignatius makes his own preference clear: if possible the confessor should be someone other than the director.[41] The *Official Directory*, drawing on Polanco, takes up this position, but with qualifications: 'In most cases it is better that the director not be the one to hear this General Confession. However, if the exercitant prefers it, or no other

---

[40]*Directory (Dávila)* and *1599 Directory* (MHSI 76, p. 506, pp. 661–3, [trans., Palmer, pp. 248, 317]). The concern of these *Directories* with the subject of anxiety (both the danger of causing and the need to relieve it) though reflecting the preoccupations of the age also draws our attention to possibilities and needs that might be found in any age or situation.

[41]*Autograph Directory* (MHSI 76, p. 70 [trans., Palmer, p. 7]).

priest is available, or any other reason requires, there is nothing to prevent the director's doing it.'[42]

FIVE MEDITATIONS

The following five meditations are ordered to the graces of life-changing contrition and gratitude [48, 55, 61, 71], deep alterations in one's very instincts of attraction and recoil [63], and the desire to live for Christ [53] and to 'amend' [61, 63]. As well as containing the subject matter through which to 'find' these graces, the text (together with parts of the subsequent additions) also provides the exercitant with practical guidance on prayer. Thus at the start of the First Week, the exercitant is introduced to an overall method, to the specific ways of praying which form the characteristic sequence of the exercitant's day, and to elements of Ignatius' language. The more significant of these materials will be touched on in the commentary of their respective positions.

God, sin and mercy

Ignatius himself did not regard these opening meditations as posing any great difficulties of interpretation, but an initial reading can easily miss features crucial for understanding them. Two points in particular should be kept in mind.

First, prayer in the Exercises is from the beginning Christocentric and Trinitarian. The exercitant makes the five meditations in the consciousness that God as Father wishes him or her to be reconciled with himself, through the saving death of Christ and the action of the Holy Spirit. This needs to be emphasized, since even the centrality of Christ, to say nothing of the place of the Father and the Spirit, are often not fully appreciated on a first reading of the text, especially when the text is read without a proper understanding of colloquy and repetition, or without reference to the Rules for Discernment.

Second, the God of the First Week is a God of mercy. Conversion can come about on different levels, and although people of varying spiritual quality might be admitted to them, the five exercises envisage primarily a spiritually mature and sensitive person, one seeking to advance 'from good to better'.[43] For a person of this kind, conversion will mean not a

---

[42]*1599 Directory* (MHSI 76, p. 663 [trans., Palmer, p. 318]). See also *Directory (Polanco)* (ibid., pp. 297, 452–3 [trans., Palmer, pp. 130, 212]).

[43]Cf. [9], [315]. As John Coventry observes, 'the exercises of the First Week were meant to be done by people of spiritual quality, not rumbustious sinners'. 'Sixteenth and Twentieth-Century Theologies of Sin', p. 58.

preliminary change of conduct prompted by fear, but the deep change of heart that can only arise out of a new personal discovery of God's mercy.

Mercy, then, is the dominant theme of the First Week Meditations, but there can be no profound sense of God's mercy without a profound sense of sin. Hence the week opens up a faith-vision of sin: sin seen as the negation of praise, reverence and service [50, 52, 58, 59], as a negative power pervading the history of free creation [50–52], as destructive of our relationship with ourselves and with the world.[44] But sin is always considered in the Exercises in the light of mercy, the mercy which is finally revealed in the Creator's commitment to sinful humanity in the cross of Jesus [53], and which can be sensed in everything – in one's experience of the world [60] and in life itself [61, 70]. This discovery, made without complacency or presumption, brings about a love-inspired conversion which is different from the conversion prompted by fear. Certainly Ignatius recognized, as does the mainstream homiletic tradition, that situations exist when fear must indeed be the first step [370]. But the First Week, where the meditation on Hell comes after and not before the person has been touched by God's love [65], is not such a situation. The essential grace of the First Week is that of a conversion arising out of the literally heart-breaking experience of being loved and forgiven.

Practical points

Giving the First Week poses numerous questions of presentation and content. How far is it in keeping with Ignatius' purpose to modify or supplement the material he provides? What place belongs to the five-meditation sequence? Is it in any case feasible to have the exercitant pray through this entire sequence on the first day, as the text seems to suggest one should [72]?

On these points, despite divergencies of detail, the general position of Ignatius and the early authorities is clear from the *Directories*. The Week should begin as nearly as possible with the exercitant making all of the five meditations.[45] For the remaining time, the norm should be the daily repetition

[44]The faith-understanding of sin, into which a person is led by the First Week Exercises, does not however dispense from a moral education. The First Week presupposes that the exercitant has received (or is receiving) such an education; indeed the Exercises themselves, as we have seen, contain elements of a moral education appropriate for an exercitant of the time in the section on the General Examen [33–42]. To live today according to the First Week perception of sin, and to be aware of the range of its applications, it is necessary to have an outlook formed by a moral education adequate for our own time. This will include among other things a contemporary understanding of the person in relation to society.

[45]The common practice in the time of the *Directories* was to start by presenting the first four exercises (first and second singly, third and fourth together) adding the

of this sequence. Nevertheless other materials might be added, consisting either in the addition of new points to the given meditations or in supplementary meditations, notably on the Last Things.[46] Today ways of presenting the First Week cover a wide range, and many go well beyond the limited flexibility of the early practice.[47] Among these it is impossible to pick out a single 'right way' of giving the First Week to contemporary exercitants; it is for the director to decide how best to help an individual realize its objectives. To do this calls for a certain familiarity with current approaches, together with sensitivity to the circumstances and needs of the individual exercitant. But to give the First Week, it is also necessary to know and understand the five meditations which constitute the First Week text. Adaptable though it is, this stage of the Exercises consists not in any way of meditating on sin and repentance, but in material and a dynamic of a particular character.

First meditation: three sins

Preparatory prayer and preludes

[45] [1] THE *FIRST EXERCISE* IS A *MEDITATION* WITH *THE THREE POWERS* ON THE FIRST, SECOND AND THIRD SINS; [2] IT CONTAINS AFTER A PREPARATORY PRAYER AND TWO PRELUDES [48] THREE PRINCIPAL POINTS AND A COLLOQUY

The *First Exercise* ... the title is concerned less with the content of the prayer than with its form, component parts and sequence.

---

fifth the second time round: cf. *Directory (Ignatius)* (MHSI 76, p. 82–3 [trans., Palmer, p. 12]), *Directory (Polanco)* (ibid., pp. 293–4 [trans., Palmer, p. 128]), *Directory (Miró)* (ibid., p. 382 [trans., Palmer, p. 168]), *Directory (1599)* (ibid., pp. 649–50 [trans., Palmer, p. 314]). One of the 'Ignatian' *Directories* insists however that the exercises should be given 'one by one ... until at the end the person is making all five'. This admits of various interpretations, but is certainly making the point that at the beginning the exercitant should not be made to feel overloaded or pressed, cf. *Directory (Ignatius)* (ibid., p. 80 [trans., Palmer, p. 11]).

[46]Ignatius himself, while insisting that further material is not needed if the exercitant finds what they want in the five meditations, recommends exercises on death, judgement and the like, if the exercitant is helped by them; cf. *Directory (Ignatius)* (MHSI 76, p. 85 [trans., Palmer, p. 13]). The *Directory* of 1599 suggests that additional matter might be used 'to forestall tedium and bring about deeper penetration of the matter' (MHSI 76, p. 650 [trans., Palmer, p. 314]). As subjects for meditation the Last Things appear frequently in the *Directories*, and they are commended in a note added by Polanco to the Latin versions of the Exercises after [71].

[47]Especially in the use of Scripture. The *Directories* contain little Scripture material, other than that already in the text. Among Old Testament materials, the sin of David is proposed for meditation by Cordeses (MHSI 76, p. 541 [trans., Palmer, p. 271]). Two Gospel texts are offered for use after the General Confession, the Prodigal Son and Lazarus (MHSI 76, pp. 391, 428 [trans., Palmer, pp. 173, 197]).

[48]In the Autograph, 'preamble'. The word 'prelude', taken from the Latin versions, is adopted in the present translation as being more familiar to contemporary exercitants and directors.

meditation In general, a 'meditation' is a prayer in which material is thought out or mentally processed, in the light of faith and in the desire to hear and respond to God's word to oneself. It is distinguished from 'contemplation', which is a prayer characterized by an affective quality and by receptiveness and simplicity.[49] Meditation is usually regarded as a 'beginner's' prayer, a prayer for the purgative way, but to understand its use in the Exercises we must realize that meditation here applies not only to method and 'level', but also to subject. Thus 'meditation' is used of every exercise (including the Two Standards and Three Classes), where the subject is a matter of truth or doctrine, while the subject of contemplation is always personal.[50]

the three powers The 'powers' or faculties of the soul (memory, understanding and will) are integral components of the human person, and they operate in all prayer, though not always as systematically and consciously as in this opening exercise, where their application constitutes a method. This consists in a three-stage sequence: (1) a summoning to consciousness of truth already held in the memory; (2) a process of exploring (or, a mediaeval image, 'masticating') this content with the mind;[51] (3) the response of the affections (or of the 'heart'). As noted earlier, when this psychological dynamic comes about in prayer, the 'thinking' stage is not study but the search for the 'interior understanding', to be distinguished from 'much knowledge' [2]. It should also be noted that the clarity and tidiness of Ignatius' exposé will not be exactly reflected in the overlap and interplay of experience itself.[52]

[46] Prayer. The *preparatory prayer* is to ask God our Lord for grace that all my intentions, actions and operations may be directed purely to the service and praise of his Divine Majesty.

**[47] [1] The first prelude is *the composition*, made by seeing the place.
[2] It should be noted here that for contemplation or meditation about visible things, for example a contemplation on Christ our Lord (who**

---

[49]In the Exercises the distinction should not however be drawn too exclusively. Discursive elements come into the later 'contemplations', and if 'meditation' begins with the intellect, it is itself a movement towards the level of the affections; indeed prayer which begins as 'meditation' may develop through prayer itself, especially colloquy and repetition, into 'contemplation' (see [64], [156]).

[50]On contemplation in the Exercises, see the comment on [101] below.

[51]But in the meditation on Hell the activity of the intellect is replaced by that of imagination.

[52]While the powers serve here to provide a prayer 'method', their use in prayer, whether explicit or implicit, has further importance than this. A large part of the process of conversion consists in the powers being taken up into, and transformed by, the Christ-life (cf. [234], [245]), and their employment in prayer is itself part of this process.

is visible), **³** the 'composition' will consist in seeing through the gaze of the imagination the material place where the object I want to contemplate is situated. **⁴** By 'material place' I mean for example a temple or a mountain where Jesus Christ or our Lady is to be found – according to what I want to contemplate.

⁵ Where the object is an invisible one, as is the case in the present meditation on sins, the composition will be to see with the gaze of the imagination, and to consider, that my soul is imprisoned in this body which will one day disintegrate, **⁶** and also my whole composite self (by this I mean the soul joined with the body), as if exiled in this valley among brute beasts.

preparatory prayer Ignatius explicitly mentions this prayer of petition every time he sets out a meditation or contemplation during the four Weeks,[53] and he insists that it must never be changed ([4] and [105]). The overall sense is clear: the exercitant asks to approach through grace ever more closely to the ideal of a life totally dedicated to the praise and service of God. There seems always, however, to have been a certain unclarity about the distinction between 'actions' and 'operations'. In the Latin texts the three elements of the Spanish are reduced to two: intentions and actions (Versio Prima), powers and operations (Vulgate). Various interpretations of the Spanish are offered by modern commentators.[54] A practically useful distinction identifies 'action' with the (inner) act of choice and 'operation' with its subsequent execution.[55]

the composition The preparation for prayer here described is denoted in the Spanish text as 'composition seeing the place' or simply 'composition' ([65], [232]). The more familiar terminology in English, 'composition of place', is taken from the Latin versions.

In imaginatively composing a place or situation corresponding to the subject of prayer, one 'composes oneself', in the sense of 'getting oneself together', or becoming recollected.[56] For the significance of the material places in the Gospel contemplations, see comments on [91], [103] and [112].

---

[53]It does not appear in the Three Ways of Praying, where the term 'preparatory prayer' is used to designate petitions that correspond to the second prelude below (cf. [244], [246], [248], [250], [251]).

[54]Dalmases, *Ejercicios*, p. 69, n. 46, refers to a distinction offered by Calveras between 'internal operations' and 'external actions', and similarly Gueydan suggests that 'actions' come about outside the person, while 'operations' pertain to the person's own bodily, intellectual, affective and spiritual life (*Exercises*, p. 55).

[55]This suggestion is proposed by Louis Puhl, *The Preparatory Prayer*, PASE, drawing on Nonell, *Ejercicios, Estudio sobre el texto de los Ejercicios*, p. 26. Cf. also Fessard, *La dialectique*, p. 50.

[56]On this point the reader is referred especially to Peters, *Spiritual Exercises*, pp. 29–30.

Here, and in a quite different way in [151] and [232], the 'place' represents an aspect of one's situation before God. Thus at the outset of the Exercises, and before coming on to consider the effects of sin in history, one puts oneself into a situation of loneliness, irrationality, and disharmony with both self and creation, which is the situation of every human being in so far as he or she is under the thrall of sin. The imagery recalls the parable of the Prodigal Son.

[48] [1] **The second prelude is to** *ask God our Lord for what I wish for and desire.*
   [2] **The petition must be adapted to the matter under consideration; thus for example in contemplating the Resurrection one asks for joy with Christ joyful,** [3] **while in contemplating the Passion one asks for grief, tears and great suffering with Christ suffering.**
   [4] **Here I will ask for a personal** *shame and confusion* **as I see** *how many have been damned* **on account of** *a single mortal sin,* [5] **and how many times I myself have deserved to be damned for ever on account of** *my numerous sins.*

[49] Note. Before all the contemplations or meditations the preparatory prayer should always be made without any change, and also the two above-mentioned preludes, which should be changed at times to suit the proposed material.

ask God our Lord for what I wish for and desire Petition is a central motif in the Exercises and takes a number of forms. Essential to the Exercises as a personal faith-venture are the wholly spontaneous petitions (cf. [54], [109]). But together with these, and especially characteristic of the Exercises, there are the forms of 'given' petition (such as the Preparatory Prayer above, the petitions of the Triple Colloquy [63, 147], and the series of eleven petitions included in the preludes to meditation and contemplation[57]). Marking as they do the stages of a journey of conversion, and being in a sense connatural with the Gospel themes or episodes with which they are associated, these can be said to correspond ultimately to the desires of the Spirit in the heart of every believer. The value of these petitions can be obscured however by over-simple interpretations. The exercitant may not always express their desires precisely as Ignatius does, or their initial reaction to a petition in the Exercises might be at first a case of 'desiring the desire', rather than of instant identification.[58]

[57]See [48, 55, 65, 91, 104, 139, 152, 193, 203, 221, 233].
[58]The Jesuit Constitutions prescribe that an applicant to the order be presented with the values of the Third Mode of Humility [167] and asked if he himself experiences such desires. If he does not, he should be asked whether he desires to experience them (*Constitutions SJ,* §102).

shame and confusion Both terms are relational, and together they represent a way of experiencing oneself before God's mercy. Hence the cause of 'shame and confusion' is not sin-awareness in itself, but the experience of the self-aware sinner in the presence of a God who is merciful and faithful (cf. [74]). One asks that through prayer this experience be deepened and intensified so as to change the heart profoundly.

how many have been damned, etc. Conscious of God's mercy, the exercitant must also be conscious that mercy is free. To help the exercitant grasp the significance of mercy at this level, Ignatius proposes a tactic which will hardly commend itself to people today, if only because of the assumptions it makes about condemnation already incurred by others. But the essential point does not depend on such assumptions. The importance of the references to Hell in the Exercises, both here and elsewhere, lies in making us alive to a possibility that confronts each of us in our freedom, and in reminding us that our salvation involves, both for ourselves and for God, a real death-or-life issue.[59]

In the Versio Prima this clause is modified to read: 'how many have perhaps been damned'. The 'perhaps' is added in the hand of Polanco.

a single mortal sin In the Exercises the term 'mortal sin' sometimes designates the 'deadly' (or 'capital') sins,[60] but here 'mortal sin' seems the natural reading.[61] Though the contrast between the 'single mortal' of the condemned individual and the exercitant's 'numerous sins' is meant to be discomfiting, 'mortal sin' must be understood in the full sense of the term, as connoting a free and radical rejection of God.[62]

[59]The primary implications of the doctrine of Hell are for ourselves. With regard to others, neither Scripture nor Tradition give grounds for certitude that any individual is in Hell, and for everyone who has departed this life we can and should hope that they are with God. For a study in depth on the meaning of Hell for Christian faith, the reader is referred to Hans Urs von Balthasar, *Dare We Hope 'That All Men Are Saved'?*

[60]The deadly, or capital, sins are the flaws or habitual evil tendencies in which sinful decisions or actions have their root. The two senses of 'mortal sin', though distinct, are closely connected, one or more of the capital sins being ordinarily the context and history of the act of freedom which constitutes a mortal sin.

[61]In the original texts, Latin as well as Spanish, 'mortal sin' clearly refers to 'capital sin' in [18] and [244]. Sometimes the appropriate translation is not absolutely clear, and even in the present case Peters considers 'capital sin' a possible and indeed preferable reading (cf. Peters, *Spiritual Exercises*, p. 190).

[62]'Mortal sin' is defined in the *Directory* of Pereyra as 'properly a treason committed against his Majesty, since by it, as far as the person can, he makes into his God the creature for which he deserts his own God, and would wish that God were not God' (MHSI 76, p. 151 [trans., Palmer, p. 52]).

my numerous sins As in [50] and [51] 'mortal sin' is not used of the exercitant. The emphasis is on 'sins' in the plural, namely the multiplicity of choices, acts and omissions, which express and endorse an egocentricity which left to itself could have had destructive effects that grace or Providence have not in fact allowed.

Three sins

One cannot delimit in advance the personal insights an exercitant might gain from pondering the three points that follow, with their scriptural and theological content. But certain broad essentials of the meditation should be noted.

Although the primary effect is to make the exercitant aware of his or her implication in the mystery of evil, the meditation does so by centring not on the exercitant's own sins, but on three situations that bring home the nature of sin in itself. In regard to each of these situations the process of meditation moves between two poles: sin as action against God, and sin in its concrete effects. Moreover in each point the material is meditated on not only so as to induce a sense of the nature of sin, but also so as to arouse, out of that sense, the feeling of 'shame and confusion', as explained above.

The theme of the history of sin can be subsequently extended through other biblical incidents[63] to include finally the effects of sin on individuals, on relationships, and within society today (always, of course, as will help a particular exercitant to find the grace of this exercise).

[50] ¹ The first point will be to bring the memory to bear on the first *sin*, which was that *of the angels*, then to bring the intellect to the same event in order to reason over it; ² then the will so that by seeking to recall and to comprehend the whole matter I may feel all the more *shame and confusion*, ³ comparing the one sin of the angels with my many sins. For while they went to Hell for one sin, how many times have I deserved Hell for so many.

⁴ When I say: 'Bring to memory the sin of the angels', I mean recall how they were created in grace, but not wishing to avail themselves of liberty in order to give reverence and obedience to their Creator and Lord, ⁵ and falling into pride, they were changed from grace to malice

---

[63]In this connection note the incidents in which the early chapters of Genesis pick up the subsequent development of human sin-history, i.e. the sin of Cain (Gen. 4:1–10), the corruption of the human race and the anger of God (Gen. 6:5–12), pride in Babel and its consequence (Gen. 11:1–9). In the *Directories* the extra meditations are seldom based on a biblical text, but as mentioned earlier an example is the sins of David (2 Sam. 11:1–27; 12:1–25).

and were cast out of Heaven into Hell. **⁶ One should next go over the subject in more detail with the understanding, and then** *arouse the affections of the heart with the will.*

sin ... of the angels Since sin can be committed by a pure spirit, sin is not essentially tied to animal passions, the instability of the human make-up, or the dynamics of human society. The essence of sin – ours and that of the angels – is, as Ignatius here defines it: the refusal to 'use' one's freedom to give reverence and obedience to one's Creator and Lord, in short the refusal to allow God to be God.

shame and confusion Though the requested grace [46] is explicitly referred to only in this first point, the object of the other two points is also to feel 'shame and confusion'.

to arouse the affections of the heart with the will Director and exercitant must be clear that the involvement of the will in prayer does not consist in trying to force emotion. What is required is a willed co-operation with, and yielding to, the action of the Spirit within the movement from understanding to affective response. Elsewhere the Exercises make clear that this response does not always come instantly (cf. [4], [322]).

[51] ¹ The second point. To bring the three powers to bear in the same way on *the sin of Adam and Eve,* **² calling to memory the long penance they did on account of that sin, and** *the corruption that came upon the human race,* **with so many people going their way to Hell.**
³ When I say: 'Call to memory the second sin, that of our first parents', I mean recall how after Adam had been created in *the plain of Damascus* **and placed in the earthly paradise, and Eve had been created from his rib, ⁴ they were forbidden to eat of the tree of knowledge. But they ate and by doing so sinned. ⁵ Afterwards dressed in tunics of skins and cast out of paradise, they lived their entire life without the original justice which they had lost, in great labours and much penance.**
⁶ Then go over the subject in greater detail with the understanding, and use the will as has been explained above [45].

the sin of Adam and Eve The first human sin, like the sin of the angels, is the refusal to 'use' the gift of freedom to allow God to be effectively God in one's life. The sin is considered as the hinge of a tragic sequence with a 'before' (earthly paradise – total harmony) and an 'after' (total disharmony with effects for the subsequent history of the human race).

In approaching the story of the fall, one must keep in mind the distinction between meditation with the powers of the soul and imaginative contemplation. Imagination, if it helps, may enter this meditation at any point, and indeed there is much in the story that appeals to imagination. But the essential is to extract the universal meaning within the story, which has to do with the nature of all human sin.

the corruption that came upon the human race It is of the nature of sin that its effects are never confined within the individual, but reach into the tissues of human society.

the plain of Damascus not Damascus in Syria, but a Damascus located by tradition in the region of Bethlehem.

[52] ¹ *The third point*. Do the same for the third sin: the particular sin of *any individual* who has gone to Hell for *a single mortal sin* and also the numberless other people who have gone to Hell for fewer sins than I have committed. ² 'Do the same', I say, with regard to such a third sin, a particular one, calling to memory the gravity and malice of sin against one's Creator and Lord, ³ reflecting with the understanding how someone who has sinned and acted against the infinite goodness has been *justly condemned* for ever. Then conclude with the will as has been said.

The third point completes the history of sin by bringing the effects of sin into the here-and-now. It also corresponds exactly to the second prelude, which is the key to its interpretation. Hence the exercitant is not required at this stage to meditate on Hell (that will be done later), but to consider a possibility, that of a human being cutting himself or herself off from God by a single decisive act of rejection or through the erosion of love by a single capital sin leading to such an act. Again this is considered in order to arouse 'shame and confusion' before the goodness of God.

any individual The situation projected onto a hypothetical stranger (who calls to mind the 'person I have never seen or known' of [185] and [339]) is a real possibility that could have been already realized for the exercitant.

a single mortal sin In both the Versio Prima and the Vulgate Polanco adds 'perhaps' and in the Vulgate he inserts a further 'perhaps' to the 'innumerable others'.

justly condemned It is of the nature of mercy and forgiveness to be undeserved. 'Do not consider what we truly deserve', says the Roman Canon of the Mass, 'but grant us your forgiveness'; the exercitant's confusion comes from realizing that this is precisely how they themselves are treated by God.[64]

Colloquy

In both meditation and contemplation the 'points' lead into the prayer that Ignatius describes in terms of familiar exchange and calls 'colloquy'. Though given a special place at the end of prayer, it is not an appendage to prayer, but its culmination; moreover it may arise at any moment in prayer, and when it does so, it is always, in a sense, a culminating moment.

In the Exercises Ignatius presents the colloquy in various ways. Sometimes he simply invites the exercitant to 'end with a colloquy', sometimes he offers brief guidelines, while the colloquy can also be the context in which he concludes an exercise with specific content or procedures (such is the case here and in the Triple Colloquies). But in whatever form the colloquy is proposed it will always be marked by the personal and spontaneous quality of conversation between friends.

In the present case it is particularly crucial to understand the meaning of colloquy in prayer in the Exercises, for meditation on the three sins is not proposed as an exercise in its own right, with its own completeness, but as a preliminary to this personal meeting with Christ on the cross, the ultimate revelation of both sin and mercy.

[53] [1] **Colloquy.** *Imagining* **Christ our Lord present before me and nailed to the Cross, make a colloquy asking how it came about that** *the Creator made himself a human being* **and from eternal life came to temporal death, and thus** *to die for my sins.* [2] **Then, turning to myself, I will ask, '***What have I done for Christ? What am I doing for Christ? What ought I to do for Christ?***'** [3] **Finally, seeing him in that state hanging on the Cross,** *go over whatever comes to mind.*

[54] [1] **A colloquy, properly so called, means speaking** *as one friend speaks with another***, or a servant with a master,** [2] **at times asking for some favour, at other times accusing oneself of something badly done, or sharing personal concerns and asking for advice about them. And then I will say an Our Father.**

imagining The mode of prayer changes and in the colloquy the exercitant enters on what will be later understood as 'imaginative contemplation'.

[64]Scripture abounds in texts which make the same point; perhaps the best known example comes from the *De profundis*, 'If you, O Lord, should mark iniquities, Lord, who could stand? But there is forgiveness with you, so that you may be revered' (Ps. 130:3).

the Creator made himself a human being The stricken figure on the Cross is none other than the 'Creator of all things'. The language recalls Phil. 2:6–11. The reference is made explicit in the Versio Prima,[65] which contains the verb (*exinanivit se*) used in the Latin New Testament of Christ's 'self-emptying' or 'self-humbling'. In the context of this first exercise, Christ's humility contrasts with the pride that is the root of sin, his use of freedom with the sinner's misuse.

to die for my sins The heart of the colloquy of the cross is here – the Creator died for my sins (the focus at this point is personal). There is an echo of Gal. 2:20: *The son of God loved me and gave himself for me*,[66] (but this is not to be understood in a way that sets the personal in conflict with the communitarian and collective).

What have I done for Christ? What am I doing for Christ? What ought I to do for Christ? It is noticeable that whenever Ignatius gives a content to the colloquy, he presumes the grace asked for in the petition and leads the exercitant a step further. Here, at least in the third question, the focus shifts from past to future, and from 'shame and confusion' to the desire to serve. Note also that these questions represent the typical movement of Ignatian response from the affective to the effective, from the response of the heart to, eventually, the response of 'doing'.

go over whatever comes to mind The general indications contained in the text open the way for the exercitant to find and to dwell upon personal thoughts.

as one friend speaks with another The conversation model brings out the spontaneous and personal character of this prayer, but too strict an interpretation of the model could lead to a limited understanding of colloquy precisely as prayer. The model points primarily to a whole quality of relationship, and does not imply that actual speaking will dominate. In any case, conversation includes listening and in the prayer of a spiritually maturing person colloquy will come increasingly to be characterized by contemplative listening. For friendship as the model of our relationship to Christ, cf. [146, 224, 231].

The conclusion of prayer: 'Our Father'

The 'Our Father', which comes at the end of each of the exercises should be regarded not as a formality, but as a way of giving a consciously Trinitarian conclusion to every time of prayer.

[65]'Let a colloquy be made considering how the Creator emptied himself (*exinanivit se*)'.

[66]Quoted in the *Directory* of González Dávila in connection with [203] (MHSI 76, p. 526 [trans., Palmer, p. 262]).

Second meditation: one's personal sin

In the previous meditation, the exercitant has been considering the history of sin as an objective reality (but in the awareness that one's personal sins involve one in this reality). The present exercise begins with the history of one's own sins. The grace consists of an intense contrition, based on the perception of oneself as a mercifully loved sinner. The sense of sin is heightened as the exercitant relates his or her personal sin to a growing understanding of the nature of sin as an offence against God and his creation, and the exercise culminates in thanksgiving for the mercy of God leading to the intention of amendment.

[55] **[1] THE SECOND EXERCISE IS A MEDITATION OF MY OWN SINS: IT CONTAINS AFTER A PREPARATORY PRAYER AND TWO PRELUDES, FIVE POINTS AND A COLLOQUY**
 [2] Prayer. The preparatory prayer should be the same.
 [3] The first prelude will be the same *composition.*
 [4] The second prelude is *to ask for what I want.* **Here it will be to ask for mounting and intense sorrow, and** *tears* **for my sins.**

[56] **[1] The first point is** *the record of my sins.* **I will call to memory all the sins of a lifetime, looking back on them from year to year or from one period to another. For this, three things will be helpful:**
 [2] (i) to see the place and house where I lived,
 (ii) the relations I have had with others,
 (iii) the occupation in which I have spent my life.

[57] **The second point. To weigh up these sins, considering** *the intrinsic foulness and malice of each deadly sin* **committed,** *quite apart from its being forbidden.*

[58] **[1]** *The third point.* **To look at who I am, diminishing myself by means of comparisons:**
 (i) what am I compared to all the human race?
 [2] (ii) what is the whole human race compared to all the angels and saints in paradise?
 [3] (iii) what can I alone be, as I look at what the whole of creation amounts to in comparison with God?
 [4] (iv) I look upon all *the corruption and foulness of my body;*
 [5] (v) I look at myself as though I were *a running sore,* **from which many sins and evils have flowed, and the most vile poison.**

[59] ¹ *The fourth point.* To consider who God is, against whom I have sinned, *going through his attributes* and contrasting them with their opposites in myself: ² his wisdom with my ignorance, his almighty power with my weakness, his justice with my injustice, his goodness with my malice.

[60] ¹ *The fifth point. An exclamation of wonder*, with intense feeling, as I reflect on the whole range of created beings. How have they ever let me live and kept me alive? ² The angels, who are the swords of divine justice, how have they borne with me, and looked after me, and prayed for me? ³ The saints, too, how have they been able to intercede and pray for me? The heavens, the sun, the moon, the stars, and the elements, the fruits, the birds, the fishes and the animals, how have they kept me alive until now?⁶⁷ ⁴ As for the earth how has it not opened to engulf me, creating new hells where I might suffer for ever?

[61] *Colloquy.* I will conclude with a colloquy about mercy, conversing with God our Lord and thanking him *for giving me life up till now*, proposing for the future *to amend my life* with his grace. Our Father.

composition As in the previous exercise.

to ask for what I want The 'shame and confusion' of the preceding meditation opens the way to a 'mounting and intense sorrow' (*crecido y intenso dolor*), words which denote a deep and powerful feeling or attitude; *tears* i.e. tears which arise from, and in a sense 'embody', the sorrow in the heart. Such tears are a gift, and constitute the second of the three levels of consolation (cf. [316]).

the record of my sins The word 'record' means literally the court record of a trial, and the exercitant comes to the exercise with a mind prepared by the image of a human tribunal (cf. [74]). But the tale of sins also summarizes a history, a personal sinful history that forms a thread woven into the sinful history of the world. However it would be a misunderstanding of Ignatius' purpose to think of this first of the five points as an invitation to rehearse one's life in fine detail. It is the overall impressions and dominant patterns that are important.⁶⁸

---

⁶⁷In the Versio Prima are added the words, 'how have they kept me alive until now?', while in the Autograph the sentence is left incomplete.

⁶⁸The second exercise of this Week is given not for the exercitant to begin examining his conscience for confession, but so that he can look in a global fashion at the many sins he has committed in his past life, and experience dismay at them, come to repentance, etc., *Directory, de Vitoria* (MHSI 76, p. 104 [trans., Palmer, p. 22]).

the intrinsic foulness and malice of each deadly sin The deadly sins are 'foul' because they disfigure human life and conduct; and they have the quality of 'malice' because they are an offence against God and his goodness.

quite apart from its being forbidden The sinful character of the deadly sins is not the result of their being forbidden; they are forbidden because of the foulness and malice they have in themselves. A person of spiritually mature insight senses this intrinsic negative quality of sin.[69]

The third point ... The fourth point Two sets of comparisons bearing respectively on the smallness of the creature in relation to God and the greatness of God in relation to the creature. They are designed to bring home not only the reality of creaturehood itself (constituted by the distance between infinite and finite being), but also the distance of creaturehood as sinful (cf. [58 [4,5]] and [59]).

corruption and foulness[70] of my body Ignatius held the body in considerable honour, but in a way that was acceptable in his day he finds in certain aspects of the body powerful metaphors to describe sin and its effects.[71]

a running sore This image contains the truth that sin is never only personal and private, but contaminates the world itself, especially the quality of other people's lives and the realm of relationships and structures.

going through his attributes Since the language is abstract and concise it is perhaps worth recalling that the function of meditation is to break open such language, asking what the words 'wisdom', 'power', 'justice', 'goodness' mean.

The fifth point. An exclamation of wonder It has been observed that the sense of unworthiness in the presence of creation itself, even indeed of physical nature, is characteristic of the incipient mystic.[72] The main point however is positive. If one can allow even nature (which does not sin) to make one

---

[69]Joseph Rickaby (*Spiritual Exercises*, p. 36) cites in this connection St Thomas Aquinas, *Contra Gentiles*, III 122: 'God is not offended by us except at what we do against our own good'. J. Veale draws attention to the value of this text for expounding the second exercise; cf. 'The First Week: Practical Questions', p. 22.

[70]The word 'foulness' translates the same word (*fealdad*) that was used in [57] of the deadly sins.

[71]The same point can be made by using other images than that proposed by Ignatius, e.g. the image of sin as a cancer cell (suggested with other possibilities by Veltri, *Orientations*, p. 127).

[72]Egan, *Ignatius Loyola the Mystic*, p. 25.

conscious of one's sinfulness, nature itself will also proclaim God's mercy and faithfulness. A literally wonderful sign of these is the simple fact that one is alive and has creation at one's service.[73] In this final point, with its mood of wonder and 'intense affection', the exercitant is already moving towards the concluding prayer of gratitude.

Colloquy Again it must be stressed that in an Ignatian meditation the colloquy is not an appendix, but a culmination. Thus all the foregoing considerations lead to a new appreciation of God's gratuitous mercy.

for giving me life One of the fundamental premises of the First Week meditations is that life itself is a sign of God's continuing fidelity.

up till now The mercy of God has a history. My life, considered above as a history of sin, is also a history of mercy.

to amend my life Amendment is the spontaneous response to a new discovery of the goodness and fidelity of God. The entire language in which Ignatius describes the 'colloquy of mercy' is suggestive of intense consolation, a note heightened still further in the Vulgate by the addition of praise: 'Lastly this meditation must be concluded by a colloquy in which I extol the infinite mercy of God, giving thanks to the best of my power, that He has preserved my life up to this day.'

Third meditation: repetition, Triple Colloquy

The Ignatian prayer of repetition is to be understood in relation to two inseparable processes: the gradual assimilation of the given material, and the development of prayer towards the simple, receptive and personal quality of contemplation. Repetition does not mean making an exercise over again.[74] Though in the repetition one might replay some detail, or even pick up on a point previously overlooked or not reached, repetition is essentially

---

[73]With regard to nature, something of the insight expressed in the fifth point can be discerned in the gentler tones of Gerard Manley Hopkins:
>   Lovely the woods, waters, meadows, combs, vales.
>   All the air things wear that build this world of Wales;
>   Only the inmate does not correspond.
In the Valley of the Elwy, ed. Norman H. Mackenzie, *The Poetical Works of Gerard Manley Hopkins*, Clarendon Press, Oxford (1990), p. 143.

[74]The distinction between repetition in the Ignatian sense and 'making again' is clear in the passage where the exercitant is instructed to make the Two Standards meditation 'Again in the morning with two repetitions' [148].

concerned not with the material given, but with one's own significant responses to it, whether positive or negative. It is a selective and subjective prayer, spacious and unhurried, typified by the 'pause', by staying put where 'I find what I want' [76].

As the exercitant moves from the first two meditations (with their repetitions) to the Triple Colloquy, the dynamic of the First Week enters a further stage of development. In the opening meditations the scale remains large: sin is sin in the singular, the mystery of iniquity that pervades history (even consideration of the exercitant's own sin is the overview of a life history). Future intention while deeply felt, is conceived in broad and indefinite terms: to do things for Christ [53], to amend one's life [61]. In the Triple Colloquy attention fastens on the particular and personal, which the grace of conversion must now penetrate, giving knowledge and changed feelings with regard to the specific sins, sinful propensities and patterns of collusion with the sinful world, which mark the life of the individual exercitant. In form the Triple Colloquy is a prayer to the Father through conscious and explicit recourse to mediation.[75] The somewhat formal procedure (to be followed without detriment to the 'conversational' character of the prayer of colloquy) helps bring home to the exercitant the seriousness of the request being made. To appreciate this form of prayer we must realize too that since both here and in the Second Week the graces being asked for have to do with living a bodily and social existence in the world, Jesus and Mary in the Exercises are not only mediators but exemplars.

[62] [1] THE THIRD EXERCISE IS A REPETITION OF THE FIRST AND SECOND EXERCISES, WITH THREE COLLOQUIES
[2] **After the preparatory prayer and the two preludes, I will repeat the first and second exercises, noting and dwelling upon the points where I have felt *greater consolation or desolation, or greater spiritual relish*.**
[3] **I will then go on to make three colloquies as follows.**

[63] [1] **The first colloquy is to be made to our Lady, so that she will *obtain grace* for me from her Son and Lord for three things:**
[2] **(i)   that I may have a *felt inner knowledge* of my *sins* and an *abhorrence* for them;**
[3] **(ii) that I may feel the *disorder* in my actions, so that finding it abhorrent, I may *amend* my life and *put order* into it.**
[4] **(iii) I will ask for knowledge of *the world*, so that finding it abhorrent I may *cut myself off* from worldly things and *vanities*. Hail Mary.**

---

[75]Namely, the mediations of Jesus and Mary; these are not of course mediations of the same kind.

⁵ **The second colloquy is the same, but to the Son, that he may obtain this for me from the Father. Then an Anima Christi.***
⁶ **The third colloquy is the same but to the Father, so that the eternal Lord Himself may grant me this. Then an Our Father.**

greater consolation or desolation or greater spiritual relish The exercitant is not being asked to dwell on thoughts caused by desolation, which would be in straight contradiction to the Rules for Discernment (cf. especially [318]), but on the aspect of the word of God, or the personal thought in relation to which they were experienced.

obtain grace Petition is at the heart of the Triple Colloquy, but it must be remembered that the prayer of colloquy is a prayer not only of petition, but of 'talking over' [54].

knowledge/abhorrence The exercitant prays for both knowledge and a changed attitude with regard to personal sins, the disorder in one's life, and the sinful world.

felt inner knowledge Literally, 'that I may feel an interior knowledge'. One prays for a 'felt' (not just 'head') knowledge, a knowledge which is 'interior', in the sense explained in connection with [2].

sins Consideration of one's sins at this point may be more specific and more focused on the here-and-now than in the first point of the Second Exercise. But the objective is still not to compile a dossier, but to be graced with 'interior' knowledge.

abhorrence is the antithesis of attraction; the exercitant prays, therefore, that the change of attitude brought about by the previous exercises will be further intensified and will extend specifically to the three areas named in the petition.

disorder The more or less habitual misdirection of the deeper desires or leanings.

amend ... put order ... cut myself off That Ignatius adds these clauses only in connection with 'disorder' and the 'world' suggests that the primary object of the Triple Colloquy is change at the level of the deep affective roots of sin and the external social influences which foster it.

the world The values of society, in so far as these are opposed to Christ and his Kingdom; together with the institutions, conventions and dynamics of

*For text, cf. *Personal Writings*, p. 359.

persuasion that embody these values and give them force. Note especially that the concept of 'world' includes the tendency of the world to rationalize its sinful characteristics and to defend them against scrutiny.[76]

vanities A now trivialized word which tends to suggest the merely 'frivolous'; it is to be understood here to mean what is ultimately 'empty', 'illusory'.

Fourth meditation: resumé

[64] ¹ THE FOURTH EXERCISE *RESUMES* THE THIRD
² By 'resumes', I mean that the understanding, carefully and *without digressing*, should range over the memory of *things contemplated* in the previous exercises. The same three colloquies should be made.

resumes Prayer moves into synthesis: a coming together of details and the emergence of meaning from the interplay between them. But it is a synthesis of things contemplated, not a speculative synthesis.

without digressing I.e. without going onto any subject other than the matter previously contemplated. It is on this matter, and on this matter precisely as penetrated and illuminated by contemplation, that the prayer is concentrated.

things contemplated As noted earlier, meditation moves from an initial 'thinking' stage to the response of the affections. The term 'contemplated' acknowledges this, implying a contemplative quality in the first and second meditations themselves, as well as in the first repetition.

Fifth meditation: Hell

The subject of the final meditation is one which needs to be present to the consciousness of the free person, who is invited to choose life but is capable of choosing death.[77] But in the First Week of the Exercises the meditation on

---

[76]The significance of these three elements could be expressed for a person making the Spiritual Exercises by saying that one finds one's 'sin' in the memory of the past, the 'disorder' in one's present self-awareness, and the 'world' in the future, as the challenge to be met with, when the Exercises are over.

[77]Even in this final meditation the perspective is still that of the personal issue in the exercitant's own life, and the effectiveness of the meditation does not depend on the numbers or even the existence of people actually in Hell. As Hans Urs von Balthasar remarks: 'If the threats of judgement and the cruel, horrifying images of the gravity of the punishments imposed upon sinners that we find in scripture and tradition have any point, then it is surely, in the first instance, to make *me* see the seriousness of the responsibility that I bear along with my freedom' (*Dare We Hope 'That All Men Are Saved'?*, p. 211); see B. Grogan, 'Giving the Exercise on Hell'.

Hell is not for Ignatius the starting-point of conversion, but a confirmation. It comes after the exercitant has had the experience of God's merciful love. Made in a climate of trust in that love, it is made too in the awareness that we are capable of refusing love. Though the petition is for the grace of fear, the meditation ends on a note of *thanksgiving* for God's loving mercy, and implicit in the thanksgiving for the past is *trust* for the future, yet a trust which must never degenerate into presumption or complacency.

There are many ways in which the subject of Hell might be approached in meditation. The approach adopted in the fifth exercise consists in a particular form of the 'prayer of the senses' which concludes the contemplative day in the Second to Fourth Weeks. However while in the later exercises the senses give access to a personal *presence*, here they lead to the interior sense of a *situation*, that of damnation. The text as it stands reflects the imagination of another age, but exercitants today might still find their own ways of meaningfully bringing the senses to bear on the subject of Hell.

[65] ¹ THE FIFTH EXERCISE⁷⁸ IS A MEDITATION ON HELL; IT CONTAINS AFTER THE PREPARATORY PRAYER AND THE TWO PRELUDES *FIVE POINTS* AND A COLLOQUY
² Prayer. The preparatory prayer should be as usual.
³ The first prelude, the *composition*, is here to see with the eyes of the imagination *the length, breadth and depth of Hell*.
⁴ The second prelude, is *to ask for what I want*. Here it will be to ask for an interior sense of the suffering undergone by the damned
⁵ so that if through my faults I should ever forget the love of the eternal Lord, at least the fear of punishments may help me not to fall into sin.

[66] The first point will be to look with the eyes of the imagination at the great flames and at souls as though in bodies of fire.

[67] The second point. To *hear with one's ears* the wailings, howls, cries, blasphemies against Christ our Lord and against all the saints.

[68] The third point. To smell with the sense of smell smoke, sulphur, filth and putrefaction.

[69] The fourth point. To *taste with the sense of taste* bitter things, such as tears, sadness, and the pangs of conscience.

---

⁷⁸The title 'Fifth ... Meditation' does not mean that every day of the First Week should necessarily include a meditation on Hell. In the time of the *Directories* the subject was commonly introduced only on the second day, as noted above, and later in the Week its place could be taken by additional subjects mentioned in the Vulgate: cf. *Directories* (MHSI 76, pp. 386, 391, 435, 541 [trans., Palmer, pp. 170, 172–3, 201, 270]).

[70] The fifth point. To feel with the sense of touch; that is to say, how those in Hell are touched and burned by the fires.

[71] ¹ Colloquy. As I make a *colloquy with Christ* our Lord, I will recall to my memory the persons who are in Hell, some because they did not believe in his coming, others because while believing they did not act according to his commandments; ² dividing them into three categories: first, those before his coming, second, those during his lifetime, and third, those after his lifetime in this world. ³ And with that I will give thanks to him for not allowing me to fall into any of these categories by putting an end to my life. ⁴ Likewise, I will thank him for his constant loving kindness and mercy towards me right *up to the present moment*. I will conclude with an Our Father.[79]

Five Points These induce the sense of an existence totally against God and totally in thrall to evil.[80]

composition ... the length, breadth and depth of Hell I.e. the three dimensions of space. Before coming on to imagine Hell as a situation, one makes oneself present to Hell as a place (which, for Ignatius, it literally was).

to ask for what I desire For a fear that might serve to reinforce 'love of the eternal Lord' (here a Christ title). Both love and fear are mentioned for the first time. At this stage the exercitant may be expected to be experiencing a very profound love for the God whose kindness has been borne in on one in the preceding meditations. The petition looks to the future, a future to which the key will be love, but in which love also will remain subject to weakness, and therefore always in need of humility. A large part of the 'grace' of this meditation is precisely to keep our love humble.

hear with one's ears Note that the blasphemies are against 'Christ our Lord'.

taste with the sense of taste As in the prayer of the senses explained below [121–126] one of the points entails an 'interior' or metaphorical sensing; [124] there it will be the senses of taste and smell, here it is the sense of taste. This interior sensing is an important key to the meaning of this kind of prayer.

[79]In both the Versio Prima and the Vulgate the following note, written in the hand of Polanco, appears between the end of the Fifth Exercise and the next paragraph [72]: 'In the opinion of the one giving the Exercises it might be of benefit to the exercitant to add other meditations: e.g. on death and other punishments of sin, on judgement, etc. It should not be thought that such meditations are not allowed, even though they are not given here.'

[80]Scripture texts on this theme include: Deut. 30:15–20; Sirach 5:4–8, 15:11–21; Matt. 7:21–28, 8:11–12, 22:13, 25:31–46; Lk. 13:22–30, 15:19–31; John 13:30.

colloquy with Christ The exercitant 'talks about' Hell with Christ himself; the points are a preliminary to this. That Ignatius lays down the broad lines of the conversation does not negate the spontaneity essential to the prayer of colloquy.

Sin is defined in relation to Christ: it consists in the refusal to believe in him and/or to follow his commandments. The numbers of the damned (assumed in Ignatius' age to be large) are classified according to their historical relationship to the Incarnation, the centre-point of history.

up to the present moment Gratitude for the past (again, life is the sign of God's loving fidelity) leads to trust for the future, and it is in the context of thanks and trust that the exercitant wishes his or her own response in the future to be supported, and saved from complacency, by a graced fear.

[72] [1] NOTE
The first exercise should be made at midnight, the second on rising in the morning, the third before or after Mass, as long as it is made before the midday meal, the fourth at the time of Vespers, the fifth an hour before supper. [2] I intend this timetable (more or less) to be applied always during the four weeks in so far as age, constitution and temperament allow the exercitant to do five exercises or fewer.

ADDITIONS

In each of the Weeks, Ignatius includes practical notes which he calls 'additions'.[81] Of the ten given here, the first, third, fourth, and fifth, together with the final note on the examen [90] remain constant throughout the Exercises. As the Exercises go on, the others are modified or replaced (cf. [130, 131, 206, 229]).

The additions represent the distillation of much experience and the text of the Exercises itself leaves no doubt about the importance Ignatius attached to careful observance of them (cf. [6, 90, 130, 160]). But they are not to be applied woodenly. They are of value in so far as they help the exercitant to 'make the Exercises better', and more specifically, to find what he or she desires. If the additions are to serve this purpose, it is necessary that account be taken of the individual, as Ignatius explains in the *Directory* dictated to Vitoria:

> In observing the rules or ten additions which are given for making the Exercises well, care should be taken to have them observed very exactly, as is directed, seeing to it that there is neither excess nor too much laxity.

[81]For further reading on the Additions, see Brian Grogan, 'To make the Exercises better'.

The exercitants' characters also need to be taken into account. Melancholic persons should not be pressed too hard, but given free rein with most of them; the same is true of persons who are delicate and not much used to such things. But careful thought must be given to what will be most helpful. I myself have employed leniency in these rules with some persons, and it did them good; with others I used considerable strictness, but as gently as possible, and I observed that by the Lord's grace this did them good also.[82]

In accommodating the additions to the individual today, the director needs also to be aware of psychological and cultural differences between a sixteenth- and late twentieth-century exercitant, and of the particular situation in which the Exercises are being made (e.g. in a retreat-house, a group, etc.). But in order to modify the additions, one needs first to appreciate their purpose. Why did Ignatius believe that these practical recommendations might 'help' the exercitant, and indeed help very significantly? One thing they 'help' to do is to integrate into the Exercises *the time outside formal prayer*. In this time, the moment of going to bed, the moment of waking and the quarter hour immediately following prayer receive special attention; but the additions also offer ways of helping the exercitant to remain in the Exercises throughout the day. As well as doing this they help the exercitant both in prayer and at other times, *to involve the whole person* in the Exercises. Everything that affects consciousness – emotions, thoughts, imagination, senses, posture, the effects of environment – all this as far as possible needs to be brought into line with the desired 'end'. Since the Spirit is working all the time throughout the Exercises, so all the time the exercitant is concerned, conscientiously, but without stress, to co-operate in that work.

[73] [1] **ADDITIONS FOR MAKING THE EXERCISES BETTER AND FOR FINDING MORE READILY** *WHAT ONE DESIRES*

what one desires For 'desire' understand both the overall desire to find God's will, to make progress, and to become free from disordered attachments, but also the particular desires, which vary as the Exercises develop.

Additions 1 to 5: aids to prayer

[2] **The first addition: After going to bed,** *as I am about to go to sleep,* **I will think for the space of a Hail Mary of the time I have to get up,**

[82]MHSI 76, p. 104 [trans., Palmer, p. 105]. The passage reappears in substance in the *1599 Directory* (MHSI 76, p. 661 [trans., Palmer, pp. 316–7]).

and *for what purpose*, **going over the exercise I have to make.**

[74] [1] **The second addition. Immediately on waking, without allowing my thoughts to stray, I will turn my attention to the subject I am about to contemplate in the first exercise at midnight. I will rouse myself to confusion for my many sins by using examples,** [2] **such as that of** *a knight coming before the king* **and his court, filled with shame and confusion for serious offences against the Lord from whom in the past he has received many gifts and many favours.** [3] **Similarly, for the second exercise, I will see myself as** *a great sinner in chains*, **about to appear, bound, before the supreme and eternal judge;** [4] **here taking as example the way in which prisoners deserving of death appear in chains before a judge in this world.** [5] **I will get dressed with thoughts like these in my mind, or others adapted to the proposed material.**

as I am about to go to sleep The integration of the whole day into the Exercises includes the integration of the exercitant's last thoughts before sleep,[83] and of their thoughts on waking. For the night only practical acts of memory and intention are commended, imagination and emotion are not mentioned. On rising however, both during the night and in the morning, the imagination is enlisted to create a preparatory mood for the meditation about to be made. Elsewhere Ignatius suggests less elaborate preparations, suited to any prayer, either within the Exercises (cf. [130, 206, 229] or indeed outside of them (cf. [239, 244, 245, 250, 258]). But the imaginative scenarios proposed here correspond to quite specific stages within the First Week sequence and are for use only in connection with the first and second meditations (cf. [88]).

for what purpose See [131, 239].

a knight coming before the king The exercitant is being prepared to pray for the grace of the first meditation, namely 'shame and confusion' before the risen Christ, Lord of the world, from whom great favours have been received. While other imagery might hold more appeal for an exercitant today, Ignatius' example illustrates clearly what he means by 'shame and confusion' in the first exercise.

a great sinner in chains Imagery preparing the exercitant to come before God with his or her 'record' of sin [56]. But note that from experiencing oneself

---

[83]For a comment on the First Addition in relation to the function of sleep, see Grogan, 'To make the Exercises Better', p. 22, n. 40; and the article by Karl Rahner referred to by Grogan, 'A Spiritual Dialogue at Evening: on Sleep, Prayer and Other Subjects'.

as a sinner confronting justice and death, the exercitant moves into a meditation which concludes with the gratitude of a sinner forgiven and granted life [61].

[75] ¹ The third addition. A step or two *before the place* where I have to contemplate or meditate, I will stand for the space of an Our Father ² and, with my mind raised up, consider how *God our Lord is looking at me, etc.*, I will then *make a genuflexion* or some other act of humility.

before the place Though the Exercises are to be made wholly in a climate of prayer, the exercitant does not pray continuously in the same way as one does during a formal 'exercise', with its definite beginning, duration and end. The beginning of prayer is marked by a mental act and by an accompanying bodily ritual.

God our Lord is looking at me One approaches prayer by recognizing oneself as here and now known by God and loved. The same verb (*mirar*) is used in [102] to describe the Divine Persons looking down on the world and planning its salvation.

etc. As always in the Exercises, with an *et cetera* like this, Ignatius invites the exercitant to discover latent meanings.

make a genuflexion The value Ignatius set upon bodily posture, together with his sense of space, are apparent in this suggested procedure, and in the addition which follows.

**[76] ¹ The fourth addition. *I will enter* upon the contemplation, *now kneeling, now lying on the ground* prostrate or face upwards, now seated, now standing, but always intent on the search for what I want.
² Two things should be noted: first, if I find what I want whilst kneeling, I will go no further, and similarly if prostrate, etc.;
³ second, *where I find what I want, I will settle down*, without any anxiety to move on, until I am satisfied.**

I will enter If the recommendation of the previous addition is followed, entry into prayer is a literal as well as a mental step.

now kneeling, now lying on the ground The fourth addition picks up and develops the link between prayer and bodily comportment and sets down a basic principle regarding the comportment of the heart and mind in prayer.

Of the various postures proposed here none is commended as more inherently appropriate than another. The criterion for posture is simply conduciveness to 'what I desire', given, as Ignatius adds in [88], suitability to place and occasion. But in all the postures mentioned the body is physically still.

where I find what I desire, I will settle down Through the given points of the Exercises the exercitant seeks what he or she desires; one seeks in order to find, and the response to 'finding' is to dwell upon what one has found. This contemplative principle[84] applies to every prayer situation, but in the Exercises it clearly has a particular bearing on repetition (cf. [62, 118, 227]).

> [77] [1] **The fifth addition.** *After finishing* **the exercise I will** *either sit down or walk around* **for a quarter of an hour while I** *see how things have gone for me* **during the contemplation or meditation.** [2] *If badly*, **I will look for the cause, and having found it, I will be sorry, in order to do better in the future;** [3] **and** *if well*, **I will thank God our Lord and proceed in the same way another time.**

After finishing The practice outlined in the fifth addition is generally known today as the 'review' of prayer. It consists in a transitional space, in which the insights and experiences of the preceding hour remain present in immediate memory, but where there is place for a monitoring and reflection which would have been inappropriate during prayer itself. In the Exercises its function is to be understood in relation to the overall process of these. Hence one reflects with reference especially to the grace sought in the preparatory prayer, and more specifically in the prelude of the current exercise. The review forms part of the exercitant's preparation for further prayer, and can serve to put him or her in touch with matter for 'repetition' [62, 118]. The time following the review is an obvious moment for the personal writing mentioned in connection with [100] below.

either sit down or walk around The omission of kneeling and lying itself indicates the distinction between the potentially more intense experience of (formal) prayer and the review following it. Walking was considered by Ignatius as positively helpful to reflection after prayer, and to calming of the mind before prayer (cf. [239]), though he did not recommend it for prayer itself.

---

[84]On this point the fourth addition provides a notable illustration of the observation made in the *1599 Directory* that in the Exercises things of great importance are often treated with deceptive brevity: (MHSI 76, pp. 509–601 [trans., Palmer, p. 301]).

see how things have gone for me In both the Autograph and the Vulgate the formulation is passive; one starts by asking what happened.

If badly Desolation or distraction in prayer or even a paucity of 'movements' (cf. [6]) do not necessarily mean that one has fallen short in the generosity, docility or discernment called for on our part in prayer. But in looking for the causes one considers this possibility, and checks one's own co-operation in prayer against the preceding additions, particularly the fourth.

if well Locating faults is not the primary object of the review. The exercitant must recognize the ways in which in the time of prayer one has truly 'sought' and (more important still) 'found' what one desired; for these graces one must take time to be grateful.

Additions 6 to 9: Helps towards sustaining the climate of the Exercises throughout the day

The process of the Exercises goes on all the time. God acts according to his sovereign freedom (cf. [330]) and his action cannot be scheduled. Insights, and the movements of consolation and desolation are not confined to set times of prayer. Indeed it is a fact of experience that in the Exercises the moments of breakthrough often occur outside the times of set prayer. As far as possible therefore, an attitude of readiness for the action of God needs to be maintained throughout the day. As helps towards maintaining this readiness the following additions propose limiting the scope of one's thoughts and feelings (Addition 6), creating a 'First Week friendly' physical environment (Addition 7), and exercising a certain restraint in one's few dealings with others (Additions 8 and 9).

> [78] [1] **The sixth addition. We should not want to think about agreeable or glad things such as final glory or resurrection, etc., because feelings of pain, grief and tears for our sins are only impeded by thoughts about joy and gladness. [2] Instead, I will keep in mind that it is my wish to grieve and to feel pain and I will rather bring to memory death and judgement.**

In the First Week, the exercitant will in fact experience a wider range of feelings than those specified here: he or she will experience affection, gratitude, wonder, and the joy of forgiveness (the joy proper to the First Week). The joyful thoughts one should wish to avoid are those, therefore, which induce the kind of joy that does *not* belong to the First Week. However Ignatius insists too on the particular importance in the First Week of 'pain, grief and tears for our sins', for only in so far as one enters into this graced sorrow (which is in fact a form of consolation, cf. [316]) will the rest be authentic.

It should be noted that the exercitant is not being told to *force* thoughts and feelings.[85] The key is desire. The exercitant's deep desire is for the sorrow that opens the way to the transforming experience of mercy. In so far as he or she is present to this desire, sorrow and the thoughts that conduce to it will be wanted, thoughts and feeling which impede these will be unwanted.

[79] The seventh addition. For the same purpose I will exclude all light, by closing shutters and doors whilst I am in my room, except in order to recite the office, to read and to eat.[86]

[80] The eighth addition. I will avoid laughing or saying anything likely to provoke laughter.

[81] The ninth addition. I will put a guard on the eyes, except to receive or take leave of someone with whom I speak.

Addition 10: Penance

Penance consists essentially not in exterior practices but in a change of heart. Thus what Ignatius calls 'interior penance' is synonymous with 'repentance'. It is characteristic of Ignatius to begin this brief treatment of penance by insisting that the value of 'exterior' penance ('practices') lies in their relationship to change of heart.

[82] [1] The tenth addition is concerned with penance, which can be divided into interior and exterior. [2] Interior penance consists in grief for one's sins with the firm determination not to commit again either those or any others; [3] while exterior penance, which is the fruit of the first, is punishment imposed on oneself for sins committed. There are *three main ways* on which this can be practised.

[85]Ignatius was well aware of the danger of 'breaking one's head' by excessive attempts at thought control. Thus in a letter to Teresa Rejadell he stresses the need for 'recreation', by which he means 'a healthy relaxation when the mind is given freedom to roam at leisure over any good or indifferent subjects that keep clear of evil thoughts', *Epp. Ig.*, No. 8 (MHSI 1, pp. 107–9 [trans., *Personal Writings*, p. 136]).

[86]Cf. [130⁴, 229⁴]. The suggestion that the First Week exercitant might shut out the sunlight, though often regarded as bordering on the inhuman, seems to have caused little difficulty to the mainly Mediterranean authors of the *Directories*. The one author who shows some reservations, Lawrence Nicolai, was a Norwegian (see MHSI 76, p. 361 [trans., Palmer, p. 158]).

three main ways Ignatius distinguishes three forms of penitential practice: fasting [83], 'vigils' [84] and various kinds of self-inflicted pain or physical discomfort [85]. The first two practices have their origin in the Bible, and both figure prominently in the life of Jesus himself. Those specified in [85] originate in the Middle Ages. They are not to be found in the apostolic Church. In the time of Ignatius, such penances were a standard characteristic of religious life; and there is a long history of self-flagellation and its often morbid and extreme forms. Heir as he was to the medieval tradition, Ignatius regarded the use of disciplines and hair shirts as something quite normal. Typically, however, he insists on moderation [86] and, as a founder, broke new ground in establishing a religious order in which neither these nor any other forms of bodily penance were imposed by rule.

[83] [1] The first regards food. In this matter, to go without the superfluous is *not penance but temperance*; [2] penance begins when we go without what is in itself appropriate, and the more this is done, the greater and better is the penance, as long as the constitution is not harmed and no serious illness results.

not penance but temperance Temperance consists in cutting down superfluities (for further comment see notes on the Rules for Eating). More than many classical spiritual masters, Ignatius regarded temperance (as distinct from penance) as an important Christian quality and the acquisition of it as an ascetical discipline in its own right. For an intemperate person, for whom the superfluous has become a personal necessity, the asceticism demanded by temperance will indeed be very considerable; but 'penance' as defined here retains its particular character. The more a person is temperate the more he or she is in a position to practise a penance which promotes and expresses deep conversion of the heart.

[84] [1] The second regards the way we sleep. Here once again it is not penance to go without the superfluous, the finer quality and more comfortable, [2] but penance begins when we go without what is in itself suitable in the way we sleep. Again, the more this is done the better, as long as the constitution is not harmed and no serious illness results, [3] and provided nothing is retrenched from needful sleep, except in order to arrive at a just mean, if we have the bad habit of sleeping too much.

[85] The third is to chastise the body, that is, to inflict sensible pain on it. This is done by wearing hair cloth, cords or iron chains next to the skin; by whipping or inflicting wounds on oneself, and by other kinds of austerities.

71

[86] [1] Note. The most practical and the safest principle in regard to penance seems to be that pain should be felt in the flesh and not penetrate to the bone, so that the result is pain and not illness. [2] Therefore it would seem more appropriate to strike oneself with thin cords, which give external pain, rather than in some other way which could cause serious internal illness.

Additional notes

[87] [1] First note. Exterior penances are practised chiefly *for three purposes*: first, to make *reparation* for past sins; [2] second, *to overcome self*, so that one's sensual nature may be obedient to reason, and all the lower parts of the self may become more submissive to the higher; [3] third, *to seek and find some grace* or gift that a person wishes for and desires. For instance, one may desire to have inner contrition for one's sins, [4] or to weep abundantly, either over one's sins or over the pains and sorrows endured by Christ our Lord; or one may desire to resolve some present doubt.

for three purposes I.e. three ways in which the body participates in conversion, which if it is to be authentic must include the whole person.

reparation Penance brings a bodily component into contrition; through it the body, as it were, says 'Sorry'.

to overcome self Conversion is a graced process of personal integration, a process which Ignatius understands in terms of the faculty theology of his time. This process has an ascetical dimension and penance is the body's involvement in this.

to seek and to find some grace Penance is the body's prayer of petition, serving both to prove and intensify the commitment and sincerity of one's desires. A desire expressed in penance is not a velleity.

[88] [1] Second note. It should be noticed that the first and second additions[87] are to be put into practice for the midnight and dawn exercises, but not for the exercises made at other times. [2] The fourth addition is never to be put into practice in church in the presence of other people, but only in private, for instance in one's own home, etc.

[89] [1] Third note. When the exercitant still does not find what he or she desires (for instance, tears, consolations, etc.), it is often very

[87]Cf. [74, 76] with comments.

profitable to make some alteration in eating and sleeping, and in other penitential practices. ² Thus *we can make changes* in our practice, by doing penance for two or three days, and then for another two or three leaving it off, for it suits some people to do more penance, and others to do less. ³ Moreover, we frequently give up penance through sensuality or because we judge falsely that the human constitution cannot bear it without serious illness. ⁴ Sometimes on the other hand, thinking that the body can endure it, we practise excessive penance. ⁵ As God our Lord knows our nature infinitely better than we do, he often allows us through such alternations to perceive what is suitable for each.

we can make changes Ignatius assumes that penance of some kind is always called for in the First Week. (In the Second Week, there are times when penance is appropriate and times when it is not, cf. [130].) Actual practice however is a highly personal matter; and indeed for some there may be days with penance and days without. But whatever the exercitant's penitential practices, they must be such as to fit in with the Exercises. Like postures in prayer they are changed or persisted in strictly in accordance with the criterion of 'help' or 'hindrance' in relation to the 'end sought'. Decisions about penance must be made in the light of an honest recognition of one's tendencies – to excess or to self-indulgence. The statement that God himself gives individuals the graces to know what is suitable for them puts these decisions in the realm of 'discernment' properly so-called. Decisions in the matter of penance are made by the exercitant himself or herself.[88]

[90] Fourth note. The particular examen[89] should be made in order to remove faults and negligences in the practice of the exercises and additions. This holds for the Second, Third and Fourth Weeks as well.

---

[88]Ignatius' own instructions are that the exercitant should be told what the Exercises have to say on the subject of penance, and if the person asks for an 'instrument' such as a discipline or hair shirt, 'or the like, the director should ordinarily offer to give him what he asks', *Directory of Ignatius* (MHSI 76, p. 80 [trans., Palmer, p. 11]). The concern of the early directors to respect the freedom and discretion insisted on by Ignatius in the matter of penance is abundantly clear from the *Directories*. There is much on the need to draw attention to penance in the case of those who play it down, but also much on the need to restrain the over-zealous. The director should know what penances the exercitant is doing.

[89]Cf. Annotation 6 [6] and Particular Examen [24–31], with notes, above.

SECOND WEEK

Content and dynamic[1]

Four categories of material make up the composition of this Second Week.

(1) The *mysteries* of the life of Christ: various subjects for contemplation drawn from the Gospels.
(2) The pieces sometimes known today as the 'Ignatian meditations' i.e. Kingdom, Two Standards, Three Classes, Three Kinds of Humility. These contain important elements of spiritual doctrine and provide a lens through which to interpret the exercises that follow them. In ways which will become apparent later they serve to advance the Second Week dynamic.
(3) The triple colloquy, introduced in the Two Standards meditation and running through the week as a central motif.
(4) The material bearing on *election*, material which is not confined to the explicit treatment [169–189], but which is to be found interspersed through the text. Thus the theme is introduced after the contemplation on the Infancy narratives [135], from which point everything is set in relationship to the election (either as immediate preparation or as background).

Through this material, the exercitant is drawn into a double process: first, ongoing growth into *the true life taught by Christ* [139]; second, the process of seeking and finding and responding to God's here-and-now word, i.e. *election*.

The election theme, as we have seen, does not imply that only people faced with critical choices can make the Exercises in their fullness. But it becomes clear in the Second Week that the Exercises, as they stand, centre upon the election, and that growth in Christ and election are proposed as mutually complementary, growth in Christ being the necessary context for election, while seeking and assenting to God's will is itself the active compo-

---

[1]Though the Second Week begins, strictly speaking, with the contemplation on the Incarnation, the exercise on the Kingdom is included in the following introductory survey since it serves itself as an introduction to the week and deals with many of its characteristic themes.

nent of such growth. It is essential that the director appreciate this in order to use the Exercises for exercitants in other situations.

In the text of the Exercises the Second Week processes come together in the following sequence:[2]

1. Contemplation of the Incarnation and the Infancy [101–134].
2. Introduction to election [135–157, 165–168].
3. Election and the contemplation of the public life [161–164, 169–189].

Towards the *true life* in Christ

In the Second Week ongoing growth in the true life of Christ is promoted by a deepening and intensifying of the exercitant's personal love for Christ, and by a focusing of mind and will on certain attitudes, or life-stances, implicit in this love.

The personal love of Christ, which is the grace of the Second Week, is a love which changes and re-orientates the whole person. It is the love by which we allow the loved-one to take over our lives, to lead us along his own ways towards his own objectives, the love by which we trust ourselves to the other's power to change us. One characteristic of such love, especially to be noted in connection with the spirituality of the Exercises, is expressed in the word 'imitation'. Christ is seen not only as teacher, but as representing a model (cf. [344]). And while conformity to the Christ-model takes an infinite variety of forms, the love supposed in the Exercises is the love of the disciple who, while seeking the signs of God's will, would prefer, on his or her side, to be more rather than less literally Christ-like in all activities, situations and way of life.

In the Second Week Exercises a person advancing through contemplation in a love of this kind is made especially aware of certain specific qualities of the true life in Christ, and experiences these as desirable. The true life will be *humble* [146, 165–167], a word which indicates a God-centredness stemming from freedom from the self-centredness of pride. It will also be marked by the liberality towards God that the language of the Exercises pinpoints in the word 'more' (*más*).[3] It is thus characteristic of the true life to desire to make offering 'of greater moment' [97], to choose the course 'more' agreeable to the Divine Goodness [151] and 'more' ordered to God's glory [152], to experience the gratuitous preferences of the third Kind of Humility [167, 168].

---

[2]Cf. Cusson, *Biblical Theology*, pp. 243–5.

[3]This insistence on the 'more' must nevertheless be dissociated from a self-driven ethic ('must try harder') with which the Ignatian *magis* is sometimes associated. We are concerned with the 'more' of Christ's invitations and of the expanding possibilities of his grace, not the 'more' of compulsion.

But the main emphasis in the Second Week is on the quality of spiritual poverty, a never out-grown mark of a follower of the true life in Christ, and one which the Exercises present especially as the condition for everything else in that life [146, 147]. Rooted in trust-love, the love of the person whose treasure and therefore heart is in Christ, spiritual poverty manifests itself in two ways. First, it is a radical non-possessiveness with regard to any creature, a freedom from any spirit of idolatry, of however subtle and sophisticated a kind, in relation to 'riches and honour'. But it also consists in a converted attitude to situations of insecurity, loss, diminishment, etc., situations entailing, in a literal or extended sense, the experience of 'actual poverty'.[4]

The person who is spiritually poor, whatever his or her personal situation, is open to, sets value on, and even desires such situations. Indeed such a person can take the risk, in faith and trust, to ask for them [147, 157]. However, humility, generosity and spiritual poverty are qualities often sought in relation to an individualistic concept of perfection. In the Exercises, on the contrary, they are sought in relation to the call made to every Christian to the service of the Kingdom, a service which is a sharing in Christ's own continuing mission in the world [95]. To imitate Christ, to lead the true life, and to grow in its qualities, one must be associated in this mission.[5] Indeed one must be associated in it not only by sharing Christ's work, but, at least as a desired ideal, by being involved in the very pattern of vulnerability and powerlessness which embodied his self-emptying.

Trinity

The spirituality of the Second Week, as of the Exercises in their entirety, is both Christocentric and Trinitarian. The immediately obvious aspect of Christology in the Second Week is of course the human reality of the Incarnation. Less obvious on a perfunctory reading, yet fundamental to the spirituality of the Exercises, is the relationship of Christ to the Trinity. The salvation of the human race is the work of the Trinity [107], which decides on the Incarnation [102]. Christ is our mediator with the Father (Triple Colloquy). The work of Christ is the work of the Father [95]. The

---

[4]To appreciate the central importance of Ignatius' doctrine on poverty of spirit we must realize that while the literal sense of 'poverty' (and of riches) must never be underplayed, these terms also hold meanings beyond the literal sense, which individuals have to find for themselves. Thus one person's 'riches' might consist in 'one's good name, activity, body, strength, beauty, talents, achievements, art, ideas, friendships, or even one's integral observance of the law', Cusson, *Biblical Theology*, p. 256.

[5]This should not be taken to imply that according to the Exercises every truly Christian life is explicitly or formally apostolic. There are other ways of being involved in Christ's work of establishing the Kingdom than by doing 'apostolic work', in the ordinary sense of the term.

exercitant therefore contemplates the life of Christ in the consciousness that the Trinitarian God is manifest in that life. Thus one is conscious that to share in the life of Christ is to share the life of the Trinity; to be involved in Christ's mission is to be involved in the work of the Trinity in the world. Moreover the Exercises in their entirety are made 'in the Spirit', who gives consolation and enlightenment together with the gift of discernment. The whole doctrine of election is founded on the principle that in the search for the will of God, the Christian is moved by the Holy Spirit.

THE KINGDOM[6]

All early commentators and the majority of modern ones holds this to be one of the major components of the Exercises, comparable in importance to the Two Standards, with which it is closely connected.[7]

The exercise gives the exercitant a new self-image. No longer the shamed knight of the First Week, the exercitant is now the knight restored to friendship and established in the relationship which will be the basis of the remaining weeks of the Exercises – a relationship in which the intimacy of personal union and participation in Christ's mission in the world are inseparably combined. And it is within the climate of positive feeling, even enthusiasm, thus engendered that the exercitant is introduced to the theme of union with Christ in the paradoxical values of poverty and humiliation.

Nevertheless, there are certain significant differences between the Kingdom and the later Ignatian meditations of the Second Week. The Kingdom is designated neither as a contemplation nor a meditation, but simply as an 'exercise' [99]. It is made formally only twice, in the course of what today we would call a 'repose day'. It contains no Triple Colloquy, and as a careful reading makes clear, the exercitant does not at this point actually *make* the concluding offering. But these differences do not imply that the Kingdom Exercise is of secondary importance. Rather they indicate that its function is preparatory. It can be described as a second Principle and Foundation.[8]

---

[6]The commonly accepted title of the exercise, 'The Kingdom', is derived from the Vulgate translation: cf. [91]. In the body of the text the word 'kingdom' does not appear in either the Autograph or the Latin versions. The meaning of the phrase 'Kingdom of God' is equally conveyed by 'reign of God'.

[7]According to Nadal, the Kingdom and the Two Standards go back in substance to the mystical experiences at Manresa: '(At Manresa) our Lord communicated the Exercises to him, and guided him in such a way that he devoted himself entirely to God's service and to the salvation of souls. The Lord showed this to him especially in two exercises, those on the King, and the Two Standards.' *Ep. et Mon. Nadal*, vol. v (MHSI, vol. 90, p. 40), *Fontes Narrativi*, vol. 1 (MHSI, vol. 66, pp. 306–7).

[8]See *1599 Directory* (MHSI 76, pp. 669–701 [trans., Palmer, p. 320]).

The exercise falls into three sections: (1) the preliminary parable [92–94]; (2) the call of Christ to the service of the Kingdom [95]; (3) two levels of response [96–98]. In this structure, it is the second section which is central: the contemplation of Christ inviting all men and women to share in his work in the world and in the cost of discipleship. The first part, the parable of the crusader king, provides an introduction to this contemplation, and is wholly subordinate to it.

The introductory parable

The introductory parable can be explained in terms of two main objectives. First, it prepares the exercitant to meet Christ in a new way, not only as personal saviour but as Lord of the universe, who calls his friends to share his work in building the Kingdom of God in the world. To convey this dimension of Christ Ignatius uses the traditional image of a king, and the parable serves to make the exercitant conscious of the human ideal that we apply transcendentally to Christ when we speak of him as 'king'. Second, by eliciting the exercitant's instinctive response to the idea of a noble but exigent human enterprise, it makes him or her aware of the resources of energy, love, ambition and idealism which Christ wishes to enlist in the service of the Kingdom.[9]

The original success of the parable in achieving these objectives is due partly to elements of Ignatius' culture: the simultaneously secular and religious character of chivalry, and the particular intimacy, compounded of friendship, loyalty and shared action, which was the mark of the lord–vassal relationship. But the parable also owes its success precisely to an unreal quality, to the fact that it converts potent social and cultural realities into the material of dreams.[10]

How should the parable be dealt with by the modern director? Though some exercitants can still take the parable as it stands, it fails for many reasons to be effective in the way it was when it touched the collective unconscious of an age. These reasons include the misapprehension that the warfare imagery is more significant than Ignatius intended.[11] The main diffi-

[9]On this function of the Kingdom Exercise, see Cusson, *Biblical Theology*, pp. 179–81.

[10]'To understand what Ignatius is trying to do in this parable, it is important to notice that no one like this king ever existed, and that Ignatius knew this as well as we do. There never had been a king or emperor of all Christendom; no Christian ruler had ever conducted a successful crusade "against all the lands of the infidels". Nor was there any likelihood that such a king would ever exist. Ignatius was deliberately appealing to dreams.' Connolly, 'Story of the Pilgrim King and the Dynamics of Prayer', Fleming, ed., *Notes on the Spiritual Exercises*, p. 104.

[11]Cf. [91] and comment.

culty however comes from the central image of the hero-king: for many today the idea of kingship has lost its magic, nor is everyone any longer stirred by the classic type of hero. The parable is also widely considered to be too masculine in tone to be generally suited for contemporary use. Hence new approaches have to be found. Among the more widely adopted current approaches, the following may be singled out for mention.[12]

(1) The director and/or exercitant create a modern parable, set in the modern world and featuring a mythical hero with contemporary appeal, e.g. a mythical campaigner for the oppressed, hungry, ignorant, etc., of the world today.[13]

(2) Instead of a mythical hero, the exercitant finds some personally inspiring person, contemporary or historical.[14]

(3) The exercitant designs his or her own parable, looking to that of Ignatius not so much for its content as for its objective of raising awareness of personal capacities. The exercitant devises whatever parable will best encapsulate the desires and ideals contained in their own history.[15]

(4) Using Ignatius' parable as a starting-point the exercitant dwells not so much on the concrete images (kings, knights, crusade, etc.) as on the ideas these images embody; he or she considers the characteristics of ideal leadership or of an ideally worthwhile enterprise, the kind of enterprise which would draw forth one's deepest capacity for commitment and unselfishness.

(5) An alternative way of introducing the exercise is devised from Scripture material.[16]

Exponents of the Exercises vary in their estimate of the importance of the

[12]A wide range of current approaches to giving the Kingdom exercise are discussed in Schmitt, 'Presenting the Call of the King'.

[13]Most modern adaptations of Ignatius' parable, like Ignatius' original, make use of situations containing already a moral or spiritual ideal, as distinct from situations illustrating, e.g. the sacrifices people are prepared to make to satisfy greed or the drive for power. On the reason why the Ignatian *a fortiori* requires that the introductory model should itself enshrine a moral ideal, see Coathalem, *Ignatian Insights*, p. 134.

[14]John Futrell suggests that exercitants who are religious 'may find it helpful in a repetition to hear the call articulated by the founder of their institute'. See Cowan and Futrell, *Handbook*, p. 68.

[15]Cf. Cusson, *Everyday Life*, pp. 66–7.

[16]It would take us too far afield here to suggest ways of doing this, but one suggestion made by Coathalem may be noted, viz. that the mythical king of Ignatius' parable be replaced by the biblical Messiah King: 'Thus the exercitant prepares to contemplate the kingship of Christ by considering an ideal of kingship coming not from chivalry, but from Old Testament messianic expectation', *Ignatian Insights*, pp. 134–5.

opening parable, but it is widely held that though the exercise is in essence a contemplation of the risen Christ, it should begin with an introduction corresponding in some way to that of Ignatius.[17] But this said, it must be kept in mind that the parable is intended to 'help' the exercitant (cf. title); and 'help' in the Exercises is to be understood with the connotation established in the Foundation – what helps it is to be used, what hinders is to be avoided.

An exercise experienced as in any way contrived, or one requiring protracted creative effort, will probably not 'help'. Sometimes therefore the purpose of the introduction might be best met simply by putting a few questions to one's past experience. When have I been energized or given purpose by a vision? Have unsuspected capacities ever been released in me by friendship? What qualities in others have inspired me or aroused my admiration? What have I experienced as so compellingly worthwhile that in pursuit of it labour and suffering have been easy to accept and even welcome?

[91] [1] *THE CALL* OF THE EARTHLY KING IS A HELP TOWARDS CONTEMPLATING THE LIFE OF THE ETERNAL KING
[2] **Prayer. The preparatory prayer should be as usual.**
[3] **The first prelude: is the *composition, made by seeing the place*. Here it will consist in seeing with the eyes of the imagination the *synagogues, towns and villages* where Christ Our Lord went preaching.**
[4] **The second prelude: to ask for *the grace I want*. Here it will be to beg Our Lord for grace not to be deaf to his call, but alert to fulfil his most holy will to the best of my ability.**

The call These lines, a summarizing sentence rather than a title, describe not only the inner development of the Kingdom Exercise itself (i.e. from the call of the human king to that of Christ), but also the relationship of the exercise as a whole to the contemplation of the Gospel. Precisely in contemplating Christ's life we find his call to ourselves.

The title in the Vulgate is somewhat different: 'A contemplation of the kingdom of Jesus Christ, from the likeness of an earthly king calling out his subjects to war.' By the use of the word 'kingdom', which does not occur in either the Autograph or the Versio Prima, attention is focused on the substance

---

[17]Carlo-Maria Martini, however, admitting himself unconvinced by attempts at rewriting the parable, suggests that we 'place ourselves right away in the presence of Jesus, the only Son of the Father, the first-born of all creation, the first-born from the dead, the definitive messiah, the saviour, the centre of history, who has given himself up for me', *Letting God Free Us*, p. 83. In this approach there is no attempt explicitly to prepare the exercitant's response to Christ's call, but the response of a generous person, will, of course, draw on the content of their own personal history and also find inspiration in models, but without any of this being explicitly conscious.

of the exercise, namely the contemplation of the Kingdom (or reign) of Christ. On the other hand, it is to be noted that neither the Autograph nor the Versio Prima use the word 'war', which appears only in the Vulgate.

composition made by seeing the place Though the subject of the Kingdom Exercise is the risen Christ, not an episode from the Gospel, the 'place', as in the Gospel contemplations, is now a real, material place (i.e. the Holy Land). The importance of this feature lies in the fact that the composition is not only an aid to recollection, but contributes to the prayer of the Exercises as a pedagogy in incarnational and apostolic spirituality. All human activity, and hence the salvific activity of Christ and that of our own service of Christ, comes about in the material world. Hence before contemplating the people, the exercitant takes cognizance of the place, which provides the words and actions of the people with their context.

synagogues, towns and villages The setting of the missionary activity of Christ's mortal life; *synagogues* is an emendation in Ignatius' own hand; the text had the word 'temples'.

the grace I want The specific form of Christ's call to the exercitant has yet to be discovered. But the search must be embarked on not only with a willingness to accomplish 'promptly and with diligence' whatever the Lord may eventually ask, but in freedom from whatever inner forces might make one 'deaf' – unable even to hear what the call is.

[92] The first point is to put before myself a human king chosen by the hand of God our Lord, to whom all Christian leaders and people pay homage and obedience.

[93] [1] **The second point. To see the way this king speaks to his people:** [2] **'It is my will to conquer the entire land of the infidel. Therefore, all who wish *to come with me* must be content with the same food as I have, *the same drink*, the same clothing etc.** [3] **Such persons must also labour with me by day, and keep watch by night, etc.,** [4] **so that they will afterwards partake with me in the victory, as they have done in the labour.'**

[94] [1] **The third point. Consider *the response that good subjects must make* to so liberal and kind a king,** [2] **and consequently, if anyone were to refuse the appeal of such a king, how deservedly such a person would incur the scorn of everyone and be reckoned a disgraceful knight.**

[95] [1] **The second part of this exercise consists in applying the above**

example of the earthly king to Christ our Lord, following the three points mentioned:
² Regarding the first point, if such a call made by an earthly king to his subjects claims our consideration, ³ *how much more is it worthy* of consideration *to see Christ our Lord*, the eternal King, with the entire human race before him, as to all and to each one in particular his call goes out; ⁴ 'It is my will *to conquer* the whole world and every enemy, and so enter into the glory of my Father. ⁵ Therefore all those who want to come with me will have *to labour with me, so that by following me in my suffering they may also follow me into glory*'.

[96] The second point: to consider that everyone possessed of *judgement and reason* will *offer their whole selves for this labour*.

[97] ¹ The third point. *Those who wish rather to respond in a spirit of love*, and *to be outstanding in every service* of their commitment to their eternal King and universal Lord, will *not only offer themselves for the labour*, ² but even *going against their own sensuality and their carnal and worldly love* they will make offerings of greater moment and greater importance. *These could be expressed in this way*:

[98] ¹ 'Eternal Lord of all things, before your infinite Goodness, and before your glorious mother and all the saintly men and women of *the court of heaven*, I make my offering, *with your favour and help*. ² My resolute wish and desire, and my considered determination – *on the sole condition that this be for your greater service and praise* – ³ is to imitate you in enduring every kind of *insult and abuse*, and utter poverty both actual and spiritual, ⁴ if your most holy majesty wishes to choose me and receive me into that life and state.'

to come with me 'with me' (*conmigo*), to be found five times in the exercise, is one of its key phrases. In the idealized Lord–knight relationship, the entire campaign is one of partnership: enterprise, final triumph, immediate hardships, all are shared.

the same drink Within the general martial image of a crusade, specific martial imagery is confined to a minimum. The call is not to 'fight' but to 'labour' and the specific hardships enumerated in the king's summons – rough clothing, poor food and sleepless nights – are redolent of pilgrimage rather than warfare, and indeed of the life of an apostle.¹⁸

¹⁸On the theme of crusade spirituality, cf. Hans Wolter, 'Elements of Crusade Spirituality'. On the subject of military imagery, commonly regarded as specially characteristic of Ignatius, it may be noted that by the time he came to write the Constitutions Ignatius' central image for the apostolate was not that of fighting a crusade, but of working in the Lord's vineyard.

the response that good subjects must make The exercitant is presumed to be of the calibre of the worthy knights of Ignatius' parable.

how much more is it worthy The key is in the *a fortiori*. Conscious of the response he or she would make to a 'sublime human dream',[19] the exercitant turns to the reality of the call of Christ, and acknowledges that this call is still *more* worthy of consideration than the already worthy call which has just been heard in imagination and found to be captivating.

to see Christ our Lord The exercitant at this point is invited to 'contemplate' – to 'see' and to 'hear' – the now risen Christ calling all people to his service. This is not a moment for analysis, simply for hearing. But to hear this direct and simple appeal is to begin to absorb the basic theological principles which undergird Ignatius' concept of union with Christ in the work of the Kingdom.[20] The risen Christ, Lord of the world, is at work throughout history bringing to completion the project inaugurated in his lifetime, the establishment of the Kingdom of God in the world and the conquest of every power that opposes it. Christ carries out his work through his disciples, and in sharing Christ's work the disciple shares in the suffering inseparable from it. As in the previous section, 'with me' (*conmigo*) is a key phrase. The disciple labours and suffers not just 'for' Christ but 'with' him.

to conquer If God is effectively to reign in his world, there is a 'world' that must be overcome, the world that is incompatible with Christ (John 17:9–26). With this world and its powers Christ must always be in conflict. What the powers of this world are, and how they work, will be made clear in the meditation on the Two Standards.

to labour with me, so that by following me in my suffering they may also follow me into glory All are called in some way to share in Christ's ongoing work of establishing the Kingdom of God in the world. And because Christ's own way is in some sense normative for all his followers, the work will be achieved, whether in foreseeable ways or not, in the face of the 'enemies of the Kingdom' and in hardship.

[19]Coathalem, *Ignatian Insights*, p. 134.

[20]'The exercise on the Kingdom is a ... summary or compendium of the life and deeds of Christ the lord in the work which the Father gave him – of which Isaiah said: "His work is before him" (Is. 62:11). The Lord himself spoke of "the work which you gave me to do" (Jn. 17:4), immediately adding what that work was: "I have glorified you on earth; I have manifested your name to those you have given me" (Jn. 17:4, 6). And he calls all to share this great and glorious work, each person according to his own degree.' *1599 Directory* (MHSI 76, pp. 668–71 [trans., Palmer, p. 320]) drawing on *Directory*, *Dávila* (ibid., pp. 508–9) [trans., Palmer, p. 250]).

judgement and reason To be understood not in the restricted sense in which we today might describe a person as 'reasonable', but rather in the sense of a well-integrated, fully functioning person, one who perceives and responds to reality in a way worthy of a human being.

offer their whole selves completely for this labour The emphasis is on the work, and on the claim that apostolic work in itself, once its nature is understood, will exercise on any reasonable person.

their whole selves I.e. the whole range of personal resources that a person of 'reason and judgement' would bring to any human enterprise perceived as truly worthwhile.

Those who wish rather to respond in a spirit of love[21] I.e. as distinct from those reacting simply with 'judgement and reason'. There is no question in this final section of a negative response corresponding to that of the *disgraceful knight* [94 [2]] of the parable. Anyone coming thus far in the Exercises is presumed to wish to respond positively to Christ's call. But there are *two levels of positive response*.

The first, rooted in 'judgement and reason', consists in a total personal commitment to the work of Christ. This is already a dedication of a high order, and of course there can be no such dedication to Jesus' work without a considerable degree of love for his person. But in the 'true life in Christ', into which the exercitant is now moving, response to the call is made on another plane, epitomized in the paradoxical desires of the prayer of oblation, desires which spring from a love of Christ beyond the reach of 'reason and judgement', and from the aspiration of the disciple to be with the master.

to be outstanding in every service ... not only offer themselves for the labour For Ignatius the 'service' of God includes commitment to God's work. That we are being pointed here to something more than the already generous dedication to Christ's work ascribed to the people of judgement and reason, does not imply that the values contained in the oblation do not in themselves enhance the quality of work done for Christ, or that in relation to the work these values are a kind of 'extra'. On the contrary, a person is 'outstanding' in their work for the Kingdom precisely to the extent to which, as well as

---

[21]The rendering given here is the more natural translation of the Spanish, but the phrase is frequently translated as 'those who wish to show greater love' (or words to that effect). The latter interpretation implies that the intended distinction is between degrees of love, rather than between love on the one hand, and 'reason and judgement' on the other. For a discussion of the two translations, see Peters, *Spiritual Exercises*, p. 76.

bringing to that work all their resources for action, their lives are imbued by the desires articulated in the prayer of offering.

going against their own sensuality and their carnal and worldly love While the Kingdom Exercise should not be read as a call to asceticism,[22] the exercitant is invited to see that authentic love must always recognize the need to resist what opposes it.[23] 'Sensual' and 'carnal' have a wider meaning in Ignatius' vocabulary than they have today, and they should be taken to refer to the entire realm of natural resistance or weakness that make for difficulty in following, or even hearing, the call of Christ.

The reference to *sensuality* and to *carnal and worldly love* makes us aware of the need for asceticism, but more importantly Ignatius is concerned to establish the relationship between two elements of radical Christianity: opposition to the 'carnal', 'sensual', and worldly, on the one hand, and on the other, love for Christ and the appeal of his call. By 'going against' the disordered, the false, the non-integrated in ourselves, we remove what hinders the abandon of intense love. At the same time nothing more effectively undermines carnal worldly love than the desires which reach out towards the imitation of Christ in poverty.

The idea is not to isolate asceticism, and then to look at it (if only for a moment) as a necessity of life to be practised in its own right: the key to the 'going-against' clause lies in the process of integration that characterizes the whole exercise. Going against the carnal and the worldly, together with the commitment of all one's natural resources to Christ's work, are integrated into a love quality which is higher than either – and all within the context of a relationship which is at once a personal union with Christ and a commitment to the establishment of God's reign in the world.

These could be expressed in this way Translated in the Vulgate as, 'each will respond somewhat in this manner'. Given the nature of Christ's call and the pattern of Christ's own life, people moved by love and the desire for outstanding service would in fact make an offering of this kind. This is not to say that the exercitant is necessarily able to make it yet. At this stage the response is observed, only later will it be made.

---

[22]The danger of reducing the whole Kingdom Exercise to a challenge to go against sensuality and carnal love is recognized by Rickaby, writing at the beginning of the century, who warns against changing the exercise into a meditation on mortification. On the contrary, the exercise is 'like the place where electricity is generated to supply the whole town; it is the generating place of enthusiasm and personal loyalty to Jesus Christ, cost what it may. Therefore the Exercise should be made in joy and elevation of spirit.' Rickaby, *Spiritual Exercises*, p. 83.

[23]For the sense of 'going against', see [13] with comment.

the court of heaven The picture evoked is that of final glory, precisely the 'glory' which Christ, his mother and the saints have attained after travelling the road of suffering.

with your favour and help The offering is a graced offering, to be made only with God's favour and help.

on the sole condition ... greater service and praise A similar qualification appears in [147, 157, 166, 167]. Though Ignatius would have us desire – to the point of earnestly asking for – the conditions that make for the more literal 'imitation of Christ', the ultimate norm of Christian desire is not the more literal, exterior imitation, but whatever in the present circumstances is more for the glory of God.

insult and abuse The order here reverses that of the Triple Colloquies, which proceed from 'spiritual poverty' (the disposition of the heart) to the concrete situations of actual poverty and contempt. The present Exercise starts with the most immediately challenging aspect of the Kingdom – the fact that out of love for Jesus and commitment to his Kingdom, a person with the resources to achieve worldly success might positively desire situations of worldly failure. What is implicit in the 'with me' [95] here becomes explicit. In the apostolate/imitation perspective of the Exercises, actual poverty is the normal situation of the apostle, and 'insults' a normal experience of one who in poverty preaches and works for the gospel.

[99] Note 1. This exercise should be made twice during the day, namely on rising in the morning and one hour before dinner or supper.

[100] Note 2. For the Second Week, as well as for the future, it will be very helpful to read from time to time from the *Imitation of Christ*, or from the Gospels or the lives of the saints.

A note on reading during the Exercises

Resource to books during the Exercises is not, and was not at the beginning, quite the simple issue that might appear from this paragraph. In the Exercises reading can cause inappropriate mood changes, impede personal discovery, and generally take over the mental space essential to the concept of the Twentieth-Annotation retreat. On the other hand, as the present paragraph makes clear, there are circumstances, at least from the Second Week on, when reading can be 'very profitable'. The approaches to reading found in the *Directories* reflect the tension between these two principles. Thus the *1599*

Directory lays down as a general rule that 'the exercitant reads nothing except what is given him in writing', adding that no books should be in the exercitant's room except the breviary or the office of the Blessed Virgin, 'in order that there be no opportunity of reading anything else';[24] but at the same time in particular cases a director will permit or even recommend the exercitant to read; and the *Directories* contain indications of the kind of reading that might be suggested in this event to a sixteenth-century exercitant.

Frequently recurring titles include St Augustine's *Confessions*, the writings of St Bernard, Denis the Carthusian on the Last Things, Luis de Granada on prayer and meditation, Tauler on the Passion.[25] Though restrictions on reading are especially necessary in the First Week, at the end of that week one of the confession manuals of the time might help the exercitant prepare for confession.[26] Among the books named in the Exercises pride of place falls to the *Imitation of Christ*, which the exercitant may readily be encouraged to read, from the First Week on. Readings from the 'lives of saints' should draw attention to models for the exercitant's own state of life. With regard to the Gospels or a life of Christ, the exercitant should read only what deals with the mysteries he has meditated on, or will meditate on that same day.[27] Any reading undertaken during the Exercises must have the same purpose as the additions: to help the person 'to make the Exercises better'. Books or passages should therefore be selected with painstaking care, and even if offered in order to 'relieve tedium', reading must meet certain norms. It must be calculated to 'nourish piety' and to arouse the affection being sought at the current stage of the Exercises. It should be made by 'dwelling upon and weighing carefully what one reads, and in entering into the suggested affections', and it should not be embarked upon 'out of appetite to know and see something new'. Care should be taken that 'the pleasure of reading is not allowed to encroach upon the time allotted to meditation or preparation for it'.

[24]'What is given in writing', i.e. material substantial to the Exercises (such as points for prayer), which was either given to exercitants in writing or dictated to them.

[25]Mention in the *Directories* of these and other substantial writings does not necessarily imply that they would be read in their entirety during the Exercises.

[26]Such a manual had been written by Polanco. This was commended for use at the end of the First Week by Ignatius himself: cf. *Directory (dictated to de Vitoria)* (MHSI 76, p. 103 [trans., Palmer, p. 23]).

[27]On the subject of reading, see especially the *1599 Directory* (cc. 3 and 21) and the *Directory of Miró* (MHSI 76, pp. 583, 683 [trans., Palmer, pp. 296–8, 323]). But see also *Directories* (MHSI 76, pp. 223, 263, 300, 359, 537–8 [trans., Palmer, pp. 89, 113, 131, 156, 157, 268]). It may be of interest here to recall the attitude of the early directors towards writing during the Exercises, as summarized in the *1599 Directory* (c. 3): the exercitant is encouraged to write what has to do with prayer and with what God communicates in or out of meditation; desires or resolutions; truths or insights; matter bearing on subjects of meditation. Things should be noted 'very briefly, not diffusely after the manner of a sermon', and once again writing must not obtrude on time for meditation or the preparation of it.

INFANCY CONTEMPLATIONS

Following the introductory exercise of the Kingdom, the Second Week proper begins with the contemplation of the Incarnation and from there goes on to selected episodes from the Lucan Gospel, together with a single episode from Matthew. For those wishing to stay longer with the Gospels of the infancy, a wider range of material is available in the supplementary texts [262–272.1]; cf. also [162].

In comparison with the later part of the Week, there is something relaxed about the mood of these opening contemplations. The material can hold immediate human appeal; certain departures from the ordinary regime are encouraged; the exigence of the Triple Colloquy is still to come. This does not mean, however, that the Infancy Contemplations should be regarded just as an interlude, and certainly not as non-essential.[28] On the contrary as set out in the Exercises, they introduce a number of basic themes.

First, the opening contemplation establishes the Trinitarian context crucial to understanding everything that follows. Christ's mission is the work of the Trinity. It proceeds from and expresses the love of the Trinitarian God for the world and the unconditional commitment of the Divine Persons to the world's redemption.

Second, within this Trinitarian context attention is centred on an implication of the Incarnation – childhood – which needs to become personally real for the exercitant if he or she is to appreciate the Incarnation for what it is. That the Word became human means that the Word became a child. The exercitant who does not encounter the human reality of Jesus' childhood lacks something essential to their knowledge and love of 'the Lord made human for me' [104]. Thus in these first days of the Second Week, the Trinitarian prayer of the exercitant takes the form of contemplating, with the complete realism characteristic of the imaginative method, the historical child, the *niño Jesús*.[29]

---

[28]For the place of the infancy contemplations, see Kolvenbach, 'Do not hide the Hidden Life of Christ'. Kolvenbach develops at some length the case for dispensing with the Infancy Contemplations and beginning the Second Week with the Two Standards and Christ's baptism; but despite the case that might be made for this, he insists that without the Infancy Contemplations something essential would be lacking to our knowledge of Christ.

[29]In connection with the Infancy Contemplations, the Christ-titles in both the main text and the Supplement vary between 'Jesus' [266, 267], 'the child' [265, 269, 270], and 'the child Jesus' [114, 134, 266, 268]; and the divine/messianic titles, 'Second Person' [102], 'Christ' [272], 'Saviour of the World' [265], 'Our Lord' [109, 116], and 'Christ Our Lord' [265, 270, 271, 272]. When referred to as 'the child', Jesus is always the passive recipient of the action or attention of others.

Third, the contemplation of the child and his entourage is permeated by the idea of fidelity to God's word and will. From the moment of his conception, Jesus exists wholly for the mission given by the Trinity [104]; in the Temple incident he responds consciously and explicitly to the Father's overriding claims [134, 272]; at Nazareth he is subject to his parents [134, 271]; Mary's 'Fiat' exemplifies supremely the grace of 'prompt and diligent response to God's call' [262] (cf. [91]). The Flight into Egypt is an act of obedience, and obedience is a detectable note in the Presentation.

Fourth, Ignatius proposes the Infancy Contemplations in a way that accentuates the themes of poverty and humiliation introduced in the Kingdom Exercise and presented now not as abstractions, but as embodied in the persons of Jesus and his parents, and in their hard and precarious circumstances. In these circumstances the exercitant is invited to see the first steps of a descending journey of love which begins in the heart of the Trinity and will conclude on the Cross (cf. [116]).

Finally, in the materials of the Third Day, the acceptance by Jesus of the normalities of work and family during the years of the hidden life and his action in the Temple in asserting the overriding claims of his Father, Ignatius sees Christ himself as modelling the two 'ways' – of 'counsels' and 'commandments' – between which the exercitant might have to choose in the election.

Going back to the beginning

Early in the Second Week the director should draw the exercitant's attention to [130] and [206] so that in moving forward through the Exercises, the exercitant continually gathers up all that has gone before, starting with the Incarnation and interpreting earlier events in the light of later ones and vice versa. The constant return to the Incarnation serves to keep the whole Second Week experience within the context of the vision proposed in the opening contemplation, the vision of a needy world in relation to the Trinity. Subsequent contemplations contain no further reference to the Trinity gazing down upon a world in need; and only the Two Standards refers explicitly to the exercitant's here-and-now world at all. But the whole week is made in awareness of the world in its relationship to the Trinity.

First Day

First Contemplation: Incarnation and Annunciation

[101] [1] FIRST DAY
THE FIRST *CONTEMPLATION* IS DEVOTED TO THE INCARNATION. IT CONTAINS THE PREPARATORY PRAYER, *THREE PRELUDES*, THREE *POINTS* AND A COLLOQUY

89

² Prayer. The usual preparatory prayer.

contemplation For the general sense of 'contemplation' in the Exercises, see comment on [45]. Here the exercitant is introduced to the imaginative contemplation of the Gospel.[30] As a method, this consists in entering imaginatively into the Church's faith memories of Jesus in such a way as to experience oneself as present to the situations and episodes of the Gospel, and in them to meet Jesus and other Gospel persons as real flesh and blood human beings. But if Gospel contemplation is an imaginative experience, it is also considerably more than this.[31] The key to its full power and challenge lies in the fact that the Gospels are the word of God. Because of this the events contemplated belong not only to the past but to the present of every believer, whom they provide with the materials of an interpersonal relationship with the Christ of the now.[32] In contemplating a Gospel narrative a believer truly in search of God and his will encounters the living Christ, who through this narrative reaches out to such persons, drawing them into union with himself, and sharing with them his own vision and desires.

three preludes For the remaining weeks, the number of preludes is increased to three by the addition of a new First Prelude, the 'history'. This is not only a summary or *aide-mémoire*, but is an invitation to be present to a reality of faith or a reality interpreted in faith; here, then, present to the saving action of the Trinity in relation to the predicament of the human race.[33]

points In the context of the Gospel contemplation, the term 'points' refers both to the division of the Gospel story into chronological steps (cf. [262–312]), and to the three aspects of the mystery explained below, namely persons, words, actions. The latter distinction must not be applied awkwardly or artificially, but the illustrations given below (and in [114–116]), indicate its value as an aid to entering into the heart of a Gospel episode.[34]

[30]The imaginative contemplation of the Second to Fourth Weeks of the Exercises belongs to a tradition originating in the Cistercian and Franciscan schools of the 12th–13th centuries. It should be noted that the meaning of 'contemplation' in this tradition is wider than in the later and more specific concepts of 'acquired' and of 'infused' contemplation, even though through the Exercises a person may come to experience the levels of prayer these latter describe.

[31]Imaginative contemplation, as understood in the Second Week of the Exercises, presupposes qualities of asceticism and self-giving love, and does not consist just in imaginative experience alone, irrespective of personal dispositions.

[32]On this dimension of imaginative contemplation, see Aschenbrenner, 'Becoming Whom we Contemplate'.

[33]See also comment on [102]. For the content of the term 'history' in the text of the Exercises, cf. [111, 137, 150, 191, 201, 219].

[34]For an additional feature in the points of the Third and Fourth Weeks, see [195–197, 223–225].

[102] ¹ The first prelude is to recall the *history* of the subject to be contemplated: in this case how the Three Divine Persons were looking down upon the face and circuit of the world, filled with people, ² and how on seeing that all were going down into Hell, they decreed in their eternity that the Second Person would become human to save the human race. ³ Thus when 'the fullness of time' came they sent the angel Gabriel to our Lady [262].

[103] ¹ The second prelude is the *composition*, made by seeing the place. Here it will be to see the vast extent and circuit of the earth with its many and various races; ² and then, in the same way, to see the particular house of our Lady and its rooms in the town of Nazareth in the province of Galilee.

[104] The third prelude is to ask for *what I want*: here it will be to ask for inner knowledge of the Lord who became human for me so that I might the better love and follow him.

[105] ¹ Note. It may be well to note here that in this and the following weeks, this same preparatory prayer should be made without any change, as was mentioned at the beginning [49], ² along with the same three preludes, adapted in form according to the proposed material.

history The matter of the contemplation combines the abstract theme of the Incarnation as divine decision with the concrete event of the Annunciation.[35]

composition This picks up the theme of the 'world', emphasizing the scale of the world and pinpointing within it the place of the Incarnation in a particular room, in a particular house, in a particular town and province.

what I desire To know better in order to love better, to love better in order to follow more faithfully – a classic summary of the purpose of all contemplation of the Gospel.[36] The knowledge is 'interior' or deep knowledge. The love leads to – and is only fully realized in – 'following', or discipleship.

Throughout the Second Week this petition will change only in the sense that one asks for the inner knowledge proper to a particular Gospel episode. Here the focus is on the fact that the Word 'has become man for me'. The

[35]The importance of the connection between Incarnation and Annunciation is stressed by Kolvenbach in the article mentioned above: 'Separating the truth of the Incarnation of the Word of God from the story of the Annunciation means falling fatally into the danger of diminishing this truth and turning it into a purely metaphysical abstract speculation' (p. 14).

[36]Today best known perhaps in the form of the prayer of St Richard of Chichester: 'Day by day, three things I pray: to know Thee more clearly, to love Thee more dearly, to follow Thee more nearly.'

words 'for me' should not be read in an exclusively individual sense, that would contradict the outward-looking, service-orientated character of the Exercises. But like the phrase 'for my sins' in the First Week [53] they bring out the unnegotiably personal relationship of each individual with Christ, which is the basis of the individual's involvement in the saving work of Jesus in the world.

[106] [1] **The *first point* is to see in turn the various persons: first, those on the *face of the earth*, in all their diversity of dress and appearance, [2] some white and some black, some in peace and others at war, some weeping and others laughing, some healthy, others sick, some being born and others dying, etc.; [3] secondly, see and consider the *three Divine Persons* as though on the royal seat or throne of the Divine Majesty, how they look down upon the face and circuit of the world and on all its people, living in blindness, going to their death and descending into Hell; [4] thirdly, to see *Our Lady* and the Angel who greets her. *I will reflect in order to draw profit* from what I see.**

[107] [1] **The second point is to hear what the persons on the face of the earth are saying – the way they talk to each other and how they swear and blaspheme, etc.; [2] in the same way to hear what the Divine Persons are saying, namely: 'Let us bring about the redemption of the human race, etc.'; [3] then what the angel and Our Lady are talking about. I will then reflect in order to draw profit from their words.**

[108] [1] **The third point is to watch what the persons on the face of the earth are doing, for instance wounding and killing one another, and going to Hell, etc.; [2] and in the same way, what the Divine Persons are doing, namely, bringing about the sacred Incarnation, etc.; [3] and similarly, what the angel and Our Lady are doing, the angel fulfilling his role of legate and Our Lady humbling herself, and giving thanks to the Divine Majesty. [4] Then I will reflect in order to draw profit from each of these things.**

first point In each point the sequence proceeds from the world, to the Trinity 'above' the world, and back to the person of Mary at the heart of the world.

face of the earth The exercitant contemplates the world in its totality, with particular emphasis on diversity of race and culture and on the tragic, fragile and violent aspects of human life. It is essential that the world thus contemplated be, or at any rate include, the exercitant's own world. Notice that in each of the points reference to *the persons on the face of the earth* includes an *et cetera*: in Ignatius' usage this is an invitation to the exercitant to develop a general idea in one's own way.

three Divine Persons In expanding the picture sketched out in the 'history' above, the points draw the exercitant into a characteristically apostolic mode of Trinitarian contemplation. Thus the exercitant contemplates the Trinity as transcendent, majestic, 'above' the world; but also as the God *of* the world, the God who in Christ enters the world. The thrust of the Exercises will be to involve the exercitant personally in God's own activity in Christ within the world. Here at the beginning of the Second Week the exercitant shares God's *vision* of the world, contemplating the world with the Persons of the Trinity and from their standpoint.

Our Lady The chosen one at the heart of the world: contrast with the immensities of God and of the universe accentuates the smallness of Mary; the comportment of the angel (the ambassador) accentuates her dignity.

I will reflect in order to draw profit With variants this expression will recur frequently in the Second and Third Weeks, and it also appears in the Contemplation to Attain Love. The words are to be understood in the context of contemplation. In this context reflection is the reflective process that opens the word of God to personal discovery [2]. The word *profit* refers to the initiative of God in acting in the exercitant: giving light or insight or 'the intimate feeling and relish of things' [2]; granting especially requested graces, and here the grace of a deepening knowledge and love of Christ [104]. But *profit* may also be the perception of some particular life-response called forth by the Gospel; and in many cases, the *profit* sought in contemplation will take the form especially of clarification regarding the discernment of God's will in the exercitant's election. On the side of the exercitant *drawing profit* consists in appropriation of God's action in oneself, letting oneself, through contemplation, be touched, enlightened, changed.[37]

[109] [1] Colloquy. At the end a colloquy is to be made. *I will think about what I should be saying* to the three Divine Persons, or to the eternal Word who has become human for me, or to his mother, Our Lady, [2] making prayers of petition, according to my inner feelings, so that I may the better follow and imitate Our Lord, thus newly incarnate. I will say an Our Father.

[37]Though Ignatius understands 'reflect' in the sense of 'ponder', or 'dwell upon' (Dalmases, *Ejercicios espirituales*, p. 203), to appreciate the sense of *reflect and draw profit* it can help to recall the different meaning of the word in 2 Cor. 3:18: 'And all of us, with unveiled faces, seeing the glory of the Lord as though reflected in a mirror, are being transformed into the same image from one degree of glory to another.'

I will think about what I should be saying The prayer of direct conversation, while familiar and spontaneous, is not merely casual. The main points pick up and explicate the themes of the petition. *Following* now becomes *imitation*. Christ is the *eternal Word*: crucial to the contemplation of the mortal life of Christ is the awareness that this human life, played out in the world and inter-meshing with its history, is precisely the human life of the *eternal Word who has just become human for me*. For the exercitant the Incarnation is an event not just of the past, but of the 'now' of the contemplation just made.

Second contemplation: Nativity

[110] [1] THE SECOND CONTEMPLATION IS ON THE NATIVITY [2] Prayer. The usual preparatory prayer.

[111] [1] The first prelude is the *history*; here, how our Lady, nearly nine months pregnant (as we may devoutly think of her) and seated on a donkey, [2] with Joseph and a servant girl,[38] taking with them an ox, set out from Nazareth for Bethlehem to pay the tribute which Caesar had imposed on all those lands [264].

[112] [1] The second prelude is the *composition* made by seeing the place. Here this will be to see with the eyes of the imagination the road from Nazareth to Bethlehem, considering the length and breadth of it, whether it is a flat road or goes through valleys or over hills; [2] and similarly to observe the place or grotto of the nativity, to see how big or small it is, how high, and what is in it.

[113] The third prelude will be the same, and in the same form, as in the preceding contemplation.

history Though the focal point of the Infancy Contemplations is the Child Jesus, special importance attaches to his entourage, especially to Mary and Joseph; since at this stage Jesus himself shows the world nothing beyond the common features of human infancy, he depends on the qualities of others to enable him to be a 'sign' in a way that will not be the case later.

composition. The cave corresponds to the 'room' or 'house' [103, 192, 220]. The road is one of the fundamental Ignatian symbols, expressing the dynamic cast of Ignatius' way of thinking, his view of life as movement and process; it also stands for the exposed, itinerant condition of the life of the apostle.

[38]The maid appears in the *Flos Sanctorum* by Jacopo de Voragine, one of the books Ignatius read on his sickbed at Loyola.

The Exercises contain many allusions, explicit or implicit, to roads and journeys. In [192], in almost identical terms as here, the exercitant is invited to imagine the road from Bethany to Jerusalem; cf. also [158] Jesus' journey from Nazareth to the Jordan, and the journey-model on which Ignatius constructs the Third Week.

[114] ¹ The first point is to see the persons namely Our Lady, and Joseph, and the servant girl, and after his birth, the child Jesus. ² Making myself into a poor and unworthy little servant, I watch them, and *contemplate* them, and as if I were present, serve them in their needs with all possible respect and reverence; ³ then I will reflect within myself to draw some profit.

[115] The second point. To watch and notice and consider what they are saying, and reflecting within myself, to draw some profit.

[116] ¹ The third point. To watch and consider *what they are doing*, e.g. their journeys and labours, so that Christ comes to be born in extreme poverty ² and, after so much toil, hunger, thirst, heat and cold, insults and affronts, he dies on the cross – and all of this for me. ³ Then I will reflect and draw some spiritual profit.

[117] Colloquy. I will conclude with a colloquy as in the preceding contemplation [109] and then an Our Father.

The *three points* bring out the process and the mood of imaginative contemplation. The exercitant is not an onlooker, outside the situation, but present within it. The word *contemplate* (the inner attention of the heart) follows the more immediate words *see, watch, notice*. The mood is one of humility (*poor, unworthy, servant*) and reverence (to the word *reverencia* is added the stronger word *acatamiento* [114]).

what they are doing. Attention is directed to the features of the story that point forward to the contemplations of Jesus' ministry and passion. The point takes up the theme of labour and suffering evoked in the Kingdom Exercise.

Third and Fourth contemplations: repetition

[118] ¹ THE THIRD CONTEMPLATION WILL BE A *REPETITION* OF THE *FIRST AND SECOND EXERCISES* ² After the preparatory prayer and the three preludes, the repetition of the first and second exercises should be made, ³ attention being always given to the *more important places* where one has experienced

insight, consolation or desolation. **At the end a colloquy should be made in the same way, with an Our Father.**

[119] Note. In this as in all subsequent repetitions the same order of procedure will be followed as in the repetitions of the First Week, changing the matter and keeping the form.

[120] THE FOURTH CONTEMPLATION WILL BE A REPETITION OF THE FIRST AND SECOND CONTEMPLATIONS MADE IN THE SAME WAY AS THE PRECEDING REPETITION

repetition As was seen above (commentary on [62]), *repetition* is a time when the exercitant's prayer grows more personal, and becomes more simple and receptive; in this way it contributes to the 'contemplative day', which begins with the opening contemplation(s) and moves through the repetitions to the culminating Prayer of the Senses (cf. [131ff.]). But the purpose of the repetition is not only to lead the exercitant into a prayer of simplicity and depth. Repetition belongs to the particular dynamic of the Exercises. Through it therefore the exercitant continues to assimilate a given piece of the word of God, in the desire that this word may involve one's life, and indeed repetition in the Second Week will often be a major part of the process of seeking God's will in an 'election'.

first and second exercises Where the day begins with two subjects, repetition may bring insight into the connection between these. Thus, here, the paschal decision of the Trinity, the Annunciation, the Incarnation, and the Nativity will be brought together in repetition into a unified vision.

more important places I.e. points that have emerged as personally important for the exercitant.[39]

insight or 'knowledge' (in the Spanish, *conocimiento*), the faith-enlightened, penetrative knowledge that Ignatius often specifies as 'interior' (cf. [104]); more specifically, insights into Christ and his ways.

consolation or desolation The typical Second Week experiences of consolation and desolation are those which occur in the search for God's will (c. [176]).[40] The mention of desolation here, as in [62], makes it clear that it is not of the essence of repetition to be an experience of unruffled tranquillity.

[39]Cf. introduction to [62].
[40]On returning to the places where desolation was found, cf. once more the introductory remarks to [62].

Fifth contemplation: Prayer of the Senses

The exercise which culminates the contemplative day is characterized by a concentrated sense-presence with a minimum of discursive thinking.[41] The sensing is bodily/imaginative and its immediate object is the physical realities of persons and things. But these are perceived not only as objects of the imaginative bodily senses, but as containing the mystery of the divine as touched by grace [124], as invested with faith-meanings already discovered in prayer (cf. [2]); and to this level one is present by an inner sensing of the mind and heart which comes about in and through the immediate imaginative sensing. It need hardly be added that the personal quality of the exercitant's prayer at this stage will depend primarily not on following a prayer method, but on his or her overall dispositions and the action of the Holy Spirit.[42]

Though the explicit and systematic focusing on the senses gives the Fifth Exercise a character of its own, the Exercise is to a considerable degree in continuity with the prayers preceding it. The three preludes are common to the entire sequence; the 'reflect-and-profit' motif, and the concluding colloquy pick up the first two Exercises; the matter is that proposed at the start of the day, now taken up at the stage to which contemplation and contemplative repetition have brought it.[43] The final prayer does not, therefore, require the mastery of some new technique; still less, entry into a realm of experience qualitatively different from that of the whole contemplative day. Though one or two aspects of the text raise questions, its overall tenor suggests a prayer that will ordinarily come quite readily at the end of a day spent seeking 'interior' knowledge of

---

[41]The *1599 Directory* sees the Prayer of the Senses as representing a drop from a more elevated to a more 'ordinary' prayer (MHSI 76, p. 677 [trans. Palmer, p. 322]). It would be generally agreed today however that in this final prayer Ignatius expects the exercitant's day to reach its peak contemplative quality. On the suppositions behind the attitude of the *1599 Directory* and the theology implicit in Ignatius' own position, see Endean, 'The Ignatian Prayer of the Senses'.

[42]A tradition going back to Polanco and particularly associated in this century with the name of Joseph Maréchal, connects the levels at which this prayer might be made with different concepts that can be conveyed by the word 'senses'. These essentially are two: the imaginative senses of 'ordinary prayer', and the 'spiritual senses', understood as a presence to divine realities without imagery, and characteristic of mystical prayer. It should be noted that in this distinction there is the same underlying assumption as in the position of the *1599 Directory* (that any prayer incorporating the imaginative senses is of an inferior kind). Ignatius himself makes no reference to this interpretation of spiritual senses, but he does imply that there can be 'an exalted form of prayer which requires concentration on an imagined sensory object', Endean, art. cit., p. 398.

[43]On the relationship of the Prayer of the Senses to 'repetition', see comment on [277].

Christ in his humanity, through contemplation of an episode or episodes of his mortal life.[44]

[121 **¹** **THE FIFTH CONTEMPLATION WILL CONSIST IN BRINGING**[45] *THE FIVE SENSES* **TO BEAR ON** *THE FIRST AND SECOND CONTEMPLATIONS* **²** **After the preparatory prayer and the three preludes, it will be** *profitable* **to pass the five senses of the imagination over the first and second contemplations in the following manner.**

[122] The first point is to see the persons with the imaginative sense of sight, meditating[46] **and contemplating their circumstances in detail, and to draw some profit from the sight.**

[123] The second point. To hear with the sense of hearing *what they say or might say,* **and to reflect in oneself and to draw some profit from this.**

[124] **¹** **The third point. To smell and to taste** *with the senses of smell and taste* **the infinite** *gentleness and sweetness of the divinity,* **and of the soul and of its virtues, and of everything else, according to whoever the person contemplated may be;** **²** **and to reflect within oneself and draw profit from this.**

[125] The fourth point. To touch with the sense of touch, for example embracing and kissing *the places where these persons tread and sit,* **always seeking to draw profit from this.**

[126] One should finish with a colloquy as in the first and second contemplation, and with an Our Father.

the five senses As the Vulgate specifies, the senses are employed according to the nature of the material in a particular contemplation or contemplations.

[44]For further reading the following are recommended, in addition to the article already mentioned: Coathalem, *Insights*, pp. 153–8; Cowan & Futrell, *Handbook*, pp. 92–3, 101–2; Ganss, *Spiritual Exercises*, pp. 163–5; Peters, *Spiritual Exercises*, pp. 87–8; Stanley, *I Encountered God*, pp. 30–2; Walsh, 'Application of the Senses'.

[45]'*bringing the senses to bear*': the more familiar terms ('apply the senses' and 'application of the senses') come from the Latin versions.

[46]It may be asked why the term 'meditating' should appear in a text dealing with the summit of the 'contemplative' day. A probable explanation suggested by Endean (art. cit., p. 401 and note 23) is that the material of the day includes details not to be found in Luke or Matthew, e.g. the donkey, the maidservant, the ox. In [111] Ignatius adds in his own hand the clause, 'as one may piously *meditate*' to the detail of Mary on the donkey; cf. also [261, 310].

Imaginative sensing will always consist primarily in seeing and hearing; these are the senses which give access to the persons and the words and actions that constitute the *points* of the earlier contemplations.

the first and second contemplations But not on the matter of these contemplations as first broached, but as at this stage already contemplated through the initial exercises and two repetitions.

profitable What God is doing in me, especially drawing me into interior knowledge, etc. (cf. on [106]).

what they say or might say Imaginative contemplation, through which one participates in an event, making it in a sense a personal experience, includes the element of graced imaginative freedom. But to belong authentically to the Ignatian Prayer of the Senses, such freedom must be related to the 'interior knowledge' that comes from contemplating the 'foundation in truth' of the scriptural word (cf. [12]).

with the senses of smell and taste Senses to be understood here not literally but as metaphors for attitudes and feelings within the experience of immediate imaginative presence through other senses.[47] The Third Point represents a movement in depth from an initially more exterior contemplation of the persons to a contemplation focusing explicitly on the reality of personal qualities perceived in the Spirit. This does not mean however that a particular text might not contain details calling also for the literal use of these senses,[48] but this is something quite different from the interior sensing described in this Third Point.

gentleness and sweetness of the divinity, etc.[49] The divinity is Christ's, whereas *the soul and its virtues* can refer equally to Christ and to other persons contemplated (e.g. Mary). The Vulgate understands *divine* in a more extended sense: 'the sweetness and delightfulness of the soul imbued with the divine gifts and virtues'.

---

[47]Hence both the Polanco version and the Vulgate specify 'a certain interior taste and smell'.

[48]For example, John 12:3 the fragrance of spikenard; John 19:29–30 the bitterness of gall.

[49]This reading is based on the comma placed after 'divinity' in the standard edition (MHSI 100, p. 234). Other editors, however, omit the comma. It should be noted that the text must not be taken to imply that the object of this inner sensing is the divinity in itself, but refers to the contemplation in faith of the entire person of Jesus.

99

the places where these persons tread and sit The Vulgate enlarges as follows: 'The fourth, by an inward touch, to handle and kiss the garments, places, footsteps and other things connected with such persons; whence we may derive a greater increase of devotion or of any spiritual good'. The significance given by Ignatius to places and objects has already been noted in connection with the Composition [112]. His silence here on other uses of touch does not however preclude other ways of involving the imaginative sense of touch which might seem to open the person to the graces of knowledge, love and commitment.[50]

Five notes

[127] NOTES
[1] First note. It should be noted that in the course of this and the following Weeks, I should read only the mystery of the contemplation that I have to make immediately; [2] thus for the time being I should not read any mystery which is not to be made on that day or at that time, so that the consideration of one mystery may not interfere with the consideration of another.

[128] [1] Second note. The first exercise on the Incarnation should be made at midnight, the second at dawn, the third at Mass time, the fourth at the time of Vespers, and the fifth before supper; [2] an hour should be spent on each of the five exercises, and the same order should be kept in all that follows.

[129] [1] Third note. This concerns the exercitant who is old or weak, or even if robust, has been left weakened in some way by the First Week. [2] In this Second Week it is better for such an exercitant, at least occasionally, *not to rise at midnight*, but to make one contemplation in the morning, another at Mass time, another before dinner, [3] and a repetition on these at the time of Vespers, and finally to make the prayer of the senses before supper.

An exercitant in a state of fatigue at the end of the First Week might do well, at least sometimes, *not to rise at midnight*. Ignatius' writings repeatedly insist that to give God our best service requires a certain level of health and energy, and hence in the Exercises his approach to the body is characterized by a constant search for the mean between indulgence on the one hand and

---

[50]Note the specific inclusion of touch in 1 John 1:1-2: 'We have heard it; we have seen it with our own eyes; we looked upon it, and felt it with our own hands: our theme is the Word which gives life.'

counter-productive stress on the other.[51] Both the exercitant and director should keep an eye on the former's energy-levels throughout the inherently taxing process of the Exercises; and particularly at the beginning of the Second Week when much of the process has still to be completed. Above all, it would be undesirable to reach the point of election drained of energy.

Neither the text of the Exercises nor the *Directories* explain the reason for night prayer, except perhaps obliquely in [8] where curtailed sleep is included in the categories of penance. Apart from the penitential aspect, sufficient explanation is found in time-honoured monastic practice and the benefits of night prayer which many exercitants discover for themselves through experience. From the beginning, a high value was set upon night prayer, but the provision made here is sufficient rebuttal of the notion that night prayer is of the quintessence of the Exercises.

[130] **¹ Fourth note. In this Second Week changes should be made to some of the additions mentioned in the First Week, namely the second, the sixth, the seventh and (partly) the tenth.**

² In the second addition: immediately on waking I will put before myself the contemplation which I have to make, with the desire to know more intimately the eternal Word Incarnate, so as the better to serve and follow him.

³ In the sixth addition, I will frequently call to mind the life and mysteries of Christ our Lord, beginning from his Incarnation as far as the place or mystery that I am engaged in contemplating.

⁴ The *seventh addition*: the room should be lightened or darkened and use made of *good or bad weather* in so far as the exercitant perceives that they can profit thereby and be helped to find what they desire.

⁵ Tenth addition. The exercitant must act in harmony with the mysteries being contemplated, as some demand penance while others do not.

⁶ In this way all ten of the additions should be very carefully observed.

[51]Numerous examples of Ignatius' concern for the maintenance of health can be found in his letters: e.g. 'With a healthy body, there is much that you can do; but with the body ill, I have no idea what you will be able to do. A healthy body is a great help, to do both much evil and much good – much evil with those depraved of mind and accustomed to sin, much good with those whose minds are set on God Our Lord and who are accustomed to good deeds', *Letter to Teresa Rejadell*, 11 Sept. 1536 (MHSI *Epp. Ig.* I, no. 8, pp. 107–9 [trans. *Personal Writings*, p. 108]). 'It sometimes happens that the "crucifixion of our former nature" [Rom. 6:6] ends up being the crucifixion of the new one as well, when weakness makes one incapable of actually living out the virtues', *Letter to Students of the Society of Jesus in Coimbra*, 7 May 1547 (MHSI *Epp. Ig.* I, no. 169, pp. 495–510 [trans. *Personal Writings*, p. 178]).

Modified *seventh addition* As in the First Week, the exercitants make the environment that will help them. In the Second Week they may be helped either by darkening the room, or by letting in the sunshine.

good or bad weather. The exercitant is not asked to be unaware of the weather, but to 'use' awareness of the weather. While pleasant weather can obviously be used to support feelings of joy or peace (as in the Fourth Week [229]), a possible 'use' of the experience of unpleasant weather to help contemplation is suggested in [116].

[131] [1] Fifth note. In all the exercises, except those at midnight and in the morning, the equivalent of the second addition should be observed as follows: [2] as soon as I recall that it is time for the exercise I have to do, before beginning I will put before myself where I am going and into whose presence, [3] and I will run briefly over the exercise to be done; then I will make the third addition and start on the exercise.

Second Day: Presentation and flight into exile

[132] [1] SECOND DAY
One should take for the first and second contemplations, the *Presentation* in the Temple [268] and the *Flight into exile in Egypt* [269] [2] two repetitions and the prayer of the senses should be made on these two contemplations, in the same way as on the preceding day.

As subjects of contemplation the *Presentation* includes the themes of poverty, compliance with the Law, the recognition of and witness to Jesus by a man and woman of prayer (Simeon and Anna), while the *Flight into exile in Egypt* introduces a further dimension of actual poverty, namely *exile*.

[133] [1] Note
Sometimes it is profitable for the exercitant, even if robust and in the right dispositions, to change the timetable from this second day until the fourth (inclusive), in order to better find what he or she desires. [2] In this case, one should make one contemplation at dawn and another at the time of Mass, then make the repetition on these at the time of Vespers and make the prayer of the senses before supper.

While the dense materials of the first day require the full five hours of prayer, from the second to the fourth day, it might be helpful to reduce the programme to four periods of prayer. This change of rhythm corresponds to the preparatory character of these days. Where the Infancy Gospels are concerned, the particular grace is one of joy, which makes it appropriate to follow the same schedule as that of the Fourth Week (cf. [227]).

Third Day: The Child Jesus in the Temple

[134] THIRD DAY
One should contemplate how the Child Jesus was obedient to his parents at Nazareth [271], and how afterwards they found him in the Temple [272]; then two repetitions should be made and the prayer of the senses.

Ignatius inverts the order of Luke to suit his own purposes, as the following section explains.

INTRODUCTION TO ELECTIONS

Fourth Day

The Fourth Day (Two Standards and Three Classes together with the preamble [135]) provides an immediate introduction to the process of election. The process itself begins on the Fifth Day, with the contemplation of the baptism in the Jordan and the consideration of the three kinds of humility [163].

The Preamble contains introductory material on 'election' and on the Two Standards. Later, there will be a more immediate preamble to the election [169]. The typical, but not the only 'election' an exercitant might have made in Ignatius' time was concerned with the two classic 'ways' of Christian life: the 'way of perfection', virtually corresponding to canonical religious life; and ordinary Christian life, known as the 'way of the commandments'. With regard to this distinction the point to be noticed here is Ignatius' insistence that since each way is modelled by Christ himself, either might prove to be God's will for the exercitant, and hence the way in which he or she is to seek personal perfection (or holiness).

A right choice supposes, to be sure, certain conditions. One's mind must be open to the Gospel, and one needs insight into the paradoxical, at first sight 'scandalous', dimension of the ways of Christ, hence the Two Standards meditation on which the exercitant is about to embark. From the Two Standards and subsequent meditations it will emerge that to find God's will and to reach holiness in whatever 'state' one might be called to, requires on one's own side certain evangelical preferences, preferences characteristic of the 'true life' in Christ. But at this point – for Ignatius takes things one step at a time – the principle must be established that for a person faced with the choice of a state of life, either option could be God's will, and all that matters finally is to know in what state God wishes one to be.

[135] ¹ P<small>REAMBLE FOR THE CONSIDERATION OF STATES OF LIFE</small>
² **The example given us by Christ our Lord of the first state of life,** *the* *observance of the commandments,* **has been considered in the contemplation of his obedience to his parents.** ³ **We have considered, too, his example of the second state, evangelical perfection, when he stayed in the Temple, leaving his adopted father and natural mother to devote himself to the exclusive service of his heavenly Father.** ⁴ **Now** *while at the same time contemplating his life,* **we shall begin** *to investigate and ask* **in which life or state the Divine Majesty wishes to avail himself of us.** ⁵ **By way of introduction to that, we shall see (in the first exercise that follows) the intention of Christ our Lord and on the contrary that of the enemy of human nature, as well as the attitudes we need to acquire in order to** *reach perfection in whatever state of life* **God our Lord may grant us to choose.**

the observance of the commandments The distinction between the way of the commandments and the way of perfection is derived from Matthew 19:20–21; 'These (commandments) I have observed from my youth' ... 'if you would be perfect ... '

while at the same time contemplating his life On the importance of continuing the contemplation of the Gospels throughout the time of election, cf. *1599 Directory*:
    'Great care should be taken that the meditations on Christ's life are diligently made at the proper times ... These meditations strengthen and illuminate the mind, lifting it up from earthly things and making it fitter to perceive and embrace God's will and to overcome all obstacles. To cease from meditation on the other hand would weaken and becloud the soul.
    This is why due time must be given to meditating divine realities as presented in the various mysteries, as well as due time to the election. Otherwise, if the mind is exclusively occupied with the thoughts of the election, its juice and flower of devotion might be easily sucked dry and exhausted and the soul enfeebled.'[52]

to investigate and ask While 'ask' suggests docility and openness (the fundamental disposition of the person making an election), 'investigate' suggests the element of active search.

---

[52]*1599 Directory*, ch. 30 (MHSI 76, p. 717 [trans. Palmer, p. 334]).

reach perfection in whatever state of life That certain kinds of life might in an objective sense be designated as 'ways of perfection' does not imply that only some Christians are called to personal perfection or to the fullness of holiness. Ignatius indeed makes it clear there that he sees perfection as a universal call. In our own time this position has been formally declared in the Second Vatican Council: 'All Christians in any state or walk of life are called to the fullness of Christian life and to the perfection of love.'[53]

Two Standards

Similar in scenario and content to the Kingdom, of which it is a development, the Two Standards puts before the exercitant a faith-vision of reality in terms of two value-systems, that of Christ and that of the enemy of human nature; while in the colloquy the exercitant is invited to make for him or herself the kind of response which in the Kingdom is only observed. As in the earlier exercise, the vision is dominated by a reality that profoundly affected Ignatius' outlook: the reality of spiritual powers in radical opposition, yet present and at work throughout the world. However, here these are present-ed not in their obvious ways of working, but in their subtleties. Thus the power of evil is shown as operating plausibly yet destructively, through the appeal of objectively legitimate *riches and honours*. And life in Christ is not just a morally correct life, but one that values the paradoxes of spiritual and actual poverty. The horizon (again as in the Kingdom Exercise) is that of the world: the minions of evil and the missionaries of Christ build respectively the worlds of Babylon and Jerusalem. But the emphasis is on the negative and positive individual qualities that place a person in one camp or the other, and on the desires that lead to these. These qualities are on the one side *pride*, to which the Evil One leads us through cupidity, and on the other *humility*, to which Christ leads us through the desire to follow in ways other than those of instinct and convention.

For an exercitant with an election to make, the Two Standards promotes the dispositions he or she needs in order to be able to hear Christ's call, whatever it might be. But it would be a mistake to think of the Two Standards as a special exercise for people preparing to make a life-choice. While such a situation might give an edge to the meditation in practice, neither the body of the meditation nor the colloquy lose their point if the exercitant is not faced with an immediate election. Essentially the Two Standards prepares the exercitant for a particular election because it invites him or her to the radical conversion of outlook and desire that constitutes the *true life* in Christ.

The graces of the Two Standards – assent to the vision, and the response

---

[53]*Dogmatic Constitution on the Church*, §40.

of self-offering – are one of the critical elements in the Exercises. Nevertheless it is important to realize that the actual day of the Two Standards is a moment in a process, coming as it does after lengthy preparation (Foundation, First Week, Kingdom, the Contemplation of the Incarnation and the Infancy of Christ) and being followed by ongoing developments both in and after the time of the Exercises. Thus as the Exercises go on, further insight into the vision is gained through contemplation of the Gospel while the response is deepened and confirmed through repetition. Nor will the exercitant's grasp of the Two Standards be complete even with the closing of the Exercises. As well as being a major juncture within the Exercises, the Two Standards is one of the permanent resources of Ignatian spirituality, and its doctrine will continue to yield meanings and applications as it is integrated with time into the person's developing experience and reflection.

In giving the Two Standards the director must be careful to find the mean between saying too much and too little, avoiding the lengthy explanations that impede 'inner perception', while at the same time giving the exercitant the guidance needed. To find this mean it will be helpful if the above distinction is kept in mind. The day of the Two Standards is not the moment to enter, at least in any detail, into the numerous theological or practical questions that the meditation might suggest. Later it may be well to do this. At the beginning it is the broad essentials that matter: to recognize the pull within ourselves between the two sets of values, two wisdoms, and to risk ourselves for the following of the poor and humble Christ of the Gospel.[54]

[136] [1] FOURTH DAY. *MEDITATION* ON THE TWO STANDARDS: THE ONE, THAT OF *CHRIST* OUR *COMMANDER-IN-CHIEF* AND OUR LORD, THE OTHER THAT OF *LUCIFER*, THE *DEADLY ENEMY OF OUR HUMAN NATURE*.
[2] **Prayer. The usual preparatory prayer.**

meditation The exercise is a 'meditation', and thus characterized by 'consideration' [141, 142, 144–146], though imagination has also a part to play [140, 143].

Christ In the title, as in the first prelude below, Christ precedes Lucifer. The order of considering the strategies does not indicate the priority of the two parts of the meditation. The object of the meditation is knowledge of, and insight into the way of Christ, and to have this it is necessary to be open-eyed about the way of the evil spirit.

---

[54]For the doctrine of the Two Standards in the New Testament, see Matt. 6:19–21; Mark 10:17–31; Luke 6:20–26; John 8:31–51; Phil. 2:1–11; Eph. 6:10–20; 1 Tim. 6:6–10; 1 Pet. 4:12–5:11; James 3:13–18; Rev. 3:15–22. But these are just a few of the many texts that could be cited in this connection.

Commander-in-Chief As in the Kingdom, Christ is a figure of conflict.

Lucifer The fallen angel of light, hence the deceiver.

deadly enemy of our human nature Underlying the whole of the Exercises is the principle that Christ leads us to a fully human existence, characterized by integration with self and with the world. Satan does the opposite, destroying freedom (cf. *traps and chains* [142]), and if given complete licence, literally dealing death. The point needs especially to be made here since the Two Standards is dealing with the Evil One working hiddenly behind a reasonable front.

[137] The first prelude is the *history*: in this case how Christ calls and desires everybody to be under his *standard*, and how Lucifer on the contrary wants everyone under his.

[138] ¹ The second prelude: the composition made by seeing the place; here it will be to behold a great plain extending over the entire region around *Jerusalem*, where the Commander-in-Chief of all the good is Christ our Lord; ² and another plain in the region of Babylon, where the enemy leader is Lucifer.

[139] ¹ The third prelude: to ask for *what I want*: here it will be to ask for knowledge of the deceits of the evil leader and for help to guard against them, ² and also for knowledge of the true life revealed by the supreme and true commander, and for grace to imitate him.

history refers not to the past but to a faith vision of the here-and-now world; 'history' not in the sense of particular events, but of an on-going process.

standards I.e. 'banners'. The term evokes the picture of two groups. Christ and anti-Christ seek to enlist all people into the assembly of their disciples.

Jerusalem I.e. the world as peaceful and just, as permeated by the values of the Kingdom. Those under Christ's standard both belong to this world, but also help to build it, as those under the standard of Satan belong to and help to build *Babylon*, symbol of the world as proud, corrupted by riches and power, the world under the sway of anti-Christ.

what I desire The grace requested is *knowledge*, that is to say, faith-enlightened knowledge of the ways in which Christ and his adversary work in human affairs. Though the meditation will conclude with an act of commitment, in the form of the Second Week Triple Colloquy, it should be noted that the importance of the Two Standards consists not only in the Triple

Colloquy, but in the *knowledge* in which the desires of the Colloquy are founded. The knowledge however is not of a speculative kind, but knowledge ordered to the *imitation* of Christ and avoidance of the deceits of anti-Christ.

The characteristic of anti-Christ is to proceed through deception, the plausible lie. Christ, the supreme and *true* leader reveals the *true* life.

< Part 1 >
[140] The first point is *to imagine* the leader of all the enemy powers as if he were seated in that great plain of *Babylon*, as though on a throne of fire and smoke, a horrible and fearsome figure.

[141] [1] **The second point is to consider how he summons forth count-less *demons*, and disperses them, some to one city and others to another,** [2] **thus covering *the entire world*, leaving out no region, no place, no state of life, nor any individual.**

[142] [1] **The third point is to consider *the speech* he makes to them; how he orders them to lay *traps and chains*,** [2] **and he tells them that first they must tempt people to *covet* wealth (this is his way in most cases), so that they might come more readily to the empty honours of the world, and in the end to unbounded pride.**
[3] **Therefore the first step is *riches*, the second *honour*, and the third *pride*; from these three steps the enemy leads people on to every other vice.**

to imagine The (to our minds) crudely depicted picture reflects Ignatius' concern to unmask the reality of a power that works hiddenly. Specific aspects of the nature of this reality and of its action in human beings are symbolized by the various details: *throne* (= power), *fire* (= destruction), *smoke* (= darkness and confusion). Integral to Ignatius' presentation of Satan is the symbol of *Babylon* – the power of evil as located not in Hell but in this world.

demons Malevolent preternatural influences, with nothing of the not-quite-serious, almost pantomime, associations that might be evoked in a modern reader. Note the contrast between the *demons* confided in by Lucifer and the *persons* in Part 2 [145]. Satan works also, of course, through people but without divulging his real purpose to them, while Christ's friends know their master's business (John 15:15).

the entire world The cosmic dimension of the work of Satan is again empha-sized. The individual is related to a society composed of *cities ... provinces, places, states of life*. No *state of life* carries protection against the strategy of the Evil One.

the speech The strategy is presented in the form of a 'briefing', an Ignatian device to aid objectivity. The exercitant must consider the strategy in the awareness precisely that it is the strategy of the Evil One, the enemy of human nature (without this awareness the strategy in itself might be interesting, but not of very great import). The strategy is proposed as something to be recognized rather than analysed, and (as noted above) this is not the moment to explore its practical applications in any degree of detail. To meditate on it requires however a certain unpacking of the operative words.

traps and chains The unseen reality, bondage, behind the appearances of the harmless and attractive.

covet The strategy is not concerned with the possession of wealth in itself, or even with every kind of desire to gain or keep a possession (such a desire can be given by God cf. [16, 155]). The desire described here is covetous desire or 'cupidity', the craving for wealth when we lack it, and the possessive clinging to it when we have it; it is the attitude that regards whatever we want as ours by right, the attitude of persons who 'put their trust in riches'.

riches/honour Taken literally the words refer to material possessions, and social and ecclesiastical status, but while this literal sense has relevance for every one in every age (and crucial implications for our own age), the terms also admit of wider application. In the wider sense, *riches* and *honour* can be anything at all that meets the inherent human need for identity, security, esteem, love. The particular significance we attach to the things, situations or relationships that for us meet these needs, the quality of our desire for these, our criteria for seeking or accepting them – all this raises the basic issue of the kind of persons we are and want to be in relation to God and others.

pride A stance in relation to God, consisting in the refusal to give praise and reverence [50], and hence a tendency, in however subtle a way, to try to establish oneself as absolute. When understood thus *pride* is clearly linked with cupidity: pride needs the things that build and affirm the self, and needing them for self-absolutization has to detach them from the praise, reverence and service of God. Once so detached, they will be easily captured by the isolated (or 'proud') me.

< Part 2 >

[143] Similarly, we are to apply the imagination to the supreme and true Commander, *Christ our Lord*.

[144] The first point is to consider Christ our Lord taking his stand in

a great plain in the region of Jerusalem in a *lowly, beautiful and attractive spot.*

[145] The second point: to consider how the Lord of all the world chooses so many persons, apostles, disciples, etc., and sends them out over the whole world to spread his sacred doctrine among people of every state and condition.

[146] [1] The third point: to consider *the speech* which Christ our Lord delivers to his servants and friends as he sends them out on this enterprise. [2] He commends them to seek to help all men and women, by attracting them, first, to the highest *spiritual poverty*; [3] and if his Divine Majesty be thereby served and should be pleased to choose them for it, not less to *actual poverty*; [4] and secondly, to the desire for *humiliation* and *contempt*. For from these two things follows humility. [5] Therefore there are three steps, first, poverty as opposed to riches, second, humiliation or contempt as opposed to worldly honour, and thirdly *humility* as opposed to pride. [6] From these three steps they can lead everyone to all the other virtues.

Christ Our Lord As in Part 1, the strategy must not be separated from its personal source, here Christ himself. Part 2 is not addressed therefore to a person in search of motivational integrity, inner freedom, or even humility for their own sake, but to a person who seeks an ever deeper and more authentic relationship with Christ.

a great plain Reminiscent of Luke 6:17 and hence of the teaching on the beatitudes and the woes (vv. 20–26), a classic source for the whole of this meditation.

lowly, beautiful and attractive spot In the Vulgate version ('established indeed in a lowly place, but very beautiful in appearance and supremely worthy of love') the final adjectives are referred to Christ.

the speech In proposing the strategy of Christ (*spiritual and actual poverty ... humiliation and contempt ... humility*) Ignatius again adopts the device of a 'briefing' (cf. [142]).

spiritual poverty denotes an attitude that does not look to riches and honour for a security cover against God, but which uses and enjoys these as gifts, and only in relation to God's service and praise. *Spiritual poverty* does not necessarily imply *actual poverty*, but it does imply openness to it. Where *actual poverty* in any form is simply unacceptable, a non-value, there is no *spiritual poverty*. Thus the Vulgate translates *spiritual poverty* as 'a spiritual attachment to poverty', For a person with possessions, spiritual poverty makes it possible to have these without being possessed by them.[55]

actual poverty ... humiliation, contempt. Like *wealth and honour* these terms are to be understood in an extended as well as in a literal sense. Here they should be taken as denoting the general characteristics of a way of life antithetical to the pursuit of wealth and status, the way of life lived out and commended by Jesus, and modelled in many different ways by his followers. Note however that *actual poverty* and *humiliation* are desired conditionally (*if his Divine Majesty be thereby served and should be pleased to choose them for it*). The phrase *humiliation and contempt* with its many variants echoes Luke 6:22 and Matthew 5:11.

humility God-centredness as opposed to the egocentricity of pride, the attitude which acknowledges one's need for God and trusts God with one's life and happiness. For the humble person, poverty in whatever form is a value because it provides the space in which to live by trust.

[147] **¹ A *colloquy* should be made *to Our Lady*, asking her to obtain for me *grace* from her Son and Lord that I be received[56] under his standard.**
² first *in the highest spiritual poverty* and also, if his Divine Majesty requires this and should be pleased to choose and receive me for it, *no less in actual poverty*;
³ second *in suffering humiliations and insults* so as to imitate him more closely, *provided*[57] *only* that I can suffer these without sin on the part of any other person and without displeasure to his Divine Majesty; and then a Hail Mary.
⁴ The second colloquy is to ask the same of the Son that he may obtain it for me from the Father, and then say an Anima Christi.
⁵ The third colloquy is to ask the same of the Father that he would grant it to me himself, and say an Our Father.

[55]'It behoves you to reflect that if you have possessions, they should not posses you, nor should you be possessed by anything temporal, but should refer them all to the Master from whom you have received them', *Letter to Pietro Contarini* (a wealthy clerical friend, nephew of Cardinal Gaspar Contarini and himself later a bishop), August 1537 (MHSI *Epp. Ig.* I, no. 13, p. 124 [trans. William J. Young, p. 32]).

[56]The Vulgate adds 'and remain'.

[57]For '*provided only that I can suffer without sin*' the Vulgate has 'praying however against others being in fault' adding: 'lest contempt of myself turn both to the damage of another and to the offence of God'.

Triple Colloquy The language reflects the petitioner's awareness that what is being asked for is a *grace* or gift. The protestation of desire, while intensely earnest, has a note of diffidence absent in the more dramatically high-key oblation in the Kingdom, and the threefold petition accentuates the seriousness of the request.

to Our Lady On Mary's role as intercessor, see comments on [63] above. She is specially significant here and in subsequent colloquies of the Second Week (see [156, 157, 158, 168]) because in her is found the fullness of 'imitation' and of understanding of the 'true life and teaching' of Christ [139, 164]).

The *grace* asked for is *to be received under Christ's standard*, a phrase which recalls the prayer 'to be placed with the Son' that Ignatius had been making prior to the vision at La Storta. It is important to keep this in mind in connection with the petition for actual poverty and actual humiliation: the request is not to be poor and humiliated, but *in and through poverty and humiliations* to be received *under Christ's standard*.

in highest spiritual poverty ... no less in actual poverty Spiritual poverty is asked for without conditions, for God certainly wishes the *highest spiritual poverty* for us all. Regarding *actual poverty* the true disciples, on their side, desire – and therefore offer themselves for – actual poverty no less than spiritual.

in suffering humiliations and insults In connection with these Ignatius makes explicit mention of the imitation of Christ.

provided only The conditions are vital criteria for discernment, for Ignatius knew very well that one can opt for or accept humiliation with results contrary to God's glory.[58] But the emphasis remains where it has been throughout the meditation, on the desire to be more, rather than less, Christlike in the very situation and condition of one's life, and not on the possible need to subordinate this desire to wider criteria of discernment. Though the

---

[58]Such would have been the case, to take one example, if Ignatius had failed to seek legal redress with regard to damaging rumours spread against himself and the companions shortly after their arrival in Rome in 1538. Writing again to Pietro Contarini, he explains: 'With the help of God, we shall never be worried if we personally are called lacking in culture, education or eloquence, or again if we are called wicked, deceivers or unreliable; but what hurt was that the actual doctrine which we were preaching should be called unsound, and that our form of life should be called evil, for ours are neither of these, but are of Christ and his Church', *Letter to Pietro Contarini*, 2 December 1538 (MHSI *Epp. Ig.* I, no. 7, pp. 134–6 [trans. *Personal Writings*, p. 148]).

provisos need to be included at this stage, the grace of the Two Standards is that of conversion to an outlook in which humiliation is positively valued, against an outlook in which the basic value is 'honour'.

[148] ¹ NOTE
This exercise should be *made at midnight and again in the morning, with two repetitions* (at the time of Mass and at the time of Vespers);
² it should always conclude with the three colloquies, with our Lady, with her Son, and with the Father. The following exercise, on the Three Classes, should be made before supper.

made at midnight and again in the morning, with two repetitions. The distinction between *making again* and *making a repetition* is clear.

Three Classes

In the final meditation of the Fourth Day, three 'cases' are put before the exercitant regarding a specific situation of choice, the first two bringing home the ways a person can evade the basic exigencies of indifference,[59] the third setting out in some detail the overall dynamics of availability to God's will. It is a meditation which might seem at first sight somewhat out of line with that of the Two Standards. In form the two Exercises are certainly quite different, and in content the Three Classes might appear even to take a step backward; for while the Two Standards concludes with the positive desire to follow Christ in poverty, the exercitant is now asked to consider cases in which freedom of choice is limited by the attraction of the world's riches.

The difference of form and the sense of abruptness that exercitants sometimes feel in making the transition to the final meditation, is partly explained by the different provenance of the two texts, which derive respectively from Loyola and the student years in Paris. But despite the differences in form, the Three Classes is closely connected with the Two Standards, and in relation to it represents in fact a step forward, the step from general vision towards the exigencies of concrete commitment. For the assumption behind it is that a 'higher' or 'spiritual' desire does not immediately eliminate the lower or instinctive desires, but that on the contrary the burgeoning of the higher desires might well heighten the sense of higher and lower in tension.

---

[59]Though the word appears only in the note [157], indifference is clearly the central theme of the whole meditation. As pointed out earlier, in connection with the Foundation, indifference in the sense of 'readiness to do whatever may prove to be God's will', is the fundamental disposition in which every choice must be approached. The preferences for the way of poverty inculcated in the Exercises from the outset of the Second Week do not replace indifference, but include it (cf. [167]).

This tension is especially likely to occur when one is faced with the ineluctable demands of bringing a general aspiration (namely, to follow Christ poor) to a specific costly choice. It was a tension of which Ignatius became especially conscious in the milieu of Paris with its preoccupations with ecclesiastical preferment.

Hence the 'cases' in which by means of an imaginative construct the exercitant is enabled to realize what might be his or her own reaction in a concrete choice between a 'poorer' and a 'richer' course, where one of the options exercises a powerful hold over the affections.[60] It should be noted, however, that the exercitant does not yet make his or her own election. Nor does the present meditation imply that if the three people are open to the Spirit they will necessarily relinquish their property. We are concerned here with one issue, central and demanding, that of freedom.

The meditation requires that serious attention be given to the 'case histories'; but it is important not to be deceived by the practical nature of the cases into playing down the quality of prayer to be expected of this final exercise of the Fourth Day. The Three Classes meditation is not only a 'reality check'. It is the prayer of a person standing before God and the whole heavenly court seeking grace to be unconditionally open to God's will [151]. And basic to it is the assumption that while, as always, the human collaborative response is vital, indifference and the desire to do God's will are first and foremost graces, to be earnestly prayed for.

If these principles are kept in mind, ordinarily the meditation will prove fairly straightforward to give, only the dense third class [155] requiring perhaps to be simplified in presentation. Regarding Ignatius' purpose-designed 'cases', they have a pointedness that should make the director slow to abandon them; on the other hand, they can be complemented by the recall of familiar Scripture texts.[61]

[149] [1] ALSO ON THE FOURTH DAY A MEDITATION IS MADE ON THE THREE CLASSES OF PERSONS TO HELP US *TO EMBRACE WHAT IS BETTER*

[60]The Three Classes, like the Two Standards, forms part of the exercitant's immediate preparation for election, the reference to election being indeed more to the fore in the Three Classes. However the point made above about the Two Standards holds also of the present meditation; it is not only a 'pre-election strategy', but an element of formation in the true life in Christ, of which listening to God's word in the choices of life is a central characteristic. But again, for an exercitant facing an immediate decision the Three Classes might well be a more critical experience than for others. On its wider reach, see J. English, *Spiritual Freedom*, pp. 164–5.

[61]For example: First Class, cf. Matt. 25:1–13 (foolish virgins); Luke 13:12–21 (rich fool). Second Class: cf. Matt. 6:24 (slave of two masters); Mark. 10:17–27 (rich young man); Luke 9:57–62 (excuses of those called); Luke 23:20 (Pilate). Third Class: cf. Gen. 22:1–9 (Abraham); Luke 2:38 (Mary); Acts 22:10 (Paul).

² Prayer. The usual preparatory prayer.

to embrace what is better The title makes clear that the entire exercise is ordered to choice, and choice made under the criterion not of the good, but of the *better*.

[150] ¹ The first prelude is the history. *Three persons* **have each acquired 10,000 ducats, but not purely and as would have been right for the love of God.** ² *They all want to be saved* **and** *to find God our Lord in peace* **by getting rid of the** *burden and obstacle* **to this purpose contained in their** *attachment* **to the acquired fortune.**

Three persons, each representing a 'class',⁶² have come into possession of a fortune, legitimately but not purely from the love of God, and each is conscious of an attachment to their new possession. The question that now arises is whether the love of God requires them to keep the possession or relinquish it, but before this question can be answered they must first deal with the powerful attachment aroused by a fortune of spectacular proportions.⁶³

They all want to be saved ... Again, it is not the possession of wealth, but the (covetous) attachment to it that, even in the case of legitimately held wealth, can finally jeopardize salvation itself.

to find God our Lord in peace ... 'Peace' here is that associated with *finding God*, not the 'certain level of peace of soul' of Annotation 18 [18].

burden and obstacle ... attachment I.e. *attachment* in so far as its effects on will and judgement constitute a *burden and obstacle* in the search to know what is more pleasing to God. For the three hypothetical people, the immediate critical question is not whether to keep or abandon a material possession, but whether to be free in relation to an attachment that prevents the question itself from being asked openly and without subterfuge.

⁶²In Spanish *binarios* (literally 'pairs'), a term used in the language of moral theology in dealing, as here, with 'cases of conscience'. It is explained in two ways: first in the literal sense of two people (e.g. Titius and Bertha of the classic moral case), but also as designating an individual (composed of the two elements of body and soul). For the latter explanation, see Gueydan, et al., *Exercices Spirituels*, p. 94 note. The familiar title 'Three Classes' is taken from the Latin translations. It is retained here since the persons, or pairs, represent 'types'.

⁶³Compared with the 50 ducats a year on which in Ignatius' opinion a student could live in Paris, 10,000 ducats represents a fabulous fortune. Cf. *Letter to Martín García de Oñaz*, brother of Ignatius, June 1532 (MHSI *Epp. Ig.* I, no. 3, pp. 77–83 [trans. *Personal Writings*, p. 118]).

Requiring as it does a positive will to relinquish should God so wish, freedom is a critical issue in itself.

[151] The second prelude: the composition made by seeing the place. Here will be to see myself standing *in the presence of God our Lord and of all his saints* that *I might desire and know* what is more pleasing to his Divine Goodness.

[152] The third prelude, to ask for what I want: here it will be to ask for *the grace to choose* what is more for the glory of his Divine Majesty and for the salvation of my soul.

in the presence of God our Lord and of all his saints As in [98] and [232] the saints or the divine court enhance the sense of solemnity. This is the setting within which Ignatius would have us approach serious decisions.

I might desire and know Desire precedes knowing. One is free to discover *what* is more pleasing to God only when one desires *whatever* may be more pleasing to him. We perceive according to our desires.

the grace to choose I.e. not only to be open in a general sense to Christ's way, but to make a concrete choice in reference to it. The desired criterion of choice is the *more*.

Note the difference between these two preludes and the petition of the Two Standards: in the Two Standards one asks to know the way of Jesus and the wiles of the enemy in order, as a life project, to imitate Christ and avoid the snares of the evil one; on the other hand here the petition is to desire God's will here and now and to choose the best.

[153] *The persons* of *the first class* would like to be free of the attachment they have to the acquired possession, so as to meet God in peace and be saved, but they take no means to bring this about until the hour of their death.

[154] [1] Those of *the second class* would like to be free of their attachment, but they want so to be free of it that they retain the thing itself. Thus God is to come to what they themselves want, [2] and there is no determination to relinquish the acquired possession in order to go to God, even if that were the better course for them.

[155] [1] Those of *the third class* want to get rid of their attachment, but they want to be rid of it in such a way that they also have no inclina-

tion either to keep the acquisition or not to keep it,[2] but all they want is simply that their wanting or not wanting should be in accordance with whatever God our Lord inclines them to want, and as might appear to be more for the service and praise of His Divine Majesty. [3] In the meantime they wish to *reckon themselves as having given the thing up totally in their hearts*; and they *draw upon all their powers* to want neither this particular thing, nor indeed anything else, unless it be solely the service of God our Lord that moves them. [4] Thus it is the desire to be better able to serve God our Lord that will move them to take the thing in question or to leave it.

the persons The text returns to the story. While aware of oneself and of one's own situation, one looks at the way the three fictitious people deal with their situation, i.e. with their desire to be free from covetous ties to a material possession about which a choice has eventually to be made.

the first class The desire to be free and the desire to keep the possession create a deadlock. Procrastination makes the situation tolerable. No *means* are taken.

the second class effectively confine the will of God to the boundaries of their own unfreedom (as opposed to expanding the boundaries of freedom in order to discern the will of God). They are unwilling to relinquish *even if that were the better course*.[64] Though Ignatius held that in the abstract it is a higher course (because more literally evangelical) to abandon wealth than to keep it, there is no implication here that this is necessarily the better course for the individual. Were this so, the election for one seeking what is more *to the glory of God* would already be decided. Ignatius is insisting on the willingness for relinquishment as necessary for indifference.

the third class (See [16] and [169].) The account describes a development through which immediate sensible or instinctive desires yield to the Spirit-given desires in and through which the will of God is found. *Desire*, indeed, is the key-word of this short paragraph, in which the word *querer* ('want' or 'desire') occurs seven times in the Spanish original. The whole process is the work of the Spirit, but this emphatically does not mean that no place is left for human initiative. Effort on our part indeed is integral

---

[64]The natural reading, adopted by the majority of translators, is 'although that would be the better state for them'. The alternative, possible, reading is adopted by Rickaby: 'they are not resolute to leave the thing to go to God – no, though that state were to prove the better for them' (*Spiritual Exercises*, p. 118). The Vulgate has: 'to draw God to their own wish rather than forsake their hindrance and move towards him by means of the more conducive state'.

to the process, but it is subsidiary to the work of the Spirit and collaborative with it.

Expressed in the text in two slightly different ways, the overall sequence (if we include elements already assumed) might be summarized as follows:

(1) Desire to be saved and to find peace with God (assumed of all three classes)
(2) Desire to be free of the affective tie to the acquired thing (assumed of all three classes)
(3) Replacement of the original disposition (i.e. hampering affective bond) by the disposition of indifference (no inclination to keep the possession or not)
(4) Interim affective space for the action of God leading the person to sense and to know God's will
(5) So that the ultimate decision might be 'caused' solely by the desire better to be able to serve God

to want the thing or not to want it Indifference is a commitment which develops from a lesser to a greater degree. Moreover the ideal is not primarily a situation in which immediate inclinations are eliminated, but a situation in which these do not prevent us from sensing the movements of the spirit or from perceiving our situation in the light of the signs of God's will.[65]

according as God our Lord shall move their will God moves the will primarily by giving a desire for the 'end', i.e. for God's greater praise and service. In making an election one may also be moved towards a specific option (here to keep or give up one's fortune) in such a way that the desire alone is evidence of God's will (the situation of the First and Second Times of election). It cannot be assumed however that given indifference, we shall always be moved in this way; but for Ignatius it is important that on our side we should have the *wish* to experience the movements of God more explicitly rather than less.

The idea of God *moving the will* is to be understood in terms of the paradox of spiritual freedom, that the more the Spirit enters one's freedom, the more one is truly free.

---

[65]'It is not stated that the affection for the created good is less strong in those of the Third Class than it is in those of the other classes. Neither is it stated that they possess stronger natural will power than others. But it does appear that a superior spiritual affection, the fruit of grace, comes in to re-establish some sort of equilibrium between the initial desire for "peace in God" and the instinctive repugnance to the ridding themselves spiritually (and effectively if God so asks) of the good that is loved.' Cusson, *Biblical Theology*, pp. 262–3.

as might appear to them personally Graced desire for a course of action must go with the perception that the course is the one most conducive to the glory of God. The ways a person may come to perceive God's will vary with the 'times of election'.

reckon themselves as having given the thing up totally in their hearts I.e. choose as far as possible to adopt the attitude of one who has already lost the thing. Only in this way is it possible effectively to achieve the equipoise constitutive of indifference.

draw upon all their powers Indifference, when it requires the mental relinquishment of an attractive object, is not attained without effort. But the emphasis is not primarily on ascetical effort. *Drawing upon all one's powers* must be interpreted in the overall context of Ignatius' insistence on Spirit-given desire as the principle both of choice and of its essential condition, indifference.[66]

[156] *Three colloquies.* **I will make the same three colloquies that were made in the preceding contemplation on the Two Standards.**

With the *three colloquies* the exercitants turn from the story to themselves. While the petitions are the same as in the Two Standards, their import and mood will correspond to the particular emphases of the Three Classes meditation. There will be a sharper awareness of the decision which has to be made, of the specific implications of the *actual poverty* for which one asks to be chosen, and of the inner obstacles to indifference.

[157] [1] NOTE
It is to be noted that when we experience either an *attachment* or a repugnance, which are against actual poverty, when we are not *indifferent* towards poverty or riches, [2] **a great help towards extinguishing such a disordered attachment is to ask in the colloquies (*even though it goes against carnal instinct*) that Our Lord should choose us for actual poverty,** [3] **and to desire, beg, and plead for this,** *provided it be for the service and praise of his Divine Majesty.*

attachment As the relevance of the three stories is borne in on them, the exercitant may become acutely aware of attachments to his or her own riches and to the fact that indifference in regard to these does not come easily. The present note is addressed to people in this situation. To avoid misunderstanding it must be stressed that the recommended response cannot be

[66]Cf. Annotation 16, with commentary.

engineered by will power, but comes about through the Spirit (and in the Spirit's time) and from a motivation of love and trust. Ignatius however takes this as read, and his concern is with the degree of commitment that may be called for on our side in order to attain the affective freedom in which to find God's will. The point is made not only by the insistence on 'going against', but by a general intensification of language in comparison with the Two Standards. The strong word *extinguish* appears only here in the whole Exercises, and *desire, beg, plead* contrast strongly with the simple *ask* of [147].[67]

indifferent Though the whole meditation is about *indifference* the word is here mentioned for the first time.

even though it goes against carnal instinct See comment on [97] above.

provided it be for the service and praise of the Divine Majesty. The eventual will of God is still being sought, and in the exercitant's prayer for the 'poorer' option there is no question of pre-empting the election. The Vulgate makes this clear by replacing Ignatius' conclusion with the reminder that we must preserve meantime, 'the liberty of our desire, whereby it may be lawful for us to go the way which is the more suitable to the service of God's will'. In Ignatius' own text this point is implicit rather than explicit.

Fifth to Twelfth Days

[158] FIFTH DAY. CONTEMPLATION ON THE DEPARTURE OF CHRIST OUR LORD FROM NAZARETH AND HIS JOURNEY TO THE RIVER JORDAN, WHERE HE IS BAPTIZED (cf. [273])

[159] **[1] First note. This contemplation should be made at midnight, and again in the morning, with two repetitions, at Mass-time and at the time of Vespers; before supper one should bring the senses to it.**
[2] Each of these five exercises should begin with the usual preparatory prayer and the three preludes, as has been explained in full in the contemplation of the Incarnation and Nativity, [3] and one should end with the triple colloquy of the Three Classes of Persons or according to the Note which follows the Three Classes.

---

[67]In connection with the concluding Note, Polanco quotes Aristotle to the effect that 'to be made straight, a stick must be bent the other way', *Polanco Directory* (MHSI, vol. 76, p. 307).

[160] Second note. The particular examen after dinner and supper should be made on faults and negligences regarding the exercises of the day and the additions. The same holds for the subsequent days.

[161] [1] SIXTH DAY. CONTEMPLATION ON HOW CHRIST OUR LORD WENT FROM THE RIVER JORDAN TO THE DESERT (INCLUSIVE) [cf. 274] The same arrangement should be kept in everything as on the Fifth Day.

[2] SEVENTH DAY. HOW ST ANDREW AND THE OTHERS FOLLOWED CHRIST OUR LORD [cf. 275]

[3] EIGHTH DAY. THE SERMON ON THE MOUNT ON THE EIGHT BEATITUDES [cf. 280]

[4] NINTH DAY. HOW CHRIST OUR LORD APPEARED TO HIS DISCIPLES ON THE WAVES OF THE SEA [cf. 280]

[5] TENTH DAY. HOW THE LORD PREACHED IN THE TEMPLE [cf. 288]

[6] ELEVENTH DAY. THE RAISING OF LAZARUS [cf. 285]

[7] TWELFTH DAY. PALM SUNDAY [cf. 287]

Notes on the mysteries

[162] [1] First note. The *number of contemplations* in this Second Week can be increased or cut down according to the time one may want to give to the week, or according to one's degree of progress. [2] To prolong the week, one can take the mysteries of the Visitation of our Lady to St Elizabeth, the Shepherds, the Circumcision of the Child Jesus, the Three Kings and others as well. [3] To shorten it, one can drop even some of the mysteries proposed, because what is given here is an introduction and a way of proceeding, with a view to *better and more complete contemplation later*.

[163] Second note. The material dealing with elections should be embarked upon from the contemplation on the Lord's departure from Nazareth and the events at the Jordan, that is from the Fifth Day, following the explanations given later.

number of contemplations Two points are clear. First, the exercitant is not strictly tied to the number or the subjects of the contemplations given in the

121

body of the text; and second, the methods (with which at this stage the exercitant will have some familiarity) are pedagogical, and designed to help the exercitant eventually to find their own way.

better and more complete contemplation later could be taken to mean that as the exercitant becomes increasingly familiar with Gospel contemplation, either in or after the Exercises, they will become less dependent on the strict methods given in the text. But other interpretations are also possible, e.g. that the *better and more complete contemplation* lies beyond the contemplation of the mysteries of Jesus' infancy and public life, i.e., either in the contemplation of the Passion and Resurrection, or in the contemplation of God in all things to be reached in the Contemplation to Attain Love.[68]

[164] [1] **Third note. Before entering on the elections it will greatly help the exercitant to embrace wholeheartedly the** *true teaching of Christ our Lord,* [2] **if he or she considers attentively the following three kinds of humility. They should be** *considered from time to time throughout the day,* **and in the same way the three colloquies should be made, as will be explained later [168]).**

true teaching of Christ our Lord I.e. as introduced in the Two Standards [145].

considered ... throughout the day The day is the Fifth Day of the Second Week (on which the process of the election begins). No set times are prescribed. The material is *considered from time to time throughout the day,* while the contemplations of the life of Christ continue according to the ordinary programme. It may also be pondered in the course of the contemplations themselves. Thus the exercise on the kinds of humility is a *consideration,* concerned with material to be thought over rather than systematically meditated.

Three Kinds of Humility

In the Two Standards, humility was proposed as a goal. Now it is proposed as a development, admitting of various levels.[69]

---

[68]Cf. Thomas, *Le Christ de Dieu pour Ignace de Loyola,* pp. 134–5.

[69]The Spanish and the Latin versions refer to 'ways' or 'kinds' of humility, not 'degrees'. The three categories represent however an ascending order, so it is not contrary to Ignatius' thought to call them 'degrees', provided we remember that the later ones include the earlier. The division of humility into degrees is a standard practice in the spiritual tradition (cf. the twelve degrees of humility in the rule of St Benedict).

For the general sense of humility, see above [146]. Here Ignatius specifies that it consists in 'self-subjection' [165]. There is nothing self-denigratory or servile about conceiving of one's relationship with God in this way. Humility is in fact nothing other than the love of God, but to call this love 'humility' is to pinpoint especially the quality of other-directedness in love, love as a handing oneself over in trust, letting God be Lord of one's being. A retreatant who made the Exercises under Ignatius in 1538, describes the modes of humility as 'kinds and degrees of the love of God, and of desiring to obey, imitate and serve his Divine Majesty'.[70]

To appreciate the general doctrine in this text, as well as to see its special relevance at this point of the Exercises, we must return to the distinction, and connection, between a 'moment' in the Exercises and the 'process' of maturation in Christ. In the Exercises the kinds of humility are considered at this point in order to enable the exercitant to check his or her here-and-now dispositions, especially in relation to the impending election. If the here-and-now context is ignored, and if the third and even the second kinds of humility are understood to describe only habitual dispositions, the exercise acquires an air of unreality; for it is a fact of experience that at moments we can be influenced by qualities of motivation or intention which are not operative in our lives all the time. On the other hand, the purpose of the Exercises is not just to help the exercitant reach an occasional peak in order to make an election, nor would there be any solidity about an election if the motivation required both for making and living it were a purely transitory experience. The Exercises are a major step in the life-process of maturing in Christ; and this maturation consists in coming increasingly to experience and respond to life habitually on the basis of the parodoxical wisdom of the third kind of humility.

However the development of the habit is one thing, and the disposition at the moment of the election in the Exercises is another; and the kinds of humility are introduced at this stage primarily to help the exercitant, and the director, to become aware of the attitudes that will exert an influence on judgement and will, as the exercitant seeks the will of God in the present moment of election. From the *Directories*, the practical implications of such a check are made clear. For admission to the election, the first kind of humility is insufficient. The second is both required and sufficient. The third is highly desirable, but not strictly necessary.[71] To sum up, the three kinds of

---

[70]From the retreat notes of Pedro Ortiz, Legate of Charles V to Paul III; cf. Cusson, *Biblical Theology*, pp. 264–5.

[71]'It must be insisted that a person entering upon the election do so with total resignation of his will, and if possible that he reach the third degree of humility ... Anyone who is not in the indifference of the second degree is not suited to enter upon the elections, and it is better to occupy him with other exercises until he reaches it'. *Directory dictated to de Vitoria (Directories*, p. 77 [trans., Palmer, p. 9]). In the *1599 Directory* this position is explained in terms of the psychology of rationalization. An exercitant's 'attitude of aversion from the more perfect way and inclination

humility can be characterized as 'love of the creature', 'love of the servant', 'love of the friend'.

< [165] THREE KINDS OF HUMILITY >

[1] *The first kind of humility* is necessary for eternal salvation. It consists in this, that as far as in me lies, I so subject and humble myself that I obey the law of God our Lord in everything; [2] so much so that even if I were made lord of all created things in this world, or even if my own life on this earth were at stake, I would not make a decision to set about breaking any law, whether divine or human, which obliges me under pain of mortal sin.

The first kind of humility Ignatius gives a positive definition, 'fidelity to the law of God', backed up by a negative definition, 'not for anything would I deliberately commit mortal sin'. The first is plainly wider than the second, but the negative definition, making explicit the concrete implications of fidelity to the law of God, is a criterion enabling us to judge our real sincerity.[72] The first mode of humility, if sincere, is not something to be disparaged, but consisting as it does in fidelity to obligations, it is not by itself an adequate attitude in which to make an election, because election is the search for the 'better for me' in a situation where obligations do not apply (cf. the Foundation).

[166] [1] *The second kind of humility* is more perfect than the first. It is present if I find myself at a point where I neither desire nor prefer to be rich rather than poor, to seek fame rather than disgrace, to desire a long rather than a short life, [2] *provided it is all the same for the service of God and the good of my soul.* Together with this I would not *make a decision* to set about committing a venial sin, even for the whole of creation or under threat to my own life.

The second kind of humility The second kind is, again, definied positively and negatively. Positively, it consists in the 'indifference' of the Foundation, whose language, with the exception of the sickness/health antonyms, is exactly reproduced. Negatively, it is an attitude such that here-and-now, neither for any gain, nor to save my life, would I decide to commit a venial sin. The essential difference between this and the first kind of humility

---

towards the more imperfect would influence his intellect to come up with reasons in agreement with his inclination. And since, as the maxim goes, whatever is received is received according to the measure of the one receiving, he could easily take to be God's will what is in fact his own' (MHSI 76, p. 689 [trans. Palmer, p. 325]).

[72]Cf. Cusson, *Biblical Theology*, pp. 267–8.

consists not in the rejection of venial as well as mortal sin, but in the total readiness to carry out the perceived desires of God even in matters where no (objective) obligation obtains.

provided it is all the same for the service of God and the good of my soul The judgement is, of course, a personal, subjective one. As I look at the situation with the desire only for the service and glory of God, it seems to me that each of two courses of action would give equal service and conduce equally to personal salvation. In that case the person in the second kind of humility remains open to whatever signs may eventually be given.

make a decision Here, as in connection with 'mortal sin' above, what is being checked is not simply restraint from actual sinful actions, but the quality of a person's values, priorities, and fundamental determination of will. Since the context is that of election, the references to sin both here and in relation to the first kind of humility also bear on the decision about to be made; in the matter of the election, the first mode of humility precludes the very possibility of a decision involving grave sin, the second the possibility of a decision involving venial sin.

Since we are concerned here with Christian (not Stoic) indifference, the second kind of humility will ordinarily include in germ the dispositions to be described below in the third kind, i.e. a positive attitude towards Christ's preferred way. The definition of the second kind of humility abstracts however from this. To the extent to which, irrespective of any personal evangelical preferences, one is *de facto* free in relation to the alternatives, one is sufficiently (though not ideally) disposed to approach the election.

[167] [1] *The third kind of humility* **is the most perfect humility. It is present when my disposition is as follows. Given that the first and second kinds of humility are included, and supposing equal** *praise and glory* **of the Divine Majesty, then,** [2] **in order to imitate Christ our Lord and to be actually more like him,** [3] **I want and choose poverty with Christ poor rather than wealth, and humiliations with Christ humiliated rather than fame,** [4] **and I desire more to be** *thought worthless and a fool* **for Christ, who first was taken to be such, rather than to be esteemed as wise and prudent in this world.**

The third kind of humility is distinguished from the second by positive preference: *I want and choose.* Moreover, preference is not only for poverty and contempt but for being reputed *worthless and a fool,* rather than *wise and prudent in this world* – categories not previously mentioned in the Exercises. The third kind of humility is the disposition of the person for whom it

125

is more desirable – not in a superficial way, but at the level of fundamental attitude – to lack, rather than to possess, riches and wordly honour; and to be accounted by the world as foolish and of little worth rather than as wise and prudent.

But in themselves such preferences – even when rooted deeply in the personality – do not necessarily manifest a profound evangelical attitude, and could indeed be spiritually or psychologically ambivalent. Hence what may appear to be the preferences of the third kind of humility may need to be tested against other marks of the authentic disposition. There are three in particular:

(1) This kind of humility is the attitude of a person deeply in love *with Christ*. Poverty, contempt, a reputation for foolishness are not preferred for themselves, or even as means of ascetical self-liberation, but as ways of following Christ and being like him. The third kind of humility is the love of Jesus, the wish to be identified with him, intensified to the point of folly.[73]

(2) It *includes* everything that has already been specified in the preceding two modes. It respects the law of God. It seeks the service of the Kingdom and one's own salvation.

(3) Its characteristic desires fall within the larger and absolutely fundamental desire that in all things God be *praised and glorified*. Any particular form of actual poverty or humiliation might or might not be for the greater glory of God,[74] and any preference for the way of poverty does not destroy the freedom to hear and to do whatever may prove to be the will of God; even if this means forgoing a course of action that one finds appealing precisely out of love.

praise and glory Words which capture the quality of 'altruism' in Ignatian spirituality – the simple desire that God be God in his world.

thought worthless and a fool Not exactly the same meaning as *humiliations* (in Spanish, *oprobrios*) which suggest particular incidents, whereas here the suggestion is rather than of an abiding situation. The antithesis – fool for Christ/esteemed as wise by the world – recalls the Pauline distinction between the wisdom of the world and the 'folly wisdom' of Christ. (1 Cor. 3:18–20; 4:10).

---

[73]The imitation motif is amplified in a famous passage in the *Constitutions* 101: See Ganss, *The Constitutions of the Society of Jesus*, pp. 107–8.

[74]As his writings frequently testify, Ignatius knew very well that one can opt for or accept poverty and humiliation in ways contrary to God's praise and glory. See the quotation from the letter to Pietro Contarini given above, [147] with note 58.

[168] [1] **Note. For anyone who desires to attain this third kind of humility it will, therefore, be very profitable to make the three** *colloquies* **mentioned for the Three Classes of persons.** [2] **In these, one should ask to be chosen, should the Lord so wish, for this third kind of humility, which is greater and better, so as the more to imitate and serve him, provided always that it may be for the equal or greater service of the Divine Majesty.**

colloquies. These mark the transition from *consideration* to *desire*.

Note on the Two Standards, Three Classes, Three Kinds of Humility

From the foregoing commentary it will be clear that these three texts represent a development. This might be summarized in terms of three elements: knowledge of Christ's way, commitment to Christ's way, and loving commitment to Christ's person. While each exercise is concerned with all three, the emphasis moves progressively from the first to the third.

In the Two Standards the fundamental grace is knowledge (but 'felt knowledge') of the antithetical ways of Lucifer and of Christ, whose way is a *sacred doctrine* [145]. The colloquy represents an initial response to this knowledge, an offering of oneself for a way of life without specific implications being necessarily confronted.

In the Three Classes, the knowledge is assumed and the emphasis is on the condition necessary for sincere commitment, namely a truly effective *indifference*. One need not be strictly in an election situation to make this exercise; but a person placed in such a situation will make the colloquy in an awareness of the specific 'actual poverty' to which they might be called, and perhaps of specific personal resistances to indifference [157].

Assuming knowledge of Christ's way and sincere commitment to it, the emphasis in the third kind of humility is on the affective quality of love. This quality is, of course, present and effective throughout the whole sequence, but here it is carried to a new level of intensity and gratuitousness. The Triple Colloquy is a prayer, itself inspired by love, for the grace of a greater love.

ELECTION

A school for life

One of the themes of the Spiritual Exercises consists in a distinctive and systematically worked-out doctrine on the subject of decision-making, and this doctrine is to be found not only in the present section but in the development of the Exercises as a whole. Basic to it is a concept of decision as relational. That is to say, a decision is seen as answering not just the question: 'What is the right thing to do?', but the question, 'What course is more pleasing to God?', and it is made not through our own resources alone, but through the working together of Creator and creature.[75] The doctrine emphasizes especially that a 'good and sound' decision requires two conditions, namely a previous disposition of availability to God's word, whatever that word might be, and the discernment of what is in fact more pleasing to God in my case.[76]

Considered from the standpoint of decision, the development of the Exercises so far can be said to have consisted in building up the preliminary dispositions: the desire to praise, reverence and serve God, indifference, affective freedom and what might be termed a general 'Christification of outlook'. From these dispositions, the present section goes on to the decision-making process itself. Its central feature is the 'times of election', in which Ignatius distinguishes three signs, or kinds of evidence, by which God shows his will.

This doctrine, with its integration of decision into both the ascetical and contemplative processes, is a doctrine for the whole of Christian life, not only for the Exercises. Indeed ultimately it is this that makes the doctrine relevant to every experience of the Exercises, even if no concrete choice at

---

[75]It must be strongly emphasized however that the process of making a decision in faith, though finalized by faith-criteria, does not bypass the ordinary requisites for decision-making. For example, nothing in the Exercises dispenses a person from gathering, and dealing with, complex and possibly unwelcome data. Nor is the 'inwardness' of the election process – attention to the quality of motivation, to movements of spirits, and to responses to the Gospel – a substitute for looking outwards, seeking to discern the word of God in events and situations and in prophetic voices that help interpret the claims these make on us. And the discernment integral to decision-making does not dispense with, but rather is helped by, the insights of modern psychology into hidden motivations. In short, God comes to us in the real, and the ways of decision in the Exercises do not allow the deliberate neglect of any reality that might bear on a specific choice. A person making a decision in faith must be open to all relevant immediate reality.

[76]In the case of decisions made in the Exercises these conditions are realized formally and explicitly; in other cases very often they are not.

all is made in the course of them. For the Exercises are a school for Christian life. More specifically they prepare for a Christian life lived according to a spirituality characterized precisely by the concern to integrate the decisions of life into a person's relationship with God. Even if the Exercises are not always choice-centred, they are always choice-orientated.

In the Exercises

With regard to choice-making during the Exercises themselves, there are obviously cases when the need to make a serious choice is clear, while in other cases it is for the exercitant and director to discern whether or not the exercitant's situation contains matter for decisions. On the general principles that govern such discernment, two antithetical points may be made.

(i) The intrinsic value of the doctrine of the Exercises on decision does not absolutely require that a serious decision be always made within the Exercises themselves. Without such a decision the experience of the Exercises is not intrinsically attenuated. For the development presented in the Exercises as the prerequisite to election is also a process of personal conversion and growth, issuing in a renewed commitment to Christ, and it remains such even if the Exercises do not involve an external decision. Indeed it is a fact of experience that for people already clear about their commitments, a process of deepening comes about in the Exercises, without the need for a serious fresh decision arising.

(ii) But if esteem for Ignatius' decision doctrine does not impose a strict 'electionist' position, it does sit uneasily with tendencies to assume without ado that in practice real choice-making is exceptional during the Exercises, rather than the norm. Such an assumption has various causes. Often it expresses a general preference for other dimensions of the Exercises.[77] It can reflect an unawareness of the wide range of matters which fall within the field of freedom and responsibility. And often it comes from failure to recognize a distinction drawn in the text between election and reformation of life.

What is the point of this distinction? In the text itself 'election'[78] denotes (at least in nuance) choices of a particularly decisive kind, such as the choice

[77]An unreflective tendency to play down election is often associated with an approach which accentuates such themes as freedom, personal growth and healing. Though it is right to stress the potential of the Exercises in these realms, concern for them sometimes serves to deflect attention from the place given by the Exercises to election or reform of life.

[78]In itself 'election' (*elección*) is the ordinary Spanish term for 'choice'. But since Ignatius uses it with a particular connotation, it is the standard practice in translations of the Exercises to use the English word 'election' rather than 'choice'.

of a 'state of life'[79] or a quasi-permanent life-situation, while 'reformation of life' refers to choices made within an already established state (cf. [189]). But behind the distinction lie wider principles. The search for God's will applies to every choice, in so far as values of the gospel are involved in it, but this must not obliterate all sense of the range and variety of our choices. Some choices are of critical intrinsic importance and likely to involve personally critical and prolonged processes. Others, while less intrinsically momentous, or more quickly made, are still sufficiently significant and challenging to constitute real encounter-points between Creator and creature, and for the principles of the Exercises to apply to them.[80] When a choice of the first kind needs to be made one should recognize its special character, but without playing down the importance of finding God in all our choices. Conversely we must seek and find God in all choices without making every choice a full-dress 'election process'.

In any specific situation the place of choice in the Exercises must be discerned on the basis of this wider understanding of the subject. If even then it is evident, as it very well may be, that no real decision needs to be made in the Exercises, a decision must not be engineered. However if choice is regarded in this wider perspective, it becomes difficult to maintain an *a priori* view that choice-making in the Exercises should be regarded as something exceptional.

Two caveats

Ignatius' doctrine on decision-making is clearly a major element in his spirituality, but its implications are easily read in over-simple or exaggerated ways, and in this connection a director should be aware that two questions in particular are less simple than they may seem.

[79]Though the text opens a wide range of possible subjects of election [170], the choice with which the Exercises are primarily concerned is that of a state of life, or more specifically, the choice between the way of the counsels or the way of the commandments. Part of Ignatius' concern in the Exercises is to re-establish the ideal of vocation in a Church where priesthood and ecclesiastical office are widely seen as steps to worldly promotion. Elsewhere however Ignatius mentions quite different possibilities for election: such as a decision in regard to 'insults and injuries', whether to accept these from God's hand when they come, or whether positively to ask for them (*Autograph Directory*, MHSI, vol. 76, [trans. Palmer, p. 10]). In any case, an 'election' might be described as a 'Choice' (with a capital C), rather than a 'choice' (with a small c).

[80]The reform of life is a 'logical consequence of the method of the Exercises ... the mark of their essential fruitfulness'. Gaston Fessard cited by Cusson, *Biblical Theology* p. 83, where the integral position of the 'reform of life' in the Exercises is defended against the thesis of Léonce de Grandmaison that the section on 'reform of life' is merely an appendix.

The first concerns certitude. Implicit in the Exercises is the contention that through the goodness of God (and not as the automatic outcome of a procedure) it is possible to attain the certitude of having found the here-and-now personal response that is 'more pleasing' to God. It is crucially important however to recognize the limits of this certitude. An election does not confer knowledge of the future. It does not guarantee ratification on the part of another or others (in the case, e.g., of a decision to marry, to enter a religious order, or to seek ordination). Nor does the exercitant's own certitude imply that another person would oppose God's will if on the same issue they were to reach different conclusions.[81]

These considerations do not evacuate the 'good and sound election' of the certitude proper to it. Even if we cannot know the outcome of our here-and-now 'yes' to God, we can trust that it is the response wished here-and-now by a God whose will works out through events and human processes. Unless and until further signs are given us, our discerned choice commits us. Moreover if this decision is not binding on anyone else, others risk stifling the Spirit if they fail to treat it with discerning respect. But it is essential to realize that the certitude which one can find through discernment is the subjective certitude of having responded to God's will here-and-now, and not to go beyond this into claims that Ignatius himself does not make.

The second question concerns the practical implications of the election doctrine of the Exercises for the decisions of daily life. As Ignatius' own decisions show, the approach to election in the Exercises provides a paradigm for these decisions,[82] so that by following the principles and methods of the Exercise a person may within the stream of daily life make a decision of the same quality as an election made in the special and normally unrepeatable situation of the Spiritual Exercises. Such, justly, is the belief in which many today seek God's will in personal or group processes of discernment. But this said, we must recognize that the context of many of our decisions is one of haste, agitation, or a general attitude falling far short of the dispositions inculcated by the Exercises. In these situations, too, the

[81]Ignatius' position is made clear in a letter to Francis Borgia in 1552, in which he explains his decision to make every effort to resist the wish of Pope Julius III and Emperor Charles V to confer a cardinal's hat on Borgia: 'If I did not act thus, I would be (and indeed am) quite certain in myself that I would not give a good account of myself before God our Lord, rather a wholly bad one.' However he goes on to say that despite his own clear conviction that it was God's will that he should oppose the nomination, he was also convinced that if others adopted a contrary view, there would be no contradiction: 'The same Spirit could inspire me to take one point of view for some reasons and inspire others to the contrary for other reasons.' MHSI, *Epp. Ig.*, vol. IV, p. 284, No 2652, trans. *Personal Writings*, p. 246.

[82]For notable examples, cf. *Deliberation of the First Fathers* (trans. Futrell, *Making an Apostolic Community of Love*, pp. 191ff.); *Spiritual Diary* (=*Discernment Logbook*), and the letter to Francis Borgia mentioned in note 81.

doctrine of the Exercises can be valuable, providing positive aid in the processes through which over time we learn from mistakes, advance from less purely motivated choices to more Spirit-filled ones, keep our horizons wide, and avoid complacency. But if one's starting-point is not that of the dispositions built up in the Exercises, the doctrine of the Exercises will be helpful only to the extent to which this is candidly recognized. Otherwise claims to have 'followed the methods of the Exercises' or to have 'practised Ignatian discernment' can have the effect of bestowing an inappropriate air of integrity or finality on questionable decisions.

Ignatius' doctrine on decision-making is therefore vulnerable to over-simple or extravagant interpretations, but awareness of this should lead not so much to a fear of dangers, as to respect for the potential of a doctrine which is a major component of the Ignatian spirituality of finding God in all things, and which is especially significant in an age growing in the sense of freedom and responsibility as elements of all Christian life.

The material on election falls into four parts: (i) an introductory statement or preamble [169]; (ii) directives regarding the scope of election [170–174]; (iii) the 'times' of election [175–188]; (iv) amendment and reform of life [189].

Preamble

[169] [1] PREAMBLE FOR MAKING AN ELECTION
[2] In every good election, in so far as it depends on us, the eye of our intention must be simple. I should look only at what I have been created for, namely, the praise of God our Lord and the salvation of my soul. [3] Therefore whatever my choice might be, it must help me towards the end for which I have been created, and I must not make the end fit the means, but subordinate the means to the end. [4] It often happens, for example, that people choose first of all to marry, which is a means, and secondly to serve God in married life, though the service of God is the end. Others, similarly, wish first to possess church benefices and then to serve God in them. [5] People like this do not go straight to God; they want God to come straight to their own disordered attachments. Consequently they make a means of the end, and an end of the means, and so what they ought to put first, they put last. [6] My objective should be in the first place to desire to serve God, which is the end, and secondly, should it be preferable for me, to accept a benefice or to marry, should one of those be better for me, since those are means to the end. [7] To sum up, nothing ought to induce me either to adopt such means or to reject them except the sole service and praise of God our Lord and the eternal salvation of my soul.

Introductory statement

Before coming onto matter for election and the ways of finding God's specific will, the text returns to the disposition which is the prerequisite to decision. The disposition is that already indicated by the Foundation [23], the Third Class [155], and the second kind of humility [166], while the examples of disordered choices recall the Second Class [154]. As in the Foundation, right intention is presented under the aspect of ends-and-means logic, rather than in the affective climate of an outlook changed by the experience of Christ. That the latter has been developing and will continue to develop throughout the election process is assumed.

[170] [1] < DIRECTIVES > REGARDING APPROPRIATE MATTERS FOR ELECTION, CONTAINING FOUR POINTS AND A NOTE
[2] **First point. It is necessary that all the matters about which we want to make an election be either morally indifferent or good in themselves, that they should *engage the person in the service of God within our holy mother, the hierarchical Church*, and should not be bad or repugnant to her.**

[171] [1] **Second point. Some things involve an unchangeable election, such as *priesthood, marriage*, etc.;** [2] **in others, such as the acceptance or relinquishment of benefices, or the acquisition or renunciation of material goods, election is changeable.**

[172] [1] **Third point. When an unchangeable election has been once made, there are no further grounds for election since it cannot be undone. Such is the case of priesthood, marriage, etc.** [2] **The only point to be observed here is that if the election has not been properly made and with due order (that is, without disordered attachments), *one should repent* and try to lead a good life within the election one has made.** [3] **Such an election *does not appear*, however, *to be a divine vocation*, since it is disordered and biased. In this many deceive themselves, making a divine vocation out of a biased or wrong election,** [4] **whereas a divine vocation is always pure and clear, without any admixture of the carnal or of any other disordered attachment.**

[173] [1] **Fourth point. *In matters where an election can be changed*, if someone has made an election in a proper and rightly ordered way, and has not yielded to the natural instinct or the spirit of the world,** [2] **there is no reason for making it over again, but rather one should try to become perfect to the best of one's ability in the election already made.**

[174] [1] *NOTE*
It should be noted that when such a changeable election has not been made sincerely and in due order, [2] **then if one wants to bear worthwhile fruits, such as will be highly pleasing to God our Lord, it will be to one's profit to make the election properly.**

In the Autograph there is no word corresponding to *Directives* in the title. In the Latin versions, the Vulgate has *Introductio*, and the Versio Prima has *Documentum*.

engage the person in the service of God within our holy mother, the hierarchical Church Many of the choices made in the Exercises (e.g. choices of a state of life) are directly concerned with a person's role in the Church. But more widely all decisions are made in the Church and involve its holiness, witness or mission; *engage in the service of God* literally, *militate* (Spanish: *militen*), a word which links the choice of the individual with the idea of Christian life as struggle, the struggle which engages the whole Church as 'militant'.[83] The juxtaposition of *holy mother* and *hierarchical* will re-appear in the Rules for a Right Attitude in the Church.[84]

priesthood, marriage There is no explicit mention here of religious life, but for Ignatius the category of an unchangeable situation would have included professed religious life, solemn religious vows being considered at the time of Ignatius as incapable of dispensation.

one should repent Although further election, in the proper sense, is precluded, it is nevertheless possible freely to commit oneself now to a situation that one is not free to abandon, 'going courageously forward in search of a divine will that I have forced to go through mine'.[85] But first the original (self-interested) motivation must be acknowledged and disowned. This principle alone will not resolve every question about a life-commitment that might arise in our own circumstances, which are not those of the sixteenth century. It is relevant, however, not only to the situations explicitly mentioned in the present text, but to the many ways in which people may find themselves exteriorly imprisoned by an ill-considered past decision. The Vulgate has: 'there remains when one has begun to repent of one's deed, to compensate the damage of the election by the good of one's life and the diligence of one's

---

[83]The Latin versions translate more freely: Versio Prima, 'be within the bosom of the Church', and the Vulgate has 'nor be otherwise than is consonant with the rules of the orthodox mother Church'.

[84]For further observations on the terms used in this paragraph, see Buckley, 'Ecclesial mysticism in the *Spiritual Exercises* of Ignatius'.

[85]Pousset, *Life in Faith and Freedom*, p. 115.

works; but to go back is by no means fitting ...'

does not appear to be a divine vocation A replacement in Ignatius' hand of the earlier, slightly more decisive, phrase 'we cannot say that it was a vocation'. In any case we surely sense here Ignatius' concern to establish a properly spiritual concept of vocation in a Church deeply marked by career clericalism.

Note In matters where an election can be chaged. The past choices in question here are truly discerned choices. Even when intrinsically changeable, these can continue to provide present assurance, guidance, knowledge of God's will. A *changeable* choice might, of course, be called into question by new signs, but in the absence of such signs need not be questioned solely because one is making the Spiritual Exercises.

Times for an election

[175] **¹** THREE TIMES IN ANY OF WHICH A SOUND AND GOOD ELECTION CAN
BE MADE

The *Three Times* are three spiritual situations, each characterized by a certain kind of evidence of God's will and by a mode of decision-making on our part corresponding to this evidence.

² *The First Time*. When God our Lord so *moves* and attracts the will that without doubting or being able to doubt, the faithful soul follows what is *shown*, just as St Paul and St Matthew did when they followed Christ our Lord.

The First Time This is defined[86] by four characteristics: (i) the experience has an 'object', something is *shown*; (ii) the will is *moved* by God himself to

---

[86]This definition is verified in Ignatius' account of a decision in his own life which, though he does not use the term, is plainly a First Time election: 'He was continuing in his self-denial whereby he didn't eat meat, and was firm on that; in no way was he thinking of making a change. One day, in the morning when he had got up, there appeared to him meat for the eating, as if he could see it with his bodily eyes, without any desire for this having been there before. And together with this there also came upon him a great assent of the will that from then on, he should eat meat. And although he could still remember this intention from earlier, he was incapable of being doubtful about this: rather he could not but make up his mind that he had to eat meat. And when he recounted this afterwards to his confessor, the confessor was telling him he should consider whether perhaps this was a temptation. But he, examining the matter well, was incapable of ever being doubtful about it, *Reminiscences*, §27 [trans., *Personal Writings*, p. 25].

follow the way shown; (iii) there is no doubt, or possibility of doubt, on either of the above points, i.e. that what is shown is God's will and that the volitional movement is from God; (iv) the situation is the same kind as the vocations of *St Paul* and *St Matthew*. The type of call given on those occasions continues through history as implied in the Vulgate: 'as we read that it happened to St Paul, St Matthew, and some others when called by Christ'.

In connection with this definition certain points should be noted. First, there is no explicit mention of consolation.[87] Second, the fact that the genuine First Time experience leaves no room for doubt does not mean that every experience which does not contain doubt is inspired by God; and hence the third characteristic does not rule out the need for reflection on one's experience, or for discernment on the part of the director.[88] Nor does the fourth characteristic imply that the experience is necessarily of the dramatic quality of the Damascus road.[89] But if the definition is vulnerable to interpretations beyond its strict content, and if the content itself leaves unanswered questions, the definition nevertheless makes clear the essential quality of the First Time and its distinctiveness in relation to the other times: it is a situation in which the evidence consists in being shown, decisively and unambiguously, the course to follow, and the response is one of simple assent.

[176] The *Second Time*. When sufficient light and knowledge is received through experience of *consolations and desolations*, and through experience of the discernment of different spirits.

[87]It is natural to assume, as most exponents of the Exercises do, that the First Time experience will ordinarily be a time of consolation, even indeed of consolation 'without preceding cause' [330]. Whether consolation (at any rate when understood as positive feelings of peace, joy, etc.) is a defining constituent of the First Time experience, as it is of the Second, is another question: cf. Toner, *Discerning God's Will*, pp. 114–21.

[88]A similar distinction is relevant to 'consolation without preceding cause' [330]. Toner suggests that although Ignatius gives no completely clear direction in the matter, it would seem desirable, whenever reasonably possible, to critically reflect on a First Time experience: cf. Toner, *Discerning God's Will*, pp. 121–7.

[89]If the First Time were by definition a dramatic incident, it would also of course be of its very nature a rare one. But God can touch a person with absolute conviction in discreet ways in and through ordinary experience. On the basis of such a distinction Toner argues (rightly, in my view) that there is an ordinary mode of the First Time which might be more common than exponents of the Exercises in the past have been willing to recognize: 'I would express a suspicion (it is no more than that) for whatever it is worth, that while the First Time experience in the dramatic form is relatively rare, many more decisions regarding God's will are of this other sort. If so this could explain why some choose to begin and to persevere in difficult enterprises (especially undertaking a vocation in life) for God without being able to formulate any communicable evidence other than simply "I am certain this is God's will for me".' Toner, *Discerning God's Will*, p. 121. Many people would probably agree with this view.

In the *Second Time*, the evidence is contained within the experiences of consolation and desolation, and the process of decision consists in discernment.[90]

consolations and desolations These words describe situations in which the deep influences of good and bad spirits manifest themselves through the interplay of feelings, thoughts and imagination.[91] The terms are used in the plural, since the Second Time is a process not a single event. Ultimately the decision is made on the criterion of tested consolation, but the process can be a difficult and stressful one, for election is a moment of conversion, entailing change, relinquishment and cost, and these are liable to produce desolate reactions. Working through these is an important element of the process.[92]

Ignatius' concern at this point is to define the Second Time rather than give advice about it. But elsewhere he has plenty to offer the director in the way of principles and practical suggestions. The *Autograph Directory* suggests two procedures: to note in prayer the respective attractions which arise out of consolation and desolation; and to offer alternative possible decisions, 'noting in which direction God our Lord gives a greater indication of his divine will'.[93] In the Exercises themselves the director's primary resource is of course the Rules for Discernment, but he or she should also keep in mind Annotation 16 and the cautionary advice contained in Annotation 14.

It must be noted however that the essence of the Second Time is discernment and that discernment can never be reduced to the application of guidelines or methods. And to guide another person in a Second-Time discernment requires on the part of directors themselves a discernment grounded in experience, empathy and wisdom.

[177] **[1] The *Third Time* is one of *tranquillity*. One considers first of all the purpose for which as a human being one is born, namely to praise God our Lord and to save one's soul. [2] Desiring this, one chooses as a means some life or state within the bounds of the Church, in order to find in it a help to the service of one's Lord and the salvation of one's**

[90]One way of explaining the process by which God's will is recognized in the experience of consolation is given by many commentators today in reference to the person's personal sense of Christ, or Christ-identity, the sense of Christ which grows with one's knowledge of Christ and commitment to him in the Christian community, and which is both focused and further developed by the Second Week contemplations.

[91]See commentary on the Rules for Discernment, especially [328–336].

[92]Nadal gives it as a principle that, 'if in decisions one experiences consolation in something, and then desolation comes, the latter is often a confirmation of the former', *Epist.* 1,4, MHSI, p. 644.

[93]*Autograph Directories* (MHSI 76, p. 77 [trans. Palmer, p. 9]). Ignatius illustrates the second approach by the simile of a court servant offering various dishes to a prince. The simile is repeated in the *1599 Directory*, ch. 27 (MHSI 76, pp. 703–4 [trans. Palmer, p. 331]).

soul. [3] I call this a 'tranquil' time in the sense that it is a situation when the soul is not moved by various spirits and has the free and tranquil use of her natural powers.

In the *Third Time* the evidence consists not in feelings, but in the stronger rational case; and the movement and enlightenment, which in the Second Time enter consciousness, are now not conscious or hardly so. The process is not totally rational in the sense that every rational person would see the case in the same way; we are still concerned with finding the best way for an individual, and there is a personal intuitive element in one's very assessment of the more reasonable case. Nevertheless the criterion is not *movement of the spirit*, but reason. The Third Time establishes a basic principle: our rational faculties, converted and graced, are capable by themselves of finding God's will, and that to do this it is not absolutely necessary to experience movements of the Spirit. The Third Time has been described as the time of 'ordinary grace'.[94]

tranquillity The term implies first an absence of any 'spiritual movements' which could of themselves determine choice, and, second, a freedom from all negative feelings (not only spiritual desolation, but ordinary emotional feelings such as worry, anger, distress, restlessness) that might obstruct rational deliberation. Tranquillity need not however imply the total absence of spiritual movements, either of ordinary or quiet consolation or slight desolation, or of the emotional fluctuations normal in a difficult search.

[178] [1] If the election is not made in the First and Second Times, there follow here two ways of making it in the *Third*.
[2]THE FIRST WAY TO MAKE A SOUND AND GOOD ELECTION IN THE THIRD TIME CONTAINING SIX POINTS

For the *Third Time*, as distinct from the First and the Second, Ignatius provides two methods or *ways*. The first, to be used outside the set periods of Gospel contemplation, and for as long and as often as the situation requires consists in six steps:

(1) I put before myself the issue (First Point).
(2) I recall the fundamental dispositions required on my side for any choice (Second Point)
(3) I pray that in the present choice the Spirit should act in my will and in my mind (Third Point).

---

[94]Coathalem, *Ignatian insights*, p. 188.

(4) Taking as criteria the service of God and the good of my soul, I consider reasons for and against each of the alternatives before me (Fourth Point).

(5) I evaluate these reasons and decisions (Fifth Point).

(6) I seek confirmation of the decision (Sixth Point).

³ The First Point is to put before myself the matter about which I want to make an election: for example, the acceptance or refusal of a position in life or a benefice, or anything else *subject to a changeable election*.

subject to a changeable election Ignatius certainly saw the Third Time as the least preferable way of choosing a state in life, but the reference here to a changeable election does not imply that he regarded this time as inappropriate or inadequate for making a life-choice. That would contradict the clear position mentioned above [177].⁹⁵

[179] ¹ The Second Point. It is necessary to keep as my objective the end for which I was created, namely to praise God our Lord and to save my soul. ² As well as this, *I need also to be indifferent* and free from any disordered attachment, so that I am not more inclined or attracted to accepting the thing before me than to refusing it, nor to refusing it rather than to accepting it. ³ Rather, I should be as though at the centre of a pair of scales, ready to follow the direction I perceive to be more to the glory and praise of God our Lord and the salvation of my soul.

I need also to be indifferent I.e. to be in a preliminary waiting-space precisely in order to become committed to a specific course. The *make myself indifferent* of the Foundation now becomes *be indifferent*.

[180] ¹ The Third Point is to ask God our Lord to be pleased to *move my will* and to *put into my mind* what I ought to do with regard to the thing before me that will be most for his praise and glory. ² I should use my intellect well and faithfully to go over the matter, and I should choose in accord with his most holy will and good pleasure.

move my will Essential for Christian choice in any time is the Spirit-given

---

⁹⁵In a letter written towards the close of Ignatius' life he insists that reason alone gives sufficient grounds for someone to enter the Society of Jesus; this clearly refers to a choice of a state in life made in the Third Time. Cf. MHSI, *Epp. Ig.*, vol. XI, No. 6327 (to Dr Vergara), pp. 184–6 [trans. *Inigo: Letters*, pp. 264–5].

desire to do God's will; and it is for this grace primarily that the exercitant prays on the threshold of a Third Time election. For Christian choice this essential act is also sufficient; if we do not find ourselves drawn by God, as in the First and Second Times, to a specific object, this does not mean that we are unable to find the will of God. So long as this is recognized, however, it is important to be open to whatever way God wishes to gift us, and hence to actions of the Spirit transcending the rational limits of the Third Time.

put into my mind I.e. through the processes proper to the Third Time, using the understanding faithfully and well.

[181] [1] The *Fourth* Point is *to consider and reason over* the advantages or benefits that would accrue to me if I held the proposed position or benefice, *solely for the praise of God our Lord and the good of my soul*; [2] and on the other hand to consider in the same way the disadvantages and dangers there would be in holding it. [3] I should do the same with the alternative and look at the advantages and benefits, and conversely at the disadvantages and dangers, in not holding it.

[182] [1] The *Fifth* Point. Having in this way thought and reasoned from every point of view on the thing before me, I shall look to see in which direction reason inclines more. [2] It is thus *according to the stronger inclination of the reason, and not according to the inclinations of sensuality* that the decision on the matter before me is reached.

The *Fourth* and *Fifth* Points deal with the deliberative stage of the process, the consideration of advantages and disadvantages.

to consider and reason over Many factors may be taken into account at this time, including the very down-to-earth ones, and an honesty in looking at all relevant considerations is crucial to the process, especially when the decision-making methods of the Exercises are applied to the often complicated decisions of daily life. But whatever considerations come into play, the criterion by which to assess an advantage or disadvantage is *solely for the praise of God our Lord and the good of my soul*. Note that the method consists not in a simple two-column list of pros and cons, but in four columns: advantages/disadvantages in accepting; advantages/disadvantages in not accepting.

according to the stonger inclination of the reason, and not according to the inclinations of sensuality The 'reasonable case' is one perceived according to the judgements of one familiar with the ways of God, and whose criterion is always the glory of God. On *reason* see [96], and on *sensuality* see [87] with notes.

[183] **¹ The Sixth Point. After such an election or decision has been made, the person who made it should turn with great diligence to prayer, coming before God our Lord, ² and offering him this election, so that his Divine Majesty may be pleased *to accept and confirm* it, if it is to his greater service and praise.**

to accept and confirm Here the confirmation⁹⁶ in question is not primarily of the will (the confirmation proper to the Third and Fourth Weeks), but confirmation of the decision as judgement. The importance of praying for confirmation, brought out strongly in this text, is further illustrated by the *Spiritual Diary*.⁹⁷ We pray for confirmation in order to be as sure of doing God's will as it is given us to be; and to counter the tendency in us to opt for hasty closure.⁹⁸

We are not told here what confirmation might mean. It is often taken to refer to an experience of consolation, and although this would transfer the process of the Third Time to that of the Second, many commentators understand confirmation in this sense. Indeed such confirmation is probably frequent, and at all events it would always seem good to ask for it. Confirming consolation is not, however, necessary for the validity of the Third-Time method.⁹⁹ Nor does its absence imply that no confirmation is given at all. Confirmation need not be limited to consolation, but might include confirmation in the form of insight still within the scope of the Third Time. If misunderstood, Ignatius' insistence on confirmation could play into a person's need for security, or into tendencies to lay down terms to God. We must ask for confirmation, but we must be content with the confirmation given us, and this may in the end be simply the negative confirmation that nothing comes up to call our decision into question.

Finally it should be added that what is confirmed is only that this present decision is God's will for me here and now; and that subsequent events,

⁹⁶For an extended analysis of Ignatius' concept of confirmation, see Toner, *Discerning God's Will*, chs 11–12, pp. 191–233, from which the comments offered here are largely drawn.

⁹⁷Although in the Exercises there is a reference to prayer only in the context of the Third Time, the *Spiritual Diary* clearly implies that prayer for confirmation is also required in order to finalize a Second Time election.

⁹⁸Indeed if we pray honestly and openly for the Lord's confirmation, we expose ourselves to the risk to 'disconfirmation'.

⁹⁹See the letter to Dr Vergara mentioned above (in relation to [178]); he has made a decision on the basis of reason rather than of consolation, but Ignatius assures him that 'when one is aiming at better and more perfect things, a sufficient impulse comes from reason itself'. At the same time Ignatius is sure that the Spirit in due course 'will teach you better than anyone else how to enjoy with the affection and carry out gently what reason dictates to be most for the service and glory of God', *Inigo: Letters*, p. 264.

whatever their effect on the outcome of this decision, cannot in themselves call it in question.[100]

[184] [1] THE *SECOND WAY* TO MAKE A SOUND AND GOOD ELECTION IN THE THIRD TIME CONTAINING FOUR RULES AND A NOTE

The *second way* in the Third Time is not a method of obtaining evidence of God's will, but rather a way of testing the quality of a felt inclination that moves us to a particular choice. The material is used by Ignatius in various ways. In the Exercises it reappears almost verbatim in the Rules for Almsgiving, where it serves to check the quality of a love that prompts almsgiving to relations or friends [377ff.]. A practice similar to that of Rule 2 was adopted by the First Companions as a preliminary to the process of deliberation.[101]

Here the method envisages a situation in which either in the course of the deliberation or as a result of it, the exercitant has moved beyond indifference and feels himself drawn to one of the alternatives of choice, but without being sure whether the motive is the love of God or a rationalization of hidden 'sensuality'. The Second Way (or method), if applied with strict honesty, enables the person either to sense that the love that moves one is indeed 'from above', or sensing that it is not, to regain the objectivity necessary for a consideration of advantages and disadvantages for the service of God.

[2] First Rule. The love which moves me and makes me choose something has to descend from above, from the love of God; [3] so that the one who makes the choice should first *sense* interiorly *that the love he or she has*, greater or less, for the object chosen *is solely for the sake of the Creator and Lord*.

sense ... that the love he or she has ... is solely for the sake of the Creator and Lord If such is the quality of the love, the exercitant will be enabled to *sense* it by applying the Rules that follow.

---

[100]Another way in which a choice might be said to be 'confirmed' is through subsequent developments, such as an apostolically successful outcome, good fruits in themselves, approval by authority, etc. Most people feel that decisions are indeed confirmed in this way, but for the difficulty of establishing such confirmation, cf. Toner, *Discerning God's Will*, ch. 12, 'Confirmation after the Finalized Decision', pp. 216–33. In any case, confirmation of this kind is not referred to in the Exercises.

[101]In the 1539 *Deliberation* on whether they should add obedience to their vows of poverty and chastity Ignatius and his companions decided that as a 'preparation of soul' each member of the group should think of himself as 'not being one of our company, into which he never expected to be received ... so that as an outsider he might freely propose his idea to us concerning the resolution of obeying or not obeying', trans. Futrell, *Making an Apostolic Community of Love*, p. 191.

[185] [1] **Second Rule.** *To look at* **a person whom I have never seen or known. Desiring for such a person full perfection, I should consider what I would tell him or her to do, what election to make for the greater glory of God our Lord and the greater perfection of his or her soul.** [2] **I should then do the same myself, and keep the rule which I lay down for another.**

To look at The device suggested to David by Nathan (2 Sam. 12:1–6) and to Simon the Pharisee by Jesus (Luke 7:41–43).

[186] Third Rule. As if I were at the point of death, to consider what procedure and what norms I would then wish to have followed in making the present election. I should make my decision taking entirely these as my rule.

[187] [1] **Fourth Rule. To look at and consider my situation on the Day of Judgement, and think how at that moment I would want to have chosen in the present matter.** [2] **I should adopt now the rule which I would then want to have observed, so that I may then be in total happiness and joy.**

[188] NOTE
Having followed the above-mentioned Rules for my salvation and eternal rest, I will make my election and offer it to God our Lord in accordance with Point 6 of the First Way of making an election [183].

[189] [1] FOR THE *AMENDMENT* AND *REFORM* OF ONE'S PERSONAL LIFE AND STATE
[2] **In the case of those already established in ecclesiastical positions or in marriage (whether they are well off in material possessions or not), the following is to be noted.** [3] **If such people lack either the occasion or any great readiness of will to make a choice about matters subject to a changeable election,** [4] **then instead of an election they can very profitably be given a framework and method by which to amend and reform themselves in their personal lives and states.** [5] **This requires that they should commit their existence, life and state to the glory and praise of God our Lord and the salvation of their souls.** [6] **In order to reach and attain this end, each one, by means of the exercises and the Ways of Election explained above, should consider and ponder** [7] **what size of house and staff to have, how to manage and direct it, how to teach it by words and example;** [8] **and with regard to income, how much should be allocated to dependants and house, how much should be given to the poor and to other good works.** [9] **In such matters one should seek nothing other than the greater**

143

praise and glory of God our Lord in and through everything. [10] Thus it must be borne in mind that a person will make progress in things of the spirit *to the degree to which they divest themselves of self-love, self-will, and self-interest.*

amendment (= correction of what is defective) and *reform* (= giving new shape to) refer to decisions within an established life-situation, while in an *election* one's life-situation is itself changed (as explained in the general remarks above).

There are two reasons why an exercitant might not make an election: (1) he or she is not at the moment faced by any sufficiently substantial issue; (2) even though the situation might contain matter for election, the exercitant has no readiness of will to deal with it (in Ignatius' time a situation raising questions about a benefice might have been a case in point).

In addition to the sixteenth-century domesticities cited by Ignatius, the *Directories* suggest other possible fields of application of this text: questions concerning apostolic ministry; disciplines of daily life with regard to eating, sleeping, study, and more generally abuses 'which if not actually sinful, are at least the source of many evils'.[102] Today the exercitant will find his or her own fields of application. The *1599 Directory* specifies that the bearing of this section of the Exercises goes beyond the Exercises themselves: 'if we tried to help and direct our neighbour by the program set out here, really outstanding results would ensue'.[103] The method is mainly, but not exclusively, that of the Third Time. The teaching in the Exercises on election therefore equips the exercitant to deal with the ordinary decisions of life.

to the degree to which they divest themselves of self-love, self-will, and self-interest The solemnity of the wording of this statement and the fact that it is also the concluding sentence of the Second Week of the Exercises suggest that Ignatius is propounding a 'Golden Rule' for life in the Spirit, rather than a help to making the kind of decisions dealt with in this last section. But this said, the sentence brings home the spiritual demands that might be contained in quite matter-of-fact choices. In the most practical, even pedestrian, decisions of life we are invited to enter the death and Resurrection of Jesus.

Note on the Times of Election

With regard to the Times of Election two obvious practical questions arise: what was Ignatius' own order of preference among them? and, how far did

---

[102] *1599 Directory*, ch. 34 (MHSI 76, p. 725, and cf. pp. 318, 469 [trans., Palmer, p. 340, and cf. pp. 142, 222]).
[103] *1599 Directory*, ch. 34 (MHSI 76, p. 726 [trans., Palmer, p. 340]).

he regard each of them as either commonplace or rare?

Ignatius' preference corresponds to the order of presentation. When not moved in the First Time, one resorts to the Second, and to the Third only when the Second is unfruitful.[104] With regard to the Third Time this does not justify the somewhat dismissive estimate of it sometimes found today.[105] But the principle is clear: a situation of choice is intrinsically preferable to the extent to which the action of God is manifest in it, and the human response consists in letting God act. But the 'preferable' is not necessarily the 'usual', and therefore Ignatius' rating of the Three Times on the scale between the extraordinary and the normal is another question. His position with regard to the First Time is not absolutely clear. Later this situation came to be seen as a limit case, beyond the bounds of practical likelihood.[106] But while this probably represents a hardening of Ignatius' own view, he certainly did not consider the First Time a commonplace occurrence. The Second Time, on the other hand, he saw as belonging to the realm of God's usual dealings with people, especially during the Exercises.[107]

The Three Times are distinct procedures and they correspond to distinct realms of spiritual experience. In each of them a valid decision can be made. But this distinctiveness does not exclude combinations. While none of the Three depends intrinsically on another for confirmation, Ignatius preferred that a decision made in one time be confirmed in another. In his own experience, the Second and Third Times seem to have combined frequently.[108]

---

[104]*Autograph Directory* (MHSI 76, pp. 76–77 [trans., Palmer, p. 9]).

[105]See previous note. It is clear that the Third Time is not only to be found among Ignatius' own decisions, but he recognized that decisions coming out of the Second Time might leave the director feeling justly uneasy and require to be transferred to the Third as a check. The Third Time method is widely commended in the *Constitutions*, and see the letter to Dr Vergara already mentioned. For a positive evaluation of the Third Time, see Toner, op. cit., ch. 14, 'What is the value of the Third Mode?', pp. 255–73; Hughes, 'Ignatian Discernment: A Philosophical Analysis'.

[106]'Because of the rarity of such cases, not much time should be spent discussing this first time', *1599 Directory*, ch. 26 (MHSI 76, pp. 700–701 [trans., Palmer, pp. 329–30]).

[107]The Second Time represents in Pousset's phrase, the 'mystical life in the duration and dullness of the everyday', Pousset, *Life in Faith and Freedom*, p. 119.

[108]See J. Toner, *Discerning God's Will*, ch. 13, 'The Relationship of the Three Modes', pp. 233–55. On combining the modes (or 'Times') Toner points out that to stress the value of this does not call into question their mutual autonomy. Indeed there are situations where it is not only possible but necessary to reach a conclusion by one mode only. Nevertheless where possible a combination of Two and Three is preferable. Notable evidence of Ignatius' own practice in this matter is to be found in the *Spiritual Diary* (especially entries for February 6, 8, 10, 16, 22), in the Letter to Francis Borgia (mentioned above, note 81), and the *Deliberation of the First Fathers* (note 101 above), in which the companions' communal discernment comes about through a combination of the Second and Third Times.

THE THIRD WEEK

The final stage of the Exercises

In the Gospel episodes of the Third and Fourth Weeks, the exercitant contemplates two antithetical single mysteries, Passion and Resurrection, each of which must be assimilated in itself, but which form a unity of faith-meaning.

It must be emphasized that these final contemplations still belong to the structure of the Exercises and are not an appendix or epilogue without organic connection with the sequence as a whole. They are connected with this sequence first in the sense that they presuppose, while at the same time enhancing, the graces characteristic of the previous weeks. But the significance of the Third and Fourth Weeks in the dynamic of the Exercises is also to be understood in relation to the Exercises as a process of contemplative development. For the transition from the Second Week mysteries to the Passion and Resurrection leads the exercitant not only into new material but also into a certain change of spiritual climate. This is pinpointed in the requested graces which in the final weeks shift from the more *external* graces of knowledge, love and committed discipleship [104] to graces of a more immediately participatory sort – suffering *with* Christ [203], joy *with* Christ [231, cf. 48]. As the Exercises move towards their culmination, there is an expectation that prayer might become a prayer of increasing intimacy.[1] To use a term not to be found in the Exercises themselves (though the concept in central to them), the exercitant aspires in the Third and Fourth Weeks to a contemplative involvement, as profound as God wishes to grant, in the 'paschal mystery' through which we participate in Christ's own Passion, death and Resurrection.

---

[1]Hence many commentators associate the final stage of the Exercises with the 'unitive way', putting into this category either both weeks, or – with the typically cautious *1599 Directory* – only the Fourth. The 'unitive way', a way of knowing and loving which are pure gift, cannot be the scheduled outcome of a process, but in the case of a person who has been through the Exercises up to this point, it is appropriate to ask and indeed hope for graces of a unitive nature (cf. [203]). For further discussion of the objectives of the final weeks of the Exercises, see Coathalem, *Insights*, pp. 194–7; 210–12, and O'Leary, 'What the Directories Say'.

Third Week: compassion, confirmation of Election

In the case of the Third Week, this more intimate and participatory grace is commonly designated by the word *compassion* (literally, 'suffering with'). First described in the opening meditation of the First Week [48] and picked up and explained in [193], [195], and notably [203], *compassion* consists in a certain spiritual empathy, such that the contemplation of the Passion is itself a passion for the one contemplating,[2] a suffering which is ours but in and through which Christ makes us sharers in his own. It can exist only as a mode of intense love. It transforms one's perception of every meaning of the Passion and the quality of every response to it, and it is the key to the contemplative union-in-action by which through his apostles Christ continues to labour and suffer in the mission of the Church in the world.

Compassion, then, is the characteristic perspective of Third Week contemplation, But to appreciate the place of the Third Week in the overall development of the Exercises, it must be related to the ways in which the mystery of the Cross and assent to it have already been integral to earlier stages of the Exercises. Thus the exercitant comes to pray the Passion in the Third Week having in the First Week contemplated the Cross as the sign of both sin and mercy; having heard the call of the King at the beginning of the Second Week; having in some way chosen for Christ against the plausible values of the world. These insights, conversions and decisions have prepared the way, then, for the particular prayer of the Third Week, and explicitly or implicitly this prayer, in turn, deepens and confirms them.

One element of the previous stage may well feature explicitly in the Third Week contemplation. For closely related to the grace of compassion is the grace of confirmation of the election, *confirmation* being understood now not as a verifying of the choice but as a strengthening of the chooser.[3] The need for such confirmation arises from the very nature of an Ignatian election. For a *good and sound election* – be its object an ecclesiastical office, marriage, priesthood, religious life or whatever[4] – is the choice of a course of action or life-situation precisely as the better form under which personally to lead *the true life in Christ*; and hence as a situation in which one is to share, whether in a foreseeable manner or not, in the dying and rising of Christ. One is confirmed in one's election to the extent to which one

---

[2]'We ask to experience sorrow not merely as our own or exclusively as Christ's own, but both as our and Christ's sorrow' Iparraguirre, *A Key to the Study of the Spiritual Exercises*, p. 84.

[3]There remains the possibility of 'disconfirmation'.

[4]In spite of the clear indications in the Exercises to the contrary [135, 169, 170] there is a tendency among commentators to imply that a 'real' election is the choice of 'the way of the counsels', and interpretations of the Third Week as *confirmation* seem often to work on this implication.

can say 'yes' to it at this level.

Though, of course, this acceptance belongs incipiently to the decision-making itself, it is not complete in an instant. Rather, it is a process needing to extend gradually into the profounder layers of the self, often, in the case of a naturally costly choice, in the face of re-awakened anxiety or reluctance. The Third Week serves especially to advance this process. To explain this some commentators appeal to the more external concept of Christ as exemplar and, on our side, to the response of resolve and determination inspired by the model set before us by Christ in the Passion. But there is also a more contemplative and passive mode of confirmation, which consists in the integration of the election, with its concrete implications, into the prayer of compassion, the contemplative sharing in Christ's own passion and death.[5] In this mode, confirmation is Christ's own action within us.

The Third Week exercitant: direction and discernment

While the direction of the Third Week exercitant may require little more than a discreetly supportive accompaniment, situations arise which call for discernment, both the exercitant's own and that of the director, if the leading of the Spirit is to be found. In this connection three aspects of Third Week prayer may be singled out.

The first is experience. Typical Third Week experiences range from the powerfully emotional to the arid and negative, and at each end of the spectrum inner reality may differ considerably from appearance. The grace of a strong compassionate emotion is indeed to be asked for in the Third Week [195, 203], but there are emotions that might look like compassion, while quite fundamentally diverging from it – feelings, for example, containing little commitment, or sense of personal sin or of personal indebtedness. But if intense emotion can be ambiguous, so can the antithetical experiences of paralysed feelings and sheer laboriousness. Behind these might lie a reluctance to contemplate the Passion at depth, or a frustrated desire for immediate satisfaction. But it may also be that precisely in enduring dryness and distraction the exercitant is drawn into a 'com-passion' which is the more genuine because not the form in which he or she would have wished for it. In interpreting the Third Week experience, it must also be borne in mind that at this stage it would be normal for an exercitant to enter the spiritual suffering of passive purification or the 'nights of the soul'.

[5]For an analysis of the process of confirmation, and especially of the relation between the psychological dynamics of confirmation and the prayer of compassion, the reader is referred particularly to Fennessy, 'Praying the Passion: The Dynamics of Dying with Christ' in Dister, ed., *A New Introduction to the Spiritual Exercises of St Ignatius*.

Another need for discernment arises from the nature of the Third Week perspective (focusing upon the Man of Sorrows in the affective climate of compassion) and the relation of this perspective with the many other foci which might be adopted in Passion prayer. While the Third Week grace of compassion extends to every meaning of the Passion and to the quality of all our responses to it, this does not necessarily mean that it is good in the Third Week itself to deal explicitly with everything that might figure in Passion prayer at another time.[6] But the Third Week guidelines are not dogmatic; and once the particular approach and its place in the dynamics of the whole Exercises are understood, and the grace of compassion is desired and sought, the actual themes, concerns, considerations that might come into prayer over and above the content of Ignatius' text will in the end be governed by a sense of an individual's need.[7]

And thirdly, discernment is sometimes needed in order to sense how far an exercitant's prayer in the Third Week should dwell on the particulars of physical suffering. A Passion-prayer which completely evaded these would, of course, be inauthentic,[8] but the degree to which an exercitant will do well to concentrate on or linger over the details of violence and bodily suffering will vary according to the person and the leading of the spirit. The text itself, while excluding a sanitized or purely spiritual contemplation of the Passion (cf. [196]) is marked by a discretion which leaves the individual free to find and follow the way which will lead most effectively to the grace of the Third Week.

---

[6]As well as the aspect of the cross focused upon in the Third Week, there is an implicit theology of the Cross in each of the previous weeks and it would be possible to pray the Passion in a First and in a Second Week mode.

[7]Thus chapter 35 of the *1599 Directory*, after recognizing that the affection of compassion should be 'earnestly petitioned, humbly longed for, and gratefully received' goes on to list other affections 'that should be cultivated at the same time – sense of sin, recognition of the goodness and wisdom of God, confirmation of hope, enkindling of love, imitation, zeal for souls. (MHSI 76, pp 726–31 [trans. Palmer pp. 341–2]). In widening the scope of the Third Week beyond the strict limits of the text the authors of the *1599 Directory* are doubtless influenced by their attitude of caution in regard to simple or passive prayer. But this said, it remains true that to recognize that the key to the week is indeed compassion, is not to exclude every other dimension of Passion prayer.

[8] The measure of the 'kenosis' (self-emptying) of God in the Incarnation, is a fidelity extending not only to death but precisely to 'death on the cross' (Phil. 2:8).

First Day

First contemplation: Bethany to the Last Supper

[190] [1] FIRST DAY
    FIRST CONTEMPLATION, AT MIDNIGHT
        HOW CHRIST OUR LORD WENT *FROM BETHANY TO JERUSALEM*
        INCLUDING THE LAST SUPPER ([289])
        IT CONTAINS THE PREPARATORY PRAYER, THREE PRELUDES,
        SIX POINTS AND A COLLOQUY
    [2] Prayer. The usual preparatory prayer

[191] [1] The first prelude is to recall *the history*: here how Christ our Lord sent two disciples from Bethany to Jerusalem to prepare the supper, and afterwards went there himself with the other disciples. [2] After eating the paschal lamb and having finished supper, he washed their feet and gave his most holy body and precious blood to his disciples. He spoke to them at length after Judas had gone off to sell his Lord.

[192] [1] The second prelude. Composition made by seeing the place. Here it will be to *consider the road* from Bethany to Jerusalem, whether it is broad or narrow, level, etc.; [2] similarly, the place of the supper, whether it is large or small and of what general appearance.

[193] The third prelude. To ask for what I want. Here it will be for *grief, deep feeling and confusion* because it is for my sins that the Lord is going to his Passion.

from Bethany to Jerusalem The formula *from/to* employed throughout the Third Week in the titles of the contemplations, accentuates the concept of the Passion as a journey, an extended way of the Cross which the exercitant is to walk step by step with Christ.

six points In this opening contemplation, while the three preludes are specific to the Last Supper, the approach modelled in the points is to be adopted throughout the Third Week. The material is broken down under the heads of 'persons, words and actions' (points 1–3), which are contemplated in the light of the three guiding considerations given in points 4–6.

the history Both here and in the supplementary text [289] the Supper is proposed as the opening act of the Passion rather than as a contemplation of the eucharistic meal. The theme of betrayal is emphasized, and in [289] the washing of the feet specifically includes Judas. All the details – the Eucharist as self-gift and as *the greatest sign of love* [289], the washing of the disciples' feet, the foretelling of the Passion [289] – highlight the themes of surrender and of sacrifice freely made.[9]

consider the road The exercitant prepares for the contemplation of Christ's journey through the Passion by imaginatively constructing two real roads, this and the road to the valley of Josaphat [202]. The language is reminiscent of the second prelude of the Nativity Contemplation at the beginning of the Second Week [112].

grief, deep feeling and confusion Before asking for a grace of union in Christ's Passion (or suffering with Christ) the exercitant resumes what is essentially the petition of the First Week, asking for shame and confusion coming from the awareness of God's gratuitous mercy to oneself a sinner [48], manifest in Christ's death *for my sins* [53]. Compassionate feelings, whatever their intensity, fall short of the true grace of compassion unless they contain the sense of involvement, of responsibility, on our side.

The present petition, however, even while returning to that of the First Week, at the same time subtly develops it, in that attention now centres more upon Christ for himself, and the sentiments are more those of friendship. The cause of confusion, regret, and grief is not so much that my sins have merited my death, as that they are the cause of Christ's death.

[194] [1] **The first point is to *see the persons* at the supper and by reflecting within myself to try and *draw some profit* from them.**
   [2] **The seond point. To hear what they are saying, and in the same way to draw some profit from this.**
   [3] **The third point is to watch what they are doing, and draw some profit.**

[195] [1] **The fourth point is to consider what Christ our Lord suffers in his human nature,[10] or *wants to suffer*, depending on the episode being contemplated.** [2] **At this point I will *draw upon all my powers* to grieve, to feel sorrow and to weep and in the same way to *work* through each of the points that follow.**

---

[9]According to available time and the need of the individual, Ignatius allows for a more extended and comprehensive contemplation of the Supper in [209] below.

[10]*suffers in his human nature* Originally, 'what the humanity of Christ our Lord suffers'. The phrase *in his human nature* (lit. 'in his humanity') is a correction made by Ignatius.

[196] The fifth point is to consider how the divine nature *goes into hiding*, that is to say, how Christ as divine does not destroy his enemies, *although he could do so*, but allows himself in his sacred human nature to suffer most cruelly.[11]

[197] The sixth point is to consider how he suffers all this for my sins, etc. and *what I myself ought to do and suffer* for him.

[198] Colloquy. To conclude with a colloquy to Christ our Lord, and at the end say an Our Father.

see the persons ... draw some profit For the persons, with their words and actions, cf. the supplementary text [289–298]. In the Third Week, the persons can *profit* the exercitant in two ways: they embody in various forms the response of compassion, or they reflect the potential in every human being to evade Jesus or to betray him. Thus consideration of the persons sharpens the sense of crisis engendered by contemplation of the Passion.

wants to suffer Jesus's Passion is significant for us because he wishes it for us out of love, wishes it at the level not of instinct (which recoils) but of will, where he freely accepts it. In the human will of Jesus, the wish and the freedom of God break into history in an act of absolute love.

draw upon all my powers ... work. Language which in no way invites an attitude of straining, but does call forth the commitment of the whole person to an undertaking that may not be easy. The situation that immediately comes to mind will be that of aridity or the sense of being blocked; but more fundamentally, the experience of contemplating the Passion will reflect the fact that the Passion was a 'labour' for Jesus.

goes into hiding In the supplementary text the notion of divinity going progressively into hiding, as the Passion moves ever more deeply into the realm of suffering, violence and degradation, is brought out by the disappearance of the usual titles of 'Christ' and 'Lord' and the replacement of these after [292] simply by 'Jesus'.

although he could do so (cf. Matt. 26:53; John 18:6–11) Stress upon the hiddenness of the divinity does not invite us, however, to contemplate the Passion as though 'hidden divinity' meant 'absent divinity'. On the contrary,

---

[11]*allows himself in his human nature* To avoid the impression that the divine and human natures are an independent pair of agents, the translation slightly expands the concision of the Spanish, which reads: 'the divinity goes into hiding ... and allows the sacred humanity to suffer'.

in the Third Week, as in the Colloquy of the Cross [53] we contemplate the self-emptying of the Creator God.[12]

what I myself ought to do and suffer To the 'do for Christ' of the First Week [53] is now added 'suffer'; to act and suffer for Christ: both must be the disciple's lifelong response to the Cross. By the Third Week, this response has acquired a certain specific content. 'Doing and suffering' recall now Christ's summons to his followers to labour with him and to share in the sufferings inseparable from his own conflict with the world's opposition to the reign of God [95]. Where a concrete decision has been made in the Second Week, the shape of the exercitant's 'doing and suffering' may be further specified by the commitments and exigencies arising out of his or her election.

[199] [1] *It should be noted*, **as has already been partly explained, that in the colloquies we should talk things over and make petitions** *according to our present situation*, [2] **depending, that is to say, on whether I am in a state of temptation or consolation, on whether I desire to have this or that virtue, on whether I want to choose in** *one direction or another*, **on whether I want to grieve or rejoice over what I am contemplating;** [3] **to sum up, I should ask for what I desire more earnestly in connection with particular things.** [4] *In this way*, **I can make a single colloquy to Christ our Lord, or if the matter or a particular devotion moves me, I can make three colloquies, one to the Mother, one to the Son, one to the Father,** [5] **in the same form indicated in the Second Week in the meditation on the Three Classes, with the note there appended.**

It should be noted In this note Ignatius provides the most complete summary to be found in the Exercises of what he means by the term 'colloquy'.

according to our present situation Literally 'according to the proposed matter'. As noted above (cf. note on Annotation 4 [4]), the expression should be taken to refer both to the subject matter of the Exercises and to the needs of the exercitant. Here the emphasis is clearly on the latter.

one direction or another I.e. in the choice of a life-state or situation.

In this way After a general summary of the nature of colloquy, Ignatius gives specific indications for the Third Week. Here the Triple Colloquy is no longer an integral motif, but can be adopted or not as seems appropriate to the exercitant.

[12]On this point, see Cusson, *Biblical Theology*, p. 299.

Second contemplation: Last Supper to the garden

[200] [1] SECOND CONTEMPLATION, IN THE MORNING, FROM THE LAST SUPPER TO THE GARDEN (INCLUSIVE) ([290])

[2] Prayer. The usual preparatory prayer.

[201] [1] The first prelude is *the history*. Here it will be how Christ our Lord with his eleven disciples came down from Mount Sion, where the supper had been taken, to the valley of Josaphat; [2] here he left eight of them in a place in the valley and the other three in a part of the garden, [3] and putting himself in prayer, his sweat became like drops of blood.[13] [4] He then prayed three times to the Father and awakened his disciples. Next, at his voice, his enemies fell to the ground, [5] and Judas gave him the kiss of peace; St Peter cut off the ear of Malchus and Christ put it back in place. [6] He was arrested as a criminal, and they led him down into the valley and up the slope to the house of Annas.

[202] The second prelude is to see the place; here it will be to consider the road from Mount Sion to the valley of Josaphat, and also the garden, whether wide, whether long, and of what general appearance.

[203] The third prelude is to ask for what I want. What is proper to prayer on the Passion is to ask for *grief with Christ in grief*, to be broken with Christ broken, for tears and interior suffering on account of the great suffering that Christ endured *for me*.

the history In a sense, the contemplation of the agony isolates the 'inner passion' and the emergence from this of the disposition which will motivate Jesus throughout his physical sufferings. In the supplementary text, attention is focused on one theme of Jesus' struggle in prayer [290].

grief with Christ in grief, etc. The Vulgate gives: 'To obtain what I desire, to ask for grief, mourning, anguish and other inward pains of that kind, that I may suffer together with Christ suffering for me.' If any single element in the Third Week text can be said to provide the keynote to the Week as a whole, it is this petition, already anticipated at the opening of the Exercises [48].

for me For Ignatius, as for other classical spiritual masters, the personal import of the Passion – that the Passion is 'for me' – is crucial, giving confi-

---

[13]*like drops of blood* corrected by Ignatius from 'similar to a sweat of blood'.

dence in God's love,[14] as well as powerfully eliciting love in response. Thus Gil González Dávila (to take a single instance from the *Directories*) citing Galatians 2:20, stipulates that 'the one meditating should make himself present to the mystery as though it is being done for him alone'.[15] But while the Third Week exercitant must dwell on the *for me* of the Passion, he or she must not privatize the Passion. A habit of mind characteristic of Ignatian apostolic spirituality is that of seeing both the human race in its totality and every individual with whom one deals in relation to the Passion and death of Christ.[16]

Notes on the Third Week

< NOTES >

[204] [1] FIRST NOTE **In this Second Contemplation after the preparatory prayer with the three preludes mentioned above, the same method of procedure for the points and colloquy should be followed as in the First Contemplation (of the Supper).** [2] **Two repetitions should be made of the First and Second Contemplations at the times of Mass and Vespers, and before supper the prayer of the senses should be made on the same two contemplations.** [3] **These are always preceded by the preparatory prayer and the three preludes, the latter being adapted to the matter under consideration, in the way mentioned and explained in the Second Week.**

[205] SECOND NOTE **In accordance with the age, constitution and temperament of the exercitant, the five Exercises or fewer should be made each day.**

[206] [1] THIRD NOTE **In this Third Week there are modifications to be made to the second and sixth of the Additions.**

[14]The *1599 Directory* cites St Augustine: 'He who has given us the greater, namely the Blood of his only begotten Son, will give also eternal glory, which is certainly less' (MHSI 76, p. 731 [trans. Palmer, p. 341]).

[15]MHSI 76, p. 526 [trans. Palmer, p. 262]. See also *1599 Directory* (loc. cit., p. 729 [trans. Palmer p. 341]).

[16]e.g. Ignatius, *Letter* 169 (7 May 1547): 'Look also at the people around you and realize that they are an image of the Holy Trinity. They have potential for the glory of Him to whom the universe is subject. They are members of Jesus Christ, redeemed through His many pains and insults, redeemed through His blood' (MHSI *Epp. Ig.* 1, p. 503 [trans. *Personal Writings*, p. 176]). Note that in connecting the Passion with each individual (as distinct from humankind as a collectivity) one is referring to the mind and intention of God. The content of Jesus' human consciousness during the Passion is another question.

[2] The second Addition. Immediately on waking, I will put before myself where I am going and for what purpose, and run briefly over the contemplation I want to make, whatever the mystery may be. [3] While getting up and dressing, I will make an effort to sorrow and grieve over the great grief and suffering of Christ our Lord.

[4] The sixth Addition. The modification here is that *I shall make no attempt to evoke joyful thoughts*, not even good and holy thoughts about such subjects as resurrection and final glory. [5] Rather, I will bring myself to grieve, to suffer and to feel broken, *calling frequently to mind* the labours, weariness and sorrows endured by Christ our Lord from the moment of his birth up to the mystery of the Passion in which I am at present engaged.

[207] FOURTH NOTE The particular examen should be made on the Exercises and on the present Additions, in the same way as in the previous Week.

I shall make no attempt to evoke joyful thoughts, etc. (cf. [78]). The knowledge of the Resurrection, without which the Passion could not be contemplated in its Christian meaning, should not issue in thoughts or feelings that at this moment could soften the stark reality of the Cross. The exercitant will pray, certainly, to share in some way in Jesus' own reaching out to the Father in hope and trust within his suffering. But he or she must not step out of the process of journeying towards Easter with the suffering Christ in order to contemplate the Passion in a mood of Easter joy.

calling frequently to mind (cf. [116], [130]) The constant recall of previous events of Christ's life enables the exercitant to interpret the more 'ordinary' sufferings of Christ's life in the light of the Cross. In addition, the practice counters the tendency to regard the Passion as an isolated sacrificial act, and to fail to relate it to a life led in vulnerability and in mounting conflict with forces hostile to his teaching and person.

Second to Seventh Days: The Passion

[208] [1] SECOND DAY
At midnight, the subject of contemplation should be the events from the garden to the house of Annas, inclusive [291]; in the morning from the house of Annas to the house of Caiaphas, inclusive [292]; [2] later the two repetitions and the Prayer of the Senses should be made, in the way that has already been said.

3 THIRD DAY
At midnight, from the house of Caiaphas to Pilate, inclusive [293]; in the morning, from Pilate to Herod, inclusive [294]; **4** and then the repetitions and the senses in the way that has already been said.
5 FOURTH DAY
At midnight, from Herod to Pilate [295], taking in and contemplating the first half of the mysteries which happened in Pilate's house; **6** then in the morning Exercise, the other mysteries which happened in the same house; with the repetitions and senses as has been said.
7 FIFTH DAY
At midnight, from the house of Pilate up to the nailing to the Cross [296]; in the morning, from the raising up on the Cross to his death [297]; then, the two repetitions and the senses.
8 SIXTH DAY
At midnight, from the taking down from the Cross up to, but not including, the tomb [298]; in the morning, from the tomb mystery (to be included) up *to the house where our Lady went* after her Son was buried.
9 SEVENTH DAY
A contemplation of the Passion as a whole in the Exercises at midnight and in the morning. **10** Then *instead of the two repetitions* and the senses, one should consider throughout the whole day, as frequently as possible, how the most holy body of Christ our Lord remained detached and separated from the soul, and where and how it was buried. **11** Likewise, one should consider the loneliness of our Lady with her grief and *exhaustion*, and also that of the disciples.

to the house where our Lady went In the house of Mary the exercitant will contemplate Jesus' first appearance after the resurrection [220]. Meantime Mary will occupy a central place in the considerations of the seventh ('tomb') day. Her presence thus provides a continuity between the death of Jesus and the Resurrection; more specifically, she is the exercitant's companion and model at this time, and her house becomes his or her own resting place. The Marian focus at this stage might also be understood in relation to John 19:26; Christ having given Mary as mother to St John and in him to the Church, the exercitant can think of him or herself as welcoming the mother into the 'house' which is one's own heart.[17]

A contemplation of the Passion as a whole See comment on [209] below.

instead of the two repetitions, etc. The materials prepare the exercitant for the Resurrection by directing attention on the realities of human experience

[17]See Decloux, 'Mary in the Spiritual Exercises'.

which the risen Christ enters and transforms – death, grief, solitude, weariness. But the exercitant should not be restricted to a literal application of the text. For many people, the day is an occasion for thoughts of death, one's own or the death of loved ones, and for allowing attitudes of sadness, fear or revolt in this regard to surface and to be touched by the death of Jesus. It can also be valuable, especially if the Third Week has seen the 'confirmation' of an election, to pray for the grace to experience oneself as 'dead' with Christ dead, 'dead', that is to say, to forces that impede the life of Christ in oneself, and especially to the desires and reluctances that could jeopardize the particular commitment made in the Exercises.

exhaustion In his or her own way, the exercitant, too, may feel 'spent' after the sustained accompaniment of Jesus along the road of his Passion.

[209] [1] NOTE
It should be noted that anyone who wants to spend more time on the Passion should take fewer mysteries in each contemplation, for instance in the first only the Supper; [2] in the second, the washing of the feet; in the third the giving of the Eucharist to the disciples; in the fourth, Christ's discourse, and so on for the other contemplations and mysteries.
[3] Again, after finishing the Passion, one can take half of the entire Passion for one full day, the other half on a second day, and the whole on the third day.
[4] On the other hand, someone wanting to spend less time on the Passion can take at midnight the Supper; in the morning, the Garden; at the time of Mass, the house of Annas; at the time of Vespers, the house of Caiaphas, and for the hour before supper, the house of Pilate. [5] In this way, without repetitions or the Prayer of the Senses one can make five different exercises each day with a different mystery of Christ our Lord in each exercise. [6] After finishing the entire Passion in this way, such a person can on another day take the whole Passion in one exercise or several, as shall seem likely to be more profitable.

The approaches to contemplating the Passion indicated in this Note differ in two ways in particular from the method and structure of the Second Week. First, repetitions are no longer an integral part of the contemplative day; one may wish now to follow the earlier pattern or one may not. Second, considerable value is set upon the contemplation of the Passion as a whole, an exercise to which there is no equivalent in the Second Week. Both features can be explained by the importance attached to the unity of the Passion, which makes the various episodes so many points of entry into the single mystery of the suffering and death of God in the humanity of Christ.

The note respects the variety of ways people may be led to pray the

Passion in the Third Week, and for this reason the alternatives proposed here should not be thought of as closing off other possibilities.[18]

RULES WITH REGARD TO EATING

The at first sight curious inclusion of these Rules in the Third Week is explained by the opening contemplation of Jesus at Supper [214]. In practice, whether and at what point they are to be given is left to the judgement of the director, who might also modify them in form.[19] Their general purpose is clear: to set the uses of food and drink in relation to the overall objective of the Exercises (cf. [1] and [23]), and more specifically to the norms of the Foundation; and to promote a contemplative attitude towards the satisfaction of a readily abused appetite. Hence the Rules can and do speak to exercitants today not only about the uses of food, but about other appetites, too, and other socially accepted forms of body abuse.

[210] [1] *RULES FOR THE FUTURE ORDERING OF ONE'S LIFE AS REGARDS EATING*
[2] **Rule one. There is less to be gained from *abstinence* in eating bread, since bread is not a food about which the appetite is usually as uncontrolled or the temptation as strong as is the case with other foods.**

[211] [1] **Rule two. Where drink is concerned, abstinence seems more appropriate than in the eating of bread; [2] so one ought to observe carefully what is beneficial and to be admitted, and what is harmful and to be cut out.**

[212] [1] **Rule three. In the matter of *more attractive kinds of food*,[20] the strictest and most complete abstinence ought to be observed, for in**

[18]For other possible schemata that a director might follow in proposing the Gospel material of the Third Week, cf. Cowan 'Moving into the Third Week', in Cowan and Futrell, *Handbook*, pp. 121–5.

[19]There is an austerity of tone about the rules that might not be helpful for a person already inclined to be over-rigorous, as the *Directories* seem to recognize. Thus we read in the *1599 Directory* that 'the rules for regulating one's diet ... should only be explained orally and not given in writing since (among other reasons) they ought not to be given to all persons in the same way, but adapted with discretion to each individual's character as well as to his physical and mental strength' (MHSI 76, pp. 732–4, repeating Polanco, p. 320, and Cordeses, p. 558 [trans. Palmer, p. 342, 144, 283]).

[20]His ideas regarding the uses of food and drink in a Jesuit community are developed in a letter written by Ignatius in the year of his death (1556) to Adrian Adriaenssens, Rector of Louvain (MHSI *Epp. Ig.*, vol. XI, No. 6454, pp. 374–5 [trans., *Inigo: Letters*, pp. 266–7]).

this matter the appetite is more inclined to excess, and temptation is more urgent. [2] Abstinence in order to avoid disorder in regard to food can be practised in two ways: (i) by getting into the habit of eating plain fare, (ii) by taking delicacies only in small quantities.

[213] [1] Rule four. Provided sickness is carefully avoided, the more one can cut back on normal intake, the sooner will one *arrive at the just mean* in eating and drinking. There are two reasons for this: [2] (i) by predisposing and adapting oneself in this way, one often experiences more of the inner lights, consolations and divine inspirations which will show one where the just mean lies; [3] (ii) if in cutting back in this way one finds oneself without the bodily strength or the inclination for spiritual exercises, it will be easy to reach a decision about what is more suitable for the sustenance of the body.

[214] [1] Rule five. While eating, one should *imagine that one is seeing Christ our Lord at table* with his apostles, and consider the way he eats and drinks, the way he looks about, the way he talks; and then try to imitate him. [2] Thus the higher part of the mind is taken up with considering our Lord and the lower with feeding the body, [3] and so one attains a more perfect harmony and order in the way one should behave and conduct oneself.

[215] [1] Rule six. At other times when eating, one can consider other things – the lives of the saints, or some religious contemplation, or some spiritual project that one has in hand; [2] for when attention is given to things like this, less pleasure and sensual enjoyment is taken in the body's food.

[216] [1] Rule seven. Above all, one should take care not to become wholly engrossed in what one is eating, and not to be carried away by one's appetite at meals; [2] instead, one should be in control of oneself, both in the manner of eating and in the quantity eaten.

[217] [1] Rule eight. To become free from disordered habits, it is very profitable *after dinner or supper*, or at some other time when one feels no appetite for food, [2] to make up one's mind how much food will be enough for the next dinner or supper; and similarly each day to decide the amount which it is fitting to eat; [3] then no matter how hungry or tempted one may be, one should not exceed this quantity, but rather, the better to overcome one's disordered appetite and the temptations of the enemy, if tempted to eat more, let one eat less.

Rules for the future ordering of one's life The Vulgate clarifies that the rules are concerned with 'a right temperance in food' (as distinct from penance, cf. [83]).

abstinence here has the sense not of avoidance but of limitation.

more attractive kinds of food In Spanish the word *manjares* can mean simply dishes or foods in general; but since a distinction is clearly implied between the matter of the present rule and that of Rule one, the more general sense is here less appropriate. In the time of Ignatius, bread was the staple diet of the poor and was considered sufficient, or largely sufficient, for nutritional needs. Rule three, therefore, refers to food other than bread, and the more a food is attractive or has a quality of luxury, the more, obviously, the rule is pertinent to it.

arrive at the just mean Here 'cutting back' is a particular application of the principle of *agendo contra*, the deliberate 'going against' a disordered tendency in order to arrive at the 'just mean'.[21]

imagine that one is seeing Christ our Lord at table, etc. In the Third Week the exercitant does this in contemplating the Last Supper.

after dinner or supper From the Ignatian *Directories*, we know how Ignatius himself applied these principles in the situation of the Exercises: 'A person making the Exercises should always be asked what he wants to eat, and then be given what he has requested, whether what he requests is a fowl or a mere morsel – whatever is according to his devotion. Thus, after dinner he should tell the person who clears the table or brings him dinner what he wants for supper. Similarly, after supper he should say what he will want for dinner the following day'.[22]

---

[21]See note on [13] above.

[22]*Dictated Directory* (MHSI 76, p. 79 [trans. Palmer, p. 11]). A similar instruction appears on p. 87 in *Second Directory* of Ignatius [trans. Palmer, p. 14].

FOURTH WEEK

The grace of joy

While the grace of the Third Week is to suffer with Christ, that of the Fourth Week is *joy*. How, in this connection, is the often loosely and ambiguously used térm 'joy' to be understood? We are concerned with paschal joy, the joy proper to Easter, the joy which springs from a still more fundamental grace, that of the faith and love that make the risen Christ, though invisible, the very core of the believer's existence.[1] The prime object of paschal joy, then, is the here-and-now reality of the risen Christ.

But this reality includes everything that Christ has brought about through his saving mission, the here-and-now-quality of life made possible for us, the ultimate hope offered us, all the ways in which the Resurrection is a message of God to and about the world.[2] Paschal joy, however, can be experienced at different levels; and the joy petitioned in the Fourth Week of the Exercises consists in the transforming experience of a joy which is a union in that of the risen Christ himself, just as suffering in the Third Week was such a sharing in the suffering of Christ.[3]

Flowing from Christ, this joy has the typical effects of consolation. Consolation always moves a person to God's service; and since the gifts of Christ accord with the life to which he calls us, this means that in the case of a person called explicitly to the apostolate, Fourth Week joy will constitute an élan towards apostolic mission, a source of strength, energy and

[1]Cf.1 Pet. 1:8–9: 'You did not see him, yet you love him; and still without seeing him you are already filled with a joy so glorious that it cannot be described, because you believe.'

[2]Cusson describes the 'joy of Christ' as having to do with 'the kingdom accomplished on this day, the new life transmitted to the entire world that has finally become capable, in principle at least, of accepting it and communicating with God. The joy of the love of the spouse welcoming the bride who has become capable of responding at this point of time to the love which for all eternity has been waiting for her in the heart of God':*The Spiritual Exercises Made in Everyday Life*, pp. 116–17.

[3]Sharing in the joy of Christ means sharing altruistically in Christ's joy for himself (i.e. in his return to the Father and his elevation to glory), but we must remember that Christ's joy is not only for himself but for us – joy in all he has achieved for us.

courage to participate in the work of the Kingdom.

In its fullness, Fourth Week joy engages the whole person, penetrates everyday experience, enhances and is supported by the ordinary joys of life [229.4], but its authenticity must always be measured in terms of depth and strength rather than emotional exhilaration. Even in the Exercises themselves it may function as it frequently does in daily life, as a leaven-like experience, subtly permeating a sorrow or heaviness which for the moment has to be borne. Yet if even in the Exercises, the uncomplicated plenitude of paschal joy may be slow to come, one prays for it with confidence, and does everything on one's own side to dispose oneself to receive it.

Fourth Week prayer: the apparitions and the Resurrection

The materials for contemplation proposed to the Fourth Week exercitant begin with Jesus's appearance to his Mother and conclude with the Ascension. In-between, post-Resurrection gospel episodes,[4] with four additional apparitions [308–311], are arranged to form a narrative sequence. In this sequence three broadly distinct emphases can be distinguished.[5]

1. Apparitions leading to personal faith and to witness [300–303.2]
2. Apparitions in which the details are more explicitly ecclesial: the Eucharist, the conferring of the Spirit and of the authority to forgive sins, the blessing on future believers, the miraculous catch of fish, the establishment of the position of Peter, the command to teach and baptize all nations [303.3–307]
3. A final series of apparitions, founded on Scripture or apocryphal, which display the munificence of the risen Christ in showing himself [308–311]

In each apparition, then, there is a particular content, consisting of specific aspects of the believer's relationship with Christ in the Church; and the purpose of the Week will be missed if this content is passed over. On the other hand, Fourth Week prayer should be spacious and in no way encumbered by detail. It

[4]This sequence includes all the apparitions of Jesus narrated in the Gospels, except the concluding appearances in Mark (16:14–18), Luke (24:44–49), and John (21:15–23), which are omitted in favour of Matthew 28:16–20 (cf. [307]). The apparition to Mary Magdalen does not appear in its fuller, Johannine, form (John 20:11–18), but is contained in the Marcan version (16: 9–11) in Ignatius' 'second apparition' [300]. It is for the director to find the gospel texts which seem best to help the exercitant; and he or she is not limited to Ignatius' selection. Texts should be selected, however, with regard to the range of content covered by the post-Resurrection Gospel narratives.

[5]For this division see Chapelle et al. *Exercises Spirituels d'Ignace de Loyola*, *'Les Apparitions'*, pp. 404–9.

must be remembered, again, that the object of contemplation in the final stage of the Exercises consists both in the specific details of the successive texts and also – and more fundamentally – in the single mystery to which each text gives access. Hence, in contemplating the persons, words and actions of each of the Fourth Week apparitions, the exercitant is present in a receptive and unencumbered prayer to the single reality of the joy-giving risen Christ.

First Contemplation: Our Lord appears to Mary

[218] **¹ FIRST CONTEMPLATION *HOW CHRIST OUR LORD APPEARED TO OUR LADY* ([299])**
² Prayer. The usual preparatory prayer.

[219] **¹ The first prelude is the history. After Christ died on the Cross his body remained separated from the soul but always united with the divinity. His blessed soul also united with his divinity, *descended into Hell*. ² From there he released the souls of the just; then, returning to the tomb and *rising again, he appeared in body and soul to his blessed Mother*.**

[220] **The second prelude. Composition seeing the place. Here it will be to see the arrangement of the holy sepulchre, and *the lodging or house of our Lady*, looking in detail at all its parts, such as her room, *oratory*, etc.**

[221] **The third prelude. To ask for what I want, and here it will be to ask for grace *to feel gladness and to rejoice intensely* over the great glory and joy of Christ our Lord.**

How Christ our Lord appeared to our Lady In the Versio Prima: 'The first apparition of Christ to the Blessed Virgin Mary' (cp. [299]); in the Vulgate 'How the Lord Jesus appeared after the Resurrection to his holy Mother'.

The Fourth Week contains no contemplation on the Resurrection as an event, and in both the Autograph and the Versio Prima the word 'resurrection' does not appear in the title; the exercitant contemplates only the risen Jesus in his appearances.

In taking the first of these as being the appearance to his Mother, Ignatius is following an ancient tradition,⁶ and the significance he attached to

---

⁶In Ludolph's Life, the risen Jesus and his mother are represented as talking to one another 'full of joy while lovingly delighting in the Lord's Paschal victory'. The tradition is referred to in the *Ejercitatorio* of Cisneros and it is commemorated in the dedication of a Church in Jerusalem. On authorities both before and after Ignatius who have defended this appearance see Cusson, *Biblical Theology*, p. 304. Both Rickaby (p. 193) and Longridge (p. 148) cite the Easter hymn of William Keble: 'while seraphs wait he talks apart with her a while'.

this tradition is evident both here and in the supplementary text [229]. In default of scriptural witness, he appeals to the exercitant's faith-understanding (with reference particularly to Matt. 15:16. Jesus' reproach to the apostles for missing the inner meaning of a parable). In the light of such understanding, the apparition should be considered not only as a moment of natural filial intimacy, but as corresponding to the place of Mary in the economy of salvation and in the Church.[7] That we are here being invited to consider Mary in this way is further suggested by the use in the Versio Prima and in the supplementary text [299] of the formal title 'Virgin Mary' in place of the more familiar 'our Lady'.

descended into Hell I.e. Jesus' descent into the shadow-world of Sheol or Hades[8] to which he brings life and the fulfilment of a long expectation. (Cf. [313] where this important moment in salvation history is included among Jesus' apparitions.)

rising again, he appeared in body and soul to his blessed Mother This phrase (resumed in both the Versio Prima and the Vulgate as 'appeared to the Blessed Virgin, his mother') suggests practically simultaneous events.[9]

the lodging or house of our Lady As in Weeks Two and Three, the opening contemplation of the Fourth Week begins with a room, the private, personal space of an individual or group. Here, note especially the similarity to the 'house of our Lady' with its 'rooms', which was the setting of the Incarnation [103].

oratory It is the man or woman of prayer who is able to welcome the risen Christ into whatever in their life is 'home'.

to feel gladness and rejoice intensely The quality of joy the exercitant prays for and hopes to experience is expressed by the double verb (in Spanish, *me alegrar* and *gozar*) and the reinforcing *intensely*, a word Ignatius does not use casually (cf. [55]).

That the joy of the Fourth Week is a 'participation' in the joy of Christ

---

[7]For the sense of this first apparition, the reader is referred especially to the article by Decloux, 'Mary in the Spiritual Exercises,' pp. 142–4, and Kolvenbach 'The Easter Experience of our Lady'. Both articles appear in *Our Lady in Ignatian Spirituality*, CIS 19 (1988).

[8]Cf. 1 Pet. 3:19, 4:6. In the current liturgical English translation of the Apostle's Creed 'descended into Hell' is rendered 'descended to the dead'.

[9]In the Cathedral Church of Manresa there is a *retablo* in which Mary is depicted as present at the tomb at the actual moment of the Resurrection.

himself is made clear in the Vulgate version: 'that we may share in the immense joy of Christ and his mother'. (Cf. [48] *in contemplating the Resurrection one asks for joy with Christ joyful.*)

[222] The first, second and third points should be the usual ones that we had for the Supper of Christ our Lord.

[223] The fourth point is to consider how the divine nature, which in the Passion seemed to go into hiding, now in this holy Resurrection appears and reveals itself *so miraculously in its true and most holy effects*.

[224] The fifth point is to look at *the office of consoler*, which Christ our Lord fulfils, and to compare it with the way friends are accustomed to console one another.

[225] Colloquy. To conclude with one or more colloquies, in accordance with the matter under consideration, and an Our Father.

As in the Third Week, the points supply a framework for the Week. 'Persons', 'words', 'actions' (points one to three) are contemplated with reference to the general interpretative principles set out in points four and five.

so miraculously in its true and most holy effects In the time of the apparitions and of the apostolic Church these might be summarized under three heads: effects in individuals (e.g. hope, vision, joy, love), in the Church (the building of the community), in the world (the progress of the reign of God through the mission of the apostles).

the office of consoler The Vulgate version reads: 'appreciate with what promptitude and abundance the Lord discharges the office of consoling his own, making a comparison with the consolation that can be given by a very great friend'.

Notes on the Fourth Week

< NOTES >
[226] [1] First note. In the following contemplations all the mysteries of the Resurrection should be gone through in the way indicated below, *up to and including the Ascension*. [2] For the rest, the same arrangement and procedure should be adopted and kept throughout the whole week of the Resurrection, as were maintained in the week of the

Passion. [3] Hence this first contemplation on the Resurrection may be taken as a guide with regard to the preludes, which are adapted according to the matter under consideration, [4] and also with regard to the five points, which remain the same. The additions given below also remain the same. [5] In everything else, for example the repetitions, five senses, and the shortening or lengthening of the mysteries, one can take as guide the arrangement of the Third Week of the Passion.

[227] [1] Second note. In this Fourth Week, it is usually more appropriate than in the three preceding weeks, to make *four exercises* and not five. [2] The first should be immediately on rising in the morning; the second at the time of Mass or before lunch in place of the first repetition; the third at the time of vespers in place of the second repetition. [3] The fourth, before supper, should be the *prayer of the senses* on the three exercises of the day; in this one should note and pause at the most important points and the places where greater movements or spiritual relish may have been experienced.

[228] [1] Third note. Though a fixed number of points, for example three or five, etc. have been given in all the contemplations, the person who is contemplating can take more or fewer points as better suits him or her. [2] For this purpose, it is very helpful before beginning the contemplation to foresee and specify the particular number of points to be taken.

[229] [1] Fourth note. In this Fourth Week, among the ten Additions, there are modifications to be made to the second, sixth, seventh and tenth:
[2] The second: immediately on waking to put before myself the contemplation I have to make, deliberately wanting to be moved and to rejoice in the great joy and gladness of Christ our Lord.
[3] The sixth: to call to mind and think about things which cause happiness, gladness, and spiritual joy, such as final glory.
[4] The seventh: *to make use of the light and the pleasures of the seasons*, for instance refreshing coolness in the summer, sunshine or the warmth of a fire[10] in the winter, *in so far as* we think or conjecture that these things might help us rejoice in our Creator and Redeemer.
[5] The tenth: instead of practising penance one should look to temperance and the just mean in everything, except where the Church's precepts about fasting or abstinence apply, for these must always be observed, if there is no legitimate impediment.

---

[10]'of a fire' has been added in both the Versio Prima and the Vulgate.

up to and including the Ascension The Fourth Annotation defines the matter of the Week in terms of both the Resurrection and Ascension; and the significance of the Ascension is accentuated by its position in the supplementary mysteries, where it is placed at the end of the series [312] coming after the appearance to St Paul [311]. The Ascension is the necessary completion of the contemplative sequence which began in the Second Week with Christ's descent 'for me' from the heart of the Trinity [104]. In the Ascension, Christ's return to the Father, we contemplate not only the completion of Christ's own journey, but God's promise to ourselves, made in and through Christ, as to the end of our own.

four exercises The better to establish a climate conducive to spiritual joy. Perhaps, too, Ignatius is recognizing the likelihood of fatigue at this stage of the Exercises.[11]

prayer of the senses Cf. the instructions on repetition in [62] and [118].

the number of points. The number of points is determined solely by the personal criterion of what 'better suits' the exercitant. One reason for reducing the number has to do with the ordinary movement of prayer in the Exercises towards contemplative simplicity. By the Fourth Week an exercitant may need very little material in order to sustain an hour's prayer (e.g. [308–310]).

to make use of the light and the pleasures of the seasons ... in so far as ... The experiences described do not automatically help the exercitant to reach the object of the Fourth Week, and might indeed be 'used' to evade it. Hence the qualifying 'in so far as' should not be ignored. But more significant is the point that joy in Christ, the grace of the Fourth Week, may be found within the immediate enjoyment of creation, an enjoyment which may indeed enhance the higher gift – joy of which the object is Christ himself. The Vulgate expands considerably on the concision of the Autograph: 'I make use of the pleasure of light and sky which shall offer itself; as in springtime the sight of green grass and flowers, or the agreeableness of a sunny spot; in the winter, the welcome of the sun or of a fire; and so of the other legitimate satisfactions of the body and mind, by which I may be able to rejoice with my Creator and Redeemer.' For other examples of making use of an environment (whether contrived or given) to 'help' the exercitant, see above [79] and [130.4].

---

[11]Cf. note above on day seven of the Third Week [208.9].

THE CONTEMPLATION TO ATTAIN LOVE

The Contemplation to Attain Love (sometimes known just as the *Contemplatio*) presents in the form of a contemplative paradigm the spirituality of finding and loving God in all things which is the lasting outcome of the Exercises. When should the contemplation be made? The text of the Exercises assigns it no special position and it can be made indeed at some level of benefit by anyone who assents to the values of the Foundation.[12] But many considerations leave no doubt that within the Exercises themselves, the *Contemplatio* is the note on which the whole process concludes. It has a contemplative quality which commends its use when the spiritual development of the four Weeks is complete;[13] its content gathers up the themes of the Exercises in their entirety, and it reaches beyond the Exercises themselves to work its insights and attitudes into the texture of everyday life. Moreover, the *contemplatio* presents Christ not as met with in the Gospel narratives but the post-Ascension Christ of the here and now.[14]

Content and dynamic

The dynamic of the exercise turns on the two meanings of the love of God, God's love for us and ours for God; and on the integration of these loves into the exercitant's uses and experience of immediate reality. God's love for us, the absolute and unconditional love by which God loves us before we love him,[15] the love by which God teaches us to love,[16] is the subject of the four points. Our love for God is the love we seek to *attain* [230], and which we request as grace

[12]On levels of spiritual maturity and the dispositions of the Contemplation to Attain Love, see the observations made above in connection with the Fifth Annotation ([5]); for the relation between the Contemplation and the Foundation, see Introduction to Foundation.

[13]In this matter, however, we discover in the *Directories* an evolving understanding of the nature of the Contemplation to Attain Love, and some early directors introduced it at various points within the Exercises, e.g. Miró Hoffaeus, and the *Short Directory* of c. 1580 (MHSI 76, pp. 221, 391, 458 [trans., Palmer, pp. 68, 75, 216]).

[14]Strictly speaking, therefore, the dynamics of the Exercises, taken in themselves, require that the Contemplation to Attain Love should be made after the contemplation of the Ascension. However, in order to allow the exercitant more time to assimilate its dense material, some directors prefer to give it *pari passu* with the Fourth Week contemplations, from the Second Day on, a procedure approved by Polanco and incorporated into the *1599 Directory*: (MHSI 76, pp. 323, 734–5 [trans., Palmer, pp. 145, 343]).

[15]Cf. 1 John 4:10.

[16]One is taught to love only by being loved, and this pattern of ordinary experience repeats the most profound models of religion: cf. Buckley, 'The Contemplation to Attain Love', p. 96.

in the petition [233] and in the prayer of radical self-offering, *Take and receive* [234]. Though of course always imperfect and in its plenitude an object of desire and aspiration, this love resembles God's own love. The grace of the exercise is to grow in loving in the way God himself loves.

But in the Contemplation to Attain Love, as in the Foundation, the Creator/creature relationship is proposed with explicit reference to the things, events, and situations of the exercitant's everyday world. In the Foundation these were the material of 'ordered use'. In the present exercise, they are the medium within which the exchange of loves itself takes place. As God, on his side, gives himself in love through all things, so our love for God includes all things, the totality of the self, everything we call our own, every element of our experience of God's world. This integration of love with immediate experience has as its context a certain vision, a perception of the world as a divine *milieu*, in which the love of God is so sensed in everything that 'nothing can come as an interference between God and his creature because everything is a means of encounter and union'.[17] Such a vision of reality, Ignatius believes, a person will experience at the end of the Exercises. But it must be stressed that such a vision is a grace, not a change of consciousness inducible by technique; and again that we are always dealing with a process of development not a definitive achievement.

The four points

The four points will be discussed singly in the commentary below, but to see how they can help the exercitant to develop a faith-vision of reality some general remarks with regard to them will be in place at this stage.

(1) Each of the points is presented both as an area of human reality and also as illustrating a mode of God's loving presence and action. Under the first aspect the points as they stand invite us to reflect:

- on our personal history;
- on the material world which is our environment (considered statically in point two, dynamically in point three);
- on our own personal qualities.

But as well as representing categories of reality in which we find God, the points also distinguish four ways in which this 'finding' comes about. That is to say, in and through his gifts we meet God as

---

[17]Cusson, *The Spiritual Exercises Made in Everyday Life*, p. 139.

- *bestowing* his gifts,
- *present* in his gifts,
- *working* in his gifts,
- *source* of his gifts.

(2) With regard to the presence and action of God within evil and sin-disfig-ured realities, it should be noted that the points do not deal with this explicitly, but concentrate on building the over-all vision, based on a positive theology of creation, which is the context in which God's presence and action in the negative aspects of reality are to be discerned. But this emphasis does not imply that in actually making the exercise one considers God's presence only in the obvious 'blessings' of life; and indeed if the presence and action of God in negative realities is not explicitly referred to in the text, it is implicit in a detail of which the significance is easily overlooked – the concept of the working and labouring God of the third point.

(3) As with many other materials in the Exercises, reflection on these points can open perceptions and lines of development of which the text itself makes no mention. In this connection, the exercitant might find it helpful to reflect on the four points in relation to the Weeks of the Exercises – an approach favoured by many mainstream commentators, who regard the points and the Weeks as mutually clarifying.[18] This approach must be based on the objec-tive content of the texts themselves but also on personal and subjective elements in the exercitant's own contemplation. Lines of correspondence between the texts themselves are not hard to find. The first point can recall the First Week themes of God's plan for humankind [51], the 'gift' of mercy [48, 61, 71], the universe as sign of God's fidelity [60]. The second point can recall God's presence in the world through the Incarnation, and the third the Passion in which the concept of the 'labouring' God finds its centre and culmination; while considered in relation to the Fourth Week, point four makes us aware that the essential 'effect' [223] of the Resurrection is to establish the possibility of the love and knowledge of union. But reflection on the points in relation to the four Weeks is not just a matter of seeking paral-lels between texts. It must be based on associations and insights coming from remembered personal graces.

---

[18]Cf. Fessard, *La dialectique des Exercises Spirituels*, vol. 1, pp. 149 ff., and Pousset, *Life in Faith and Freedom*, p. 196 (note). For possible ways of working out the connection, see Buckley, 'The Contemplation to Attain Love', pp. 100–103; Cowan and Futrell, *Handbook* pp. 133–4. See also *Place Me With Your Son*, Maryland Province of the Society of Jesus. p. 104, where it is suggested that the points be made by reviewing the graces of the four Weeks.

The contemplation

[230] ¹ CONTEMPLATION TO *ATTAIN LOVE*
² *Note. It will be good to notice two things at the start.*
First: love ought to find its expression in *deeds rather than in words*.

[231] ¹ Second: love consists in *mutual communication*. That is to say, the lover gives and communicates to the loved one what they have, or something of what they have, or are able to give; and in turn the one loved does the same for the lover. ² Thus the one who possesses knowledge will give it to the one without it, and similarly with *honour or wealth*. Each gives to the other.

³ Prayer: The usual prayer.

[232] The *first prelude is the composition*, which here is to see *how I am before God our Lord*,¹⁹ and the angels and the saints interceding for me.

[233] The second prelude. *To ask for what I want*. Here, it will be to ask for *interior knowledge* of all the good I have received, so that acknowledging this with gratitude, I may be able to love and serve his Divine Majesty *in everything*.

attain love The word *attain* is used in the sense not of 'obtain' but rather of 'reaching to' or 'arriving at'. The *love* to be 'attained' is a growing love on our part for God. The word *attain* carries overtones of endeavour, and indeed the whole exercise, consisting as it does in a kind of 'pedagogy of love', proposes ways of furthering the development of love on our side. Ultimately, however, the love here sought is a gift and incommensurate with our own endeavours. In the Vulgate the title reads: 'Contemplation for arousing spiritual love in ourselves'.

<hr>

¹⁹There is no absolute consensus among commentators on whether the titles in the Contemplation to Attain Love – *God our Lord, Divine Majesty, Lord and God* – refer primarily to Christ or primarily to the Trinity. Hugo Rahner maintains that the whole text refers to Christ. In the view of Peters, 'In Ignatius' vision, the risen life of Christ merges into that of the blessed Trinity ... from the Fourth Week onward the Trinity dominates the life of the exercitant ... Ignatius wants his exercitant to realize that he lives in the presence of *Dios nuestro Señor, who is Father, Son and Holy Spirit.*' Stanley suggests that the first three Points refer to Christ, the fourth to the Trinity. See H. Rahner, *Ignatius the Theologian, p. 134*; Peters, *The Spiritual Exercises, pp. 157–8*; Stanley, *I Encountered God*, p. 294.

deeds rather than in words Cf. 1 John 3:18. In Ignatius' view, 'action' is a defining characteristic of love; without expression in acts, love lacks an essential completeness. The fundamental 'act' of love is the choice to give oneself to God, and the prayer *Take and receive* is precisely such an act (and not just saying words). This act of love then extends itself into the deeds of service.

mutual communication The mutual communication here described is that which characterizes the love of friendship, a love which is spontaneous and which is directed on each side towards the good or pleasure of the other. In friendship, the giver's generosity does not coerce, but simply gives the experience of being loved; and the desire of the beloved to give in return comes not from a sense of being put under obligation but from the wish to give, which is of the essence of friendship. Nor in friendship is there any question of loving the other for their gifts and not for themselves, still less of loving only on the condition of receiving gifts.

For friendship as model of the Creator/creature relationship see [54], [224]; for mutual communication between God and his creature as the situation towards which the whole dynamic of the Exercises tends, see [15]

honour or wealth Here, and again in the prayer of offering [234], the theme of honour and wealth reappears. At this point, however, these are seen not as potential obstacles to love but as the very material of sharing.

first prelude … composition Since the exercise has to do with the here-and-now, the first prelude of the Second to Fourth Weeks, the 'history', disappears.

how I am before God our Lord etc. The similar but not identical 'composition' in the Three Classes served to accentuate the solemnity of the exercitant's situation. Here one is made aware rather of the entire invisible world – God, angels, saints – as the always present and supportive ambience of one's prayer and entire life.[20]

to ask for what I want In stating the graces to be prayed for, the petition summarizes the objectives and development of the exercise in the following sequence: (i) knowledge, (ii) gratitude and increasing love, (iii) service in everything.

interior knowledge In other words, a Spirit-enlightened vision that perceives immediate reality in its relationship to God.

---

[20]Compare [151]: *see myself standing in the presence of God our Lord and of all his saints* (Three Classes) and [232]: *see how I am before God our Lord and the angels and the saints interceding for me* (Contemplation to Attain Love).

in everything A key phrase of the *Contemplatio* – God shows his love in and through everything, I aspire to find and love God in everything. In the Vulgate one begs 'for the grace through which, seeing deeply into the immensity of his benefits bestowed on me, to devote myself totally to his love, worship and service.'

[234] **[1] The first point is to bring to memory the benefits received – *creation, redemption* and *particular gifts* – [2] pondering with deep affection *how much God our Lord has done for me*, how much he has given me of what he possesses, and further, how according to his divine plan, it is the Lord's wish, as far as he is able, to give me himself. [3] Then I shall reflect within myself and consider what, in all reason and justice, I ought for my part to offer and give his Divine Majesty, that is to say, all I possess and myself as well, saying, as one making a gift *with heartfelt love*:**
[4] *Take Lord and receive* all my *liberty, my memory, my understanding and my entire will*, all that I have and possess. [5] You gave it all to me; to you I return it. All is yours, *dispose of it entirely according to your will. Give me only the love of you, together with your grace* for *that is enough for me*.

creation and redemption – God's universal gifts to humankind considered with reference to oneself: thus by gift God created me, and has redeemed me.

particular gifts The first point is often – and valuably – taken as an occasion to recapitulate the salient events of one's personal faith-history. But the consideration of 'particular gifts' can also take other forms, e.g. the recall of gifts received during the Exercises themselves.

how much God our Lord has done for me, etc. God's love for us – expressing itself in action for us, in sharing what he has, and (as far as can be) in the gift of himself – is the model of our own love, which expresses itself in deeds of service, in the gift of *all I have and possess*, and indeed in the gift of my very self.

with heartfelt love (literally, 'with much affection'). Such an offering is the spontaneous expression of love, but a love of more than ordinary totalness and intensity.[21] The Vulgate adds 'with words of this kind or similar ones'.

---

[21]It is the intensity of love, with the resulting élan and spontaneity that makes the difference between this offering, as it might be made at the end of the Exercises, and the generous dispositions with which are a 'benefit' at the moment of beginning the Exercises. (cf. note on [5]).

Take ... and receive Take, on my side an act of handing over, of unconditional surrender, made in love and trust; and *receive*, because, nevertheless, I cannot command God to take my gift, and acknowledge that he must wish to receive it. The offering expressed by the two terms consists in the love-inspired entrustment to God of everything, and hence does not necessarily entail a sense of specific possible implications. Nevertheless, according to one's perception of God's will or invitation at a given moment, it may bring into focus some particular disposition: e.g. indifference in the face of choice; commitment to work for God's Kingdom fully as his instrument; acceptance of diminishment, loss or death.[22]

liberty Note that the prayer of offering begins by singling out liberty (even though this is implicit in 'will'). The dedication of one's freedom to God and to his will has been the main objective of the Exercises.

my memory, my understanding and my entire will In general, the handing over of the powers of the soul represents the surrender of the whole self, but the total gift of self may involve special awareness of particular components of the self in addition to the 'powers of the soul', e.g. gifts for leadership, or friendship, one's sexuality, one's creative talents, and so on.

dispose of it entirely according to your will Compare the definition of the purpose of the Exercises given in the first Annotation: 'to seek and find the divine will in regard to the disposition of one's life'. The sense is clarified by the Vulgate: 'Whatever I have or possess, you have bestowed upon me; to you I restore it all, handing it over to be governed entirely by your will.' In asking God to *dispose of* the powers of the soul, we ask him, then, to take these to himself, to take them under his control, to deploy them as he wishes.

give me only love of you together with your grace. Various translations of this line are possible. The translation here follows the Vulgate (a version both approved and used by Ignatius). This removes an ambiguity in the Spanish original 'give me only your love', making it clear that the love referred to is our love for God,[23] the love which is our part in the mutual exchange between the loving God and his loved creature, the 'love of the Divine Majesty in everything' asked for in the second Prelude [233]. 'Your grace' seems best understood not as an addition to the love of God, but precisely as the grace to love God.[24]

---

[22]But where the powers of the soul are concerned, the words *Take and receive* contain no implication that one might under any circumstances positively ask God to take these away.

[23]Thus, in the phrase 'your love' the sense of 'your' is similar to that of 'his' in, for example, 'his love and praise' [15].

[24]Cf. Gueydan et al., *Exercises spirituels*, p. 141. In *Personal Writings* the phrase is rendered 'Give me the grace to love you'.

that is enough for me. In the Vulgate, 'with that I am rich enough'.

[235] [1] **The second point. To see how God *dwells in creatures*: in the elements giving being; in the plants giving growth; in the animals giving sensation; and in humankind granting the gift of understanding;** [2] **and so how he dwells also *in me*, giving me being, life and sensation and causing me to understand. To see, too, how he makes a temple of me, as I have been created in the likeness and image of his Divine Majesty.**
[3] **Again, to reflect within myself in the way indicated in the first point or in some other way I feel to be better. The same procedure is to be observed in each of the following points.**

dwells in creatures The statement as it stands, like the statements in the Foundation, has a scholastic air and can appear at first sight somewhat passionless. But processed by contemplation, the statement becomes a vision and an experience. As Ignatius writes in a letter to Francis Borgia: 'when persons go out of themselves and enter into their creator and Lord, they enjoy continuous instruction, attention and consolation; they are aware how the fullness of our eternal God dwells in all created things, giving them being and keeping them in existence with his infinite being and presence.'[25]

in me God's presence in subhuman reality is ordered to his presence in the human person, and indeed to his presence in this person precisely as 'graced', i.e. as a temple of the Holy Spirit.

[236] [1] **The third point. To consider how *God works and labours* on my behalf in all created things on the face of the earth; 'that is, he acts in the manner of a person at work;**[26] [2] **as in the *heavens*, *elements*, plants, fruits, cattle, etc. giving being, conserving life, granting growth and sensation, etc. Then to reflect within myself.**

God works and labours From a 'static' image of presence, attention is shifted to the 'dynamic' image; God is present in the world through a continuous process. Various ways of reading this point suggest themselves. First, God's sustaining and co-operative action in physical nature can serve as a model for divine love as a continuous process within the unfolding of every human life-

---

[25]MHSI *Epp. Ign.*, No. 101, vol. i, pp. 339–40 [trans. *Personal Writings*, p. 161].

[26]In Ignatius' original this phrase is in Latin: *habet se ad modum laborantis*. Possibly Ignatius wished to protect his (analogous) concept of a labouring God against literal readings of it, that could be interpreted as impugning the doctrines of divine immutability and impassibility.

story. The point can be considered, too, as a pendant to the principle of 'ordered' use set out in the Foundation; while we 'use' creatures for God's praise, reverence and service, God himself continuously 'uses' his creation in order to give himself to us, and through all things to meet our needs and to enrich us. It must always be remembered that in the Exercises, the word here translated as 'work' (even without the reinforcing 'labours') carries an over-tone of 'toil' even suffering.[27] Thus, the God who works and labours in nature is also the God who carries out the work of the Kingdom in the face of all that opposes it, in a toil and labour in which in a sense Christ suffers throughout history.[28]

heavens, elements, etc. A similar overview of nature (but making a different point) figures in the second meditation of the First Week [60]. The Vulgate, however, is unusually sparing of detail on this third point, and simply states a general principle leaving it to the exercitant to find his or her own application: 'The third point is to contemplate the same God and Lord, working, and in a manner labouring, in his creatures for my sake; in as much as he gives and preserves in them what they are, have, are capable of, and do.'

[237] [1] The *fourth point*. To see how all that is good and every gift *descends from on high*. Thus, my limited *power* descends from the supreme and infinite power above – and similarly with *justice*, good-ness, pity, mercy, etc. – as *rays* descend *from the sun* and *waters from a fountain*. [2] Then to finish by reflecting within myself, as has been said. Finally, a colloquy and an Our Father.

The *fourth point*, in which attention concentrates on God as Source, raises the exercise to a further contemplative level of awareness, and expands the vision of God in relation to all reality to a universal scale. Thus in consider-ing the material here located, one's own higher faculties and one's mental and moral qualities, one is led to contemplate the attributes of God himself as the all-powerful, kind, pitiful and merciful Source not only of these partic-ular gifts but of all good things.

descends from on high Whereas in points two and three, God is 'in' his gifts, here the gifts point to God in himself, the 'above' from which their goodness descends. Note, too, that the *for me* of each of the previous points is here not

[27]For the link between work and suffering, see [95.5], the call of the King to 'labour with' Christ, and to 'follow him in hardship in order to follow him in glory'; also [116], the work of Joseph and Mary and the future labours of Jesus; and [206], recall of the labours and fatigues of Jesus' life. For a discussion of the third Point in relation to the Passion see Fessard, *Dialectique*, vol. i, pp. 157–60.
[28]See Buckley, 'The Contemplation to Attain Love', p. 104.

to be found. *For me* still belongs, to be sure, to the reality contemplated in the fourth point, but it is now presumed, and explicit attention is centred upon the being of God and his attributes.

power ... justice, etc.[29] Again, in the First Week similar material was used in a quite different context, i.e. the list of divine attributes in [59] which served to diminish the exercitant by reinforcing the contrast between the exercitant's sinfulness and the goodness of God. Here, attention is not on one's own deficiency in these qualities; on the contrary, because one appreciates them in oneself they can raise one's mind to a sense of the nature of God who is their source and in whom they exist in an 'eminent' way.

rays ... from the sun ... waters from a fountain. The language has strong Trinitarian associations:[30] *sun* recalls the Father of Light from whom all good things descend;[31] *rays from the sun* will remind those familiar with Ignatius' *Autobiography* of the second of the Manresa illuminations – the vision of the creation of the world under the particular form of the creation of light, and also of Ignatius' claim frequently to have seen Christ 'as the sun'.[32] In Scripture,[33] in much spiritual tradition, and at least implicitly in Ignatius' own writings (cp. the vision at the Cardoner) water is a symbol of the Spirit.

THREE WAYS OF PRAYING

In these Ways of Prayer, two distinct kinds of material provide content for consideration, meditation or contemplation. In the First Way, the material consists in the decalogue, the capital sins and contrary virtues, the powers of the soul and the senses – in short, the essentials of God's project for the whole spiritual and sensate human person. In the Second and Third Ways, prayer formulae of the Church comprise the content of two types of personal prayer of a more contemplative quality.

Basic to each of the Ways is the interrelation of content and prayer, the content giving to the prayer matter and direction, the prayer in turn bringing

---

[29]In the qualities selected and in the order of their presentation, the exercitant might note an insight into his or her own use of his gifts to co-operate in God's work. To this work we bring 'power', the capacity to create, or to effect change, but power is to be exercised, as God exercises power, with justice, goodness, pity and mercy.

[30]The language of this fourth point is discussed at some length in reference to St John's Gospel by Stanley, *I encountered God*, pp. 304–9.

[31]James 1:17.

[32]Cf. *Reminiscences*, §29, 99 [trans., *Personal Writings*, pp. 26, 63].

[33]Cf. John 4:14.

faith-penetration to the content. In the First, however, the emphasis is more on the education of outlook and in the Second and Third more on prayer as such. Thus the First Way promotes an ever deepening insight into, and understanding of, the moral essentials of converted life by means of prayerful Christ-centred reflection on these. The Second and Third Ways have the purpose of adding other forms of mental prayer to those proposed in the Exercises themselves, forms which tend to promote a contemplative simplicity in prayer,[34] but which also open a person, precisely in contemplative prayer, to the teaching of the Spirit through the prayers of the Church.

The Three Ways: the Fourth Week and beyond

Though the Fourth Annotation connects them with the Fourth Week, the Ways are not integral to the Exercises as such; they are included in the Fourth Week because they provide for the exercitant's impending return to ordinary life, while at the same time fitting in with the spiritual climate of the Week itself. To make such claims for all three of the Ways might appear, however, to run up against Ignatius himself, who especially commends the First to people of limited capacity or aspiration.[35] But the suitability of the First Way to people of this kind does not mean that they alone benefit from it. A 'way' or 'method' is not necessarily tied to a level of spiritual maturity or prayer development; and the First Way is amenable to use at many different levels – that of the 'pre-exercitant', of the Eighteenth Annotation exercitant, of the exercitant of the First Week, and also of a person returning to daily life from the full Exercises.[36] While always retaining its fundamental and never to be outgrown purpose – the integration into prayer

[34]In his or her subsequent life, the exercitant will continue to develop and personalize, as appropriate, 'ways of prayer' contained in the Exercises themselves, e.g. the examen, meditation, imaginative contemplation, decision-making through prayer, finding God in created realities. In making available an additional resource, the Three Ways do not of themselves override these.

[35]Cf. *Constitutions*, Part vii, ch. 4, no. 649 (trans., Ganss, p. 283): 'The Spiritual Exercises should not be given in their entirety except to a few persons ... But some examinations of conscience and methods of prayer (especially the first of those which are touched on in the Exercises) can also be given far more widely; for anyone who has good will seems to be capable of these exercises'. The origins of the First Way of prayer go back to Ignatius' early apostolic ministry in Alcalá, from which emerged the 'Eighteenth Annotation Exercises', of which the First Way of prayer forms a substantial part.

[36]See Walsh, 'Application of the senses', p. 61. Among the *Directories*, that of Polanco is the first to recognize that the First Way of prayer can be offered to people at different levels (MHSI 76, pp. 323–4 [trans., Palmer, pp. 145–6]). See also MHSI 76 (Dávila) p. 528 [trans., Palmer, p. 264]; (Cordeses) p. 561 [trans., Palmer, p. 284]; (*1599 Directory*) pp. 737–9 [trans., Palmer, p. 344].

of the moral basics of fidelity – it takes different forms according to the maturity of the person using it; and adopted by a person matured, sensitized, and converted through the full Exercises, it will yield vision and insight of a quality far beyond the horizons of those who might nevertheless benefit from it at a more basic level of development.

Once their nature and purpose are understood, the potential of all the Three Ways becomes evident. As the *Directories* make clear, however, they are a resource, not a prescription; they are to be used in ways that suit the individual.[37] Their use, though highly commended, is not absolutely insisted on, and account must be taken of other forms of prayer that might help a person after the Exercises.[38] But without falling into over-simple claims for them, a director should fully appreciate the value of all Three Ways as an immediate resource for the post-exercitant in his or her search for the paths of prayer into which the Spirit is now guiding them; and as a means in their own right of maintaining amid the circumstances of daily life the contemplative spirit of the Exercises and their integrated vision of all reality in relation to God.

Note on giving the Three Ways

On the practical question of incorporating the Three Ways into the Fourth Week, a picture of the early directors' approach is provided by the *Directories*, particularly that of Polanco and the *1599 Directory*. The general principles underlying this approach can be briefly summarized. The place for the Three Ways was an assigned space of two or three days after the Contemplation to Attain Love. During this space, the exercitant was not required, however, to rehearse everything. Thus, it might not be necessary to go through all five prayers of the Second and Third Ways, but once seen to have grasped the method, the exercitant could be told to continue with it later. In connection with the First Way, on the other hand, it was considered desirable, time permitting, to go through all the various procedures; but if this could not be done within the Exercises, the exercitant should leave with an adequate account in writing of those omitted.[39]

[37]The exercitant should be recommended to use in the future whichever method of prayer he or she has experienced to be most helpful; since they are suitable to 'one more than another according to personal differences or even according to different situations of the same person at different times', *Directories, Polanco* (MHSI 76, p. 326 [trans., Palmer, p. 147]).

[38]'We should not imagine that < the recommendation of the three methods > excludes such other methods as are often taught by the Holy Spirit and employed by spiritually experienced persons,' *1599 Directory* (MHSI 76, p. 741 [trans., Palmer, p. 345]; cf. p. 326 (Polanco), p. 413 (Miró) [trans., Palmer, pp. 147, 187].

[39]*Directories, Polanco* (MHSI 76, pp. 323–6 [trans. Palmer, pp. 144–7]); *1599 Directory* (MHSI 76, pp. 735–42 [trans. Palmer, pp. 343–5]).

There are, of course, many ways of introducing the Three Ways to an exercitant and Ignatius' purpose would seem to be essentially met if the exercitant returns to his or her ordinary life having had some experience of the Three Ways as prayer. There seems no reason why, if circumstances permit, they should not be introduced and practised during the days following the close of the Exercises.

The First Way

[238] ¹ THREE WAYS OF PRAYING[40]
< THE FIRST WAY OF PRAYING >
² The first way of praying is concerned with the *Ten Commandments* and the *Seven Deadly Sins*, the *Three Powers of the Soul* and the *Five Senses* of the Body. ³ This way of praying *aims more* at providing a framework, a method and certain exercises through which to prepare oneself and to make progress in order that one's prayer may be acceptable to God, rather than by giving any framework and method for prayer properly so-called.

Ten Commandments ... Seven Deadly Sins ... Three Powers of the Soul ... Five Senses. These are all categories employed in the confession manuals of the time to assist self-examination in preparation for the sacrament. Here Ignatius uses these categories in a more general perspective.[41]

aims more, etc. In what sense can the First Way be said to be a *preparation* for prayer rather than itself *prayer properly so-called?* No doubt, part of the answer lies in the distinction drawn in the Third Annotation between prayer addressed directly to a person and prayer of a more abstract or reflective kind. The Second and Third Ways are prayers in the former sense (cf. [257, 258]), while the First contains substantial elements of 'meditation' and indeed 'consideration'. In his introduction to the First Way Ignatius makes us aware, too, that it is not only one form of prayer among others, but that it is ordered to the fidelity and perseverance which are the basis of authenticity of every prayer.

But this said, it must be added that the present paragraph could easily give a misleading impression of the quality of the First Way of praying,

---

[40]The title in the Autograph reads: *Three ways of praying, and first on the commandments*. For clarification, the second part of this title has been transferred to [239] below.

[41]Within the exercises the First Way of prayer can serve, nevertheless, as an aid to the General Confession: *Directories, Cordeses* (MHSI 76, p. 534 [trans., Palmer, p. 266]).

which contains the prayer of 'colloquy' [243] and of 'imitation' [248]. Moreover, in reading the paragraph, especially in relation to the Fourth Week, one should remember the point made in the Introduction above, that these exercises can be made at many levels.

[239] [1] < (1) On the Commandments. >
< An Addition. > First of all, an equivalent of the Second Addition of the Second Week[42] should be made; that is to say, before entering into prayer I will *allow the spirit to rest a little,* **by sitting down or** *strolling about,* **as seems best to me, while considering where I am going and for what purpose. [2] This same Addition is to be observed at the start of each of the Ways of praying.**

allow the spirit to rest a little These instructions suggest a pause amid the activities of daily life. Note that while *strolling about* can be a helpful preliminary to prayer, as well as favourable to reflection after it (cf. [77]), in proposing postures for prayer itself Ignatius never includes bodily movement (cf. [76]).

[240] [1] A *preparatory prayer[43]* **should be made, in which, for example, I ask God our Lord for grace to be able to know my failings in relation to the Ten Commandments. [2] I should ask, as well, for grace and help to do better in the future, and for a** *perfect understanding of the Commandments* **so that I may keep them better for the greater glory and praise of his Divine Majesty.**

preparatory prayer Of the three elements of petition in this prayer, the first two (knowledge of failings and grace to amend) correspond to the Second Point of the General Examen [43]. It is the third (perfect understanding of the Commandments themselves) that reveals the specific character of the present exercise. The focus is no longer on one's own sins. The Commandments (and subsequently the Deadly Sins, the Powers of the Soul and the Senses) are proposed as matter for consideration *in themselves*. The object of the exercise is insight – insight into the wisdom and purpose of God, but, of course, a personal insight giving a deepening self-knowledge.

perfect understanding of the Commandments The exercitant prays for the insight that makes the difference between conforming to imposed canons of behaviour, and acting according to an interiorized vision of reality.

---

[42]*Second Addition of the Second Week* This is an erroneously worded reference to [131], which adapts to the Second Week the Third Addition of the First Week [75].
[43]Not the preparatory prayer of the four Weeks of the Exercises [46].

Such understanding is not easily acquired, or lightly to be requested. It is a matter of graced perception and develops as one grows in the Spirit. Since the same preparatory prayer is to be used for each form of the First Way [244, 246, 247], the subjects in relation to which one prays for *perfect understanding* will be in turn the Seven Deadly Sins, the Powers of the Soul and the Senses.

[241] [1] **For this First Way of praying, a suitable procedure is to** *consider and think over* **the first Commandment – how have I kept it? How have I failed to keep it? –** [2] **staying with this consideration as a rule for the** *time it takes to say three Our Fathers* **and three Hail Marys.** [3] **If in this time I discover failings, I ask forgiveness and pardon for them and say an Our Father. The same procedure should be repeated for each of the Ten Commandments.**

[242] [1] **First note. It should be noted that on finding that one is not in the habit of sinning against a particular Commandment under consideration, there is no need to spend long over it.** [2] **But according as one offends more against a Commandment or less, so one should spend more time or less in the consideration and examination of it.** [3] **This norm holds good for the deadly sins as well.**

[243] [1] **Second note. After going over all the Commandments in this way, having acknowledged my sin in regard to them and asked for grace and help to do better in the future,** [2] **I should end with a colloquy to God our Lord, adapted to the matter under consideration.**

consider and think over The starting point is objective – the Commandments (or later, Sins, Powers, Senses) considered in themselves.[44] One begins with elements of a vision of reality in its natural relationship to God, and it is with reference to this vision that one then turns to consider oneself (not only negatively but also positively).

time it takes to say three Our Fathers Taken at this pace, the prayer not only covers each Commandment in particular, but leaves a cumulative impression of the decalogue as a whole. As the note [242] makes clear, however, this

---

[44]Cf. the general approaches suggested in the *1599 Directory*. With regard to the Commandments the exercitant is recommended to 'consider a given commandment in itself – how good and just and holy it is ... how profitable is its observance'; on the Deadly Sins, he or she can 'examine how evil they are and how rightly forbidden ... how harmful if they are not avoided'; in the case of the Powers of the Soul and the Senses, one can reflect 'how noble and essential for us each of them is ... the purpose for which they were given ...' (MHSI 76, p. 737 [trans. Palmer, p. 344]).

order of time should not be followed with a rigidity that disregards the person. In connection with this and the other sections of the First Way, the early tradition recognized the value in some cases of a more flexible and spacious approach to time than that proposed here.[45]

[244] [1] (2) On the Deadly Sins
[2] With regard to the Seven Deadly Sins,[46] after the Addition, one should make *the preparatory prayer* in the way already mentioned. [3] The only change is that here the subject matter is Sins to be avoided, whereas beforehand it was Commandments to be observed. [4] The same order and rule should be followed as already explained, and the colloquy made.

[245] For a better knowledge of one's fault's in relation to the Seven Deadly Sins, one should look at their *contraries*; and similarly, and more surely to avoid these Sins, one should resolve and endeavour by means of devout exercises to acquire and keep the Seven Virtues opposed to them.

the preparatory prayer In the preparatory prayer (cf. [240]) one asks, again, for the grace of *perfect understanding* – in this case the kind of understanding already gained at a certain level through the survey of the Deadly Sins in the Second Meditation of the First Week [57].

contraries, I.e. humility (pride); generosity (avarice); chastity (lust); patience (anger); temperance (gluttony); charity (envy); diligence (sloth).

[246] [1] (3) On the Powers of the Soul
[2] With regard to the Three Powers of the Soul, the same order and rule are to be followed as for the Commandments, making the Additions, the preparatory prayer, and the colloquy.

The Vulgate adds a clarification: 'For the three powers of the soul one follows the same procedure, making the addition, the prayer and examining each of them'. The prayer consists, then, in an 'examination' of the Powers, a reflection on the nature and purpose of each, leading to appreciation and gratitude.

---

[45]Thus Polanco recommends that those able for it should meditate at length on the particular commandments of the decalogue, devoting indeed a single prayer period to each (MHSI 76, p. 325 [trans., Palmer, pp. 146–7]). Miró relates the time specification to the Fourth Addition (where I have found what I want, stay there) and to [254] below. See also the *1599 Directory* (MHSI 76, p. 739 [trans., Palmer, p. 345]).

[46]In Spanish, *los siete pecados mortales*, but here the sense of *pecado mortal* is unequivocal. (cf. note on [48] above).

Note, too, that for someone making this prayer during the Fourth Week, or after the Exercises, no consideration of the Powers of the Soul can be dissociated from the self-offering of the Contemplation to Attain Love, in which these powers are handed over to Christ [234].

In the context of such reflection one also adverts in this prayer to the quality of one's own life, as a creature endowed with memory, understanding, and will.

[247] ¹ (4) On the Five Bodily Senses.
² Method. With regard to the Five Bodily Senses, the same procedure is to be kept, changing only the *subject matter*.

The *subject matter* is now myself as sensate. The ways I lead my life as sensate are examined in the light of a developing appreciation of this dimension of human existence, a perfect understanding of the fact that precisely as sensate we are made for God's glory and praise.

[248] ¹ Note. Whoever wishes to *imitate* Christ our Lord *in the use of the senses*, should commend themselves to his Divine Majesty in the preparatory prayer, then *after considering each Sense* say a Hail Mary or an Our Father. ² And whoever wishes to imitate *Our Lady* in the use of the Senses, should commend themselves to her in the preparatory prayer, so that she may obtain that grace from *her Son and Lord*, and then *after considering each Sense*, say a Hail Mary.

imitate Not mentioned in the outline [238], imitation does not add a new theme to the First Way of prayer; rather, it is another way of approaching the fourth of the themes prescribed, i.e. the *perfect understanding* of the person as sensate in relation to God's project and purpose. This theme is now approached in the context of the Christian's graced imitation of the sensate life of Christ himself. The 'imitation of Christ' is a total quality of life, a quality consisting not in external mimicry, but in a transformation of one's inner experience by the assimilation of Christ's own experience. Here one seeks to be taken into this experience in prayer, and hence to promote the further development of it in one's life. Such a prayer consists in contemplating the Christ of the Gospels as in the Exercises themselves, seeking the grace 'to feel with the Incarnate Word, as he reveals himself, looking and hearing, touching and tasting, in the gospel word.'⁴⁷ Since this grace belongs to the properly contemplative climate of the Fourth Week, the two approaches to the Senses clearly represent different levels at which the First Way of praying can be made and experienced.

---

⁴⁷Walsh, 'Application of the Senses', p. 64.

185

in the use of the Senses That Ignatius singles out the Senses for imitation does not mean, of course, that the exercise plays down the imitation of Christ in the Powers of the Soul. But by homing in on the Senses, he insists that it is the whole person – the person as bodily and sensate as well as endowed with the higher Powers – that must be assimilated into Christ.

our Lady In Mary alone is the ideal of imitation fully realized and for this reason an exercitant might ask for the grace to experience themselves as sensate, and to lead their sensate lives in a way that participates in Mary's own imitation.

her Son and Lord Her *Son* because he is her child, her *Lord* because he is her God, the two aspects of Mary's relationship with Christ which combine to give her own 'imitation' its unique and normative quality.

after considering each Sense In the article cited above, James Walsh draws attention to specific instances of the evangelists reporting sense experience: e.g. Matt. 6:28–29 (sight); Matt. 17:6 (hearing); Mark 7:33 (touch); John 19:29–30 (taste); John 12:3 (smell).[48]

The Second Way

The Second and Third Ways of praying while, like the First, opening up insight and forming outlook, have the purpose of helping the exercitant develop a contemplative and simple prayer.

[249] THE SECOND WAY OF PRAYING CONSISTS IN *CONTEMPLATING THE MEANING* OF *EACH WORD* IN A PRAYER.

[250] Addition. In this Second Way of praying, the addition will be the same as in the First Way.

[251] Prayer. The preparatory prayer will be appropriate to the person to whom the prayer is directed.

[252] [1] The Second Way of praying is as follows. One either kneels or sits down, according as one feels better disposed and experiences more devotion. *Keeping the eyes closed*, or fixed on one spot, without allowing the gaze to wander, one says the word 'Father', [2] staying with this word for as long as one finds meanings, comparisons, relish and consolation in considerations related to it. [3] One should do this for

[48]Ibid., p. 65.

each word of the Our Father, or for any other prayer which one may wish to take for praying in this way.

[253] First rule. One should spend an hour on the whole of the *Our Father*, keeping to the procedure just given; when this is finished the *Hail Mary*, the *Creed*, the *Soul of Christ*, and the *Hail Holy Queen*, should be said vocally or mentally in the usual way.

[254] *Second rule*. If in contemplating the Our Father one finds in one or two words rich matter for reflection and much relish and consolation, there should be no anxiety to go further, even though the whole hour is spent on what has been found. When the hour is up, the remainder of the Our Father should be said in the usual way.

[255] [1] *Third rule*. If a complete hour has been spent on one or two words of the Our Father, a person wanting to go back to the same prayer on another day, should say those one or two words in the usual way, [2] and then begin the contemplation on the word immediately following them, in the manner explained in Rule Two.

[256] First note. It should be noted that when the Our Father has been completed – either in one day or several – the same procedure should be followed with the Hail Mary, and then with the other prayers, so that over a period of time one will always be exercising oneself in one of them.

[257] Second note. When a prayer is ended, one should turn to the person to whom the prayer has been addressed, and in a few words ask for the *virtues or graces for which one feels greater need*.

contemplating The word 'contemplate' which is found in the Autograph in the running title at the head of the page[49] and twice in the text [254, 255] indicates the character of this Second Way of Praying. Other words in the text, 'devotion' [252], 'relish', 'consolation' [252, 254], serve further to underline this contemplative character. It should be noted that the kind of contemplation here referred to presumes, as does all authentic Christian contemplation, the knowledge and love of Jesus developed through the contemplation of the Gospels.[50]

[49]*Oración contemplando* (= 'prayer made by contemplating').
[50]A person is shown the Second Way of prayer 'after having become thoroughly experienced in the life and mysteries of Christ', *Directories, Mercurian* (MHSI 76, p. 252 [trans. Palmer, p. 107]).

meaning Integral to both this and the following ways of prayer is the given content of the prayer formulae on which they are based. Through contemplation this 'given' is internalized and made personal, becoming the *inner perception* [2], or *inner knowledge* [63] [118] which the Exercises have already identified as the fruit of meditation and contemplation.

each word Not always to be understood literally, as it will often be appropriate to take a few words grouped according to sense.[51]

Keeping the eyes closed In the Ninth Addition, control over the eyes is generally commended to a person making the Exercises [80], but while obviously of particular advantage in any time of prayer, only here is the practice explicitly mentioned in the Exercises in this connection. Special attention to this point might be called for if a person is praying amid the personal effects and potential distractions of their own home.

Our Father ... Hail Mary ... Creed ... Soul of Christ ... Hail Holy Queen All are 'prayers of the Church', either 'official', or at least consecrated by usage, with which an exercitant of the time might be expected to be familiar. But other materials might lend themselves equally well to this exercise, e.g. liturgical prayers, or passages of Scripture, notably psalms.[52]

Second and third rules Even though one rests with just one or two words, these belong to the prayer as a whole, and they must not be completely divorced from its overall content and sequence.

virtues or graces for which one feels greater need Petition is no longer for a grace proper to a stage in a spiritual pedagogy. The graces now asked for are those which the individual finds in prayer itself that they personally need here and now.

The Third Way

[258] [1] THE THIRD WAY OF PRAYING BY RHYTHM
[2] **Addition. This will be the same as for the First and Second Ways of praying.**
[3] **Prayer. The preparatory prayer should be the same as for the Second Way.**

---

[51]Cf. *Directories, Polanco* (MHSI 76, p. 325 [trans. Palmer, p. 146]), *1599 Directory* (MHSI 76, p. 739 [trans. Palmer, p. 345]).
[52]*Directories* (MHSI 76, p. 252 [Mercurian], p. 325 [Polanco], p. 414 [Miró], p. 739 [*1599 Directory*]; trans. Palmer, pp. 107, 146, 187, 345).

4 The Third Way of praying consists in *praying mentally with each intake or expulsion of breath*, by saying one word of the Our Father or of any other prayer being said, so that only a *single word* is pronounced between one breath and the next. **5** In the interval between each breath attention is especially paid to the meaning of that word, to *the person to whom one is praying* or to one's own lowliness or to the distance between the other's grandeur and one's own *lowliness*.

6 One goes through the other words of the Our Father, keeping to the same arrangement and rule, and then say the other prayers, i.e. Hail Mary, Soul of Christ, Creed, and Hail Holy Queen in the usual way.

[259] Rule 1. On another day or at another time when one wants to pray, the Hail Mary should be said rhythmically and then the other prayers in the usual way. Subsequently one should take the other prayers in turn and follow the same procedure.

[260] Rule 2. Whoever wants to remain longer on the prayer by rhythm can recite all the prayers mentioned above, or fewer of them, but keeping the same system of rhythmic breathing already explained.

The account of the third way is largely self-explanatory, but a few remarks may be in place.

praying mentally with each ... breath Not only an easy means of pacing the recitation of words, but a way of integrating prayer into one's very consciousness and one's very bodily rhythms.[53] For this, while the breathing should be deliberate and steady, it should also be normal breathing, not altered in depth or pace for the purpose of prayer.

single word, or again phrases or small groups of words as the sense might indicate.

the person to whom one is praying Words, though still integral to the method,

[53]While the Third and Second Ways are distinct, one might be led into a way of praying which is not strictly speaking either the Third or the Second, but a form of the Third approximating to the Second. This would be the case of a rhythmic prayer in which the intervals were considerably wider than that between one breath and the next. While recognizing, however, that one might pray with wider intervals, the *1599 Directory* insists that the normal procedure is that described in the text (MHSI 76, p. 741 [trans. Palmer, p. 147]). Cf. *Directories, Polanco* (loc. cit., p. 325 [trans. Palmer, p. 188]). *Miró* (loc. cit., p. 414 [trans. Palmer, p. 345]).

direct the attention onto persons, so that of the three methods this is in fact the most immediately relational. It is this that makes it properly contemplative prayer (not just a restful devotional exercise).

lowliness Something of the sense of *lowliness* (in Spanish, *bajeza*) is conveyed by its use in [289] to describe St Peter's confusion at the washing of the feet, and in the use of the corresponding verb in [324] in connection with the need to remain humble in consolation. The concept is essential to the sense of reverence, which in turn is the expression of an authentic sense of creaturehood.

NEW TESTAMENT MATERIALS FOR CONTEMPLATION

Of the following fifty-one episodes, a number are included in the body of the Exercises [132, 134, 158, 161, 208, 226], and in these cases, as we have already seen, the *points* given here can provide the exercitant with content, supplementary material or particular lines of approach for contemplating these episodes. Other materials are added in order to help directors, without setting them limits, to find texts suited to an exercitant's needs.

Summaries such as these were clearly of more importance in the sixteenth century than today, when it is hardly thinkable that an exercitant would not possess their own New Testament. Nevertheless, a director today should be familiar with this section of the Exercises, in which details of language, emphasis or selection, though owing much to the influence of Ludolph of Saxony's *Life of Christ*, afford valuable insight into the mind of Ignatius himself. The section also provides models of the summarizing of essentials recommended in the Second Annotation.

It should be noted that whereas in the body of the Exercises, points were divided according to *persons, words and actions*, they are here the salient events in a narrative. In practice, the two approaches come together, the events being contemplated (as relevant and always without artificiality) under the aspect of persons, words and actions.

[261] **[1] THE MYSTERIES OF THE LIFE OF CHRIST OUR LORD**
[2] Note. In the following mysteries, all the words between quotation marks are from the Gospel itself,[1] the other words are not. [3] For most of the mysteries, three points are given, to make it easier to meditate or contemplate the mysteries.

[262] **[1] THE ANNUNCIATION OF OUR LADY. LUKE 1:25–38**
[2] First. The angel St Gabriel, greeting Our Lady, gave her to understand the conception of Christ our Lord: [3] 'The angel, entering where Mary was, greeted her saying to her, "Hail Mary, full of grace; you

---

[1]Ignatius, translating from the Latin Vulgate, gives the Gospel words in Spanish: these are translated here into English.

will conceive in your womb and bear a son."'

[9] Second. The angel confirms what he said to Our Lady by indicating the conception of St John the Baptist, saying to her: '"And behold, Elizabeth, your relative, has conceived a son in her old age."'

[5] Third. Our Lady replied to the angel: '"Behold the handmaid of the Lord; may it be done to me according to your word."'

[263][1] THE VISITATION OF OUR LADY TO ELIZABETH. LUKE 1:39–56

[2] First. When Our Lady visited Elizabeth, St John the Baptist, in his mother's womb, became aware of her visit: [3] 'And when Elizabeth heard the greeting of Our Lady, the child felt joy in her womb: [4] and Elizabeth, full of the Holy Spirit, cried out in a loud voice and said, "Blessed may you be among women, and blessed be the fruit of your womb."'

[5] Second. Our Lady sings the canticle, saying '"My soul magnifies the Lord."'

[6] Third. 'Mary was with Elizabeth about three months, and then she returned to her house.'

[264][1] THE NATIVITY OF CHRIST OUR LORD. LUKE 2:1–14

[2] First. Our Lady and her husband Joseph go from Nazereth to Bethlehem: 'Joseph went up from Galilee to Bethlehem, to acknowledge his subjection to Caesar,[2] with Mary his spouse and wife, a woman already pregnant.'

[3] Second. 'She bore her first-born son, and wrapped him in clothes, and placed him in the manger.'

[4] Third. 'There came a multitude of the heavenly army, which said, "Glory to God in the heavens."'

[265] [1] THE SHEPHERDS. LUKE 2:8–20

[2] First. The birth of Christ our Lord is made known to the shepherds by the angel: '"I declare to you a great joy, because today the Saviour of the world has been born."'

[3] Second. The shepherds go to Bethlehem: 'They came with haste and found Mary and Joseph and the child placed in the manger.'

[4] Third. 'The shepherds went back, glorifying and praising the Lord.'

[266] [1] The Circumcision. Luke 2:21

[1] First. They circumcised the Child Jesus.

[2] *Second*. 'The name by which he is called is Jesus, the name given to

---

[2]*subjection to Caesar* mentioned only in the Autograph, echoes the comment of Ludolph that though Mary had conceived the King of Heaven and Earth, she and her husband wished to obey the imperial decree.

him by the angel before he was conceived in the womb.'
³ Third. They gave the child back to his mother, who felt compassion at the blood that flowed from her son.

[267] ¹ THE THREE KINGS, THE MAGI. MATTHEW 2:1–12
² First. The Three Kings, the Magi, came guided by a star to adore Jesus saying, '"We saw his star in the East, and we have come to adore him."'
³ Second. They adored him and offered him gifts: 'Prostrating themselves on the ground, they adored him and presented him with gifts: gold, incense and myrrh.'
⁴ Third. 'They received a reply while they were asleep, that they should not return to Herod, and they returned to their region by another way.'

[268] ¹ THE PURIFICATION OF OUR LADY AND THE PRESENTATION OF THE CHILD JESUS. LUKE 2:22–29
² First. They bring the child Jesus into the Temple, so that he can be presented to the Lord as a first-born, and they offer for him 'a pair of turtle doves or two young pigeons'.
³ Second. Simeon, coming into the Temple, 'took him in his arms, saying "Now, Lord, let your servant go in peace."'
⁴ Third. Anna, 'coming afterwards, confessed the Lord and talked about him to all who were waiting for the redemption of Israel.'

[269] ¹ THE FLIGHT INTO EGYPT. MATTHEW 2:13–15
² First. Herod wanted to kill the child Jesus, and so he killed the innocents. Before their death, the angel warned Joseph to fly into Egypt. '"Rise up and take the child and his mother and fly into Egypt."'
³ Second. He left for Egypt. 'Rising up at night, he left for Egypt.'
⁴ Third. He stayed there until the death of Herod.

[270] ¹ THE RETURN OF OUR LORD FROM EGYPT. MATTHEW 2:19–23
² First. The angel warned Joseph to return to Israel: '"Rise up, take the child and his mother, and go into the land of Israel."'
³ Second. He rose up and came into the land of Israel.
⁴ Third. As Archelaus, the son of Herod, was ruling in Judea, he withdrew to Nazareth.

[271]¹ THE LIFE OF CHRIST OUR LORD FROM THE AGE OF TWELVE TO THE AGE OF THIRTY³ LUKE 2:51–52

² First. He was obedient to his parents. 'He grew in wisdom, age and grace.'

³ Second. It seems that he practised the trade of a carpenter, as St Mark indicates in chapter six with the remark, '"Is this man not by any chance that carpenter."'⁴

[272]¹ CHRIST'S COMING INTO THE TEMPLE WHEN HE WAS AGED TWELVE. LUKE 2:41–50

² First. Christ our Lord, at the age of twelve, went up from Nazareth to Jerusalem.

³ Second. Christ our Lord stayed in Jerusalem and his parents did not know it.

⁴ Third. After three days had gone by, they found him disputing in the Temple, and sitting in the midst of the doctors; and when his parents asked him where he had been, he replied: '"Do you not know that it is fitting for me to be in things that are my Father's?"'

[273]¹ THE BAPTISM OF CHRIST. MATTHEW 3:13–17

² First. Christ our Lord, after having said farewell to his blessed mother, came from Nazareth to the river Jordan, where John the Baptist was.

³ Second. St John baptized Christ our Lord, and when he wanted to excuse himself, judging that he was unworthy to baptize Christ, the latter said to him: '"Do this on the present occasion, because it is necessary for us to fulfil in this way all that is just."'

⁴ Third. 'The Holy Spirit came and the voice of the Father from heaven asserting: "This is my beloved son with whom I am very satisfied."'

[274]¹ THE TEMPTATIONS OF CHRIST. LUKE 4:1–13; MARK 4:1–11

² First. After he had been baptized, he went to the desert, where he fasted forty days and forty nights.

³ Second. He was tempted by the enemy on three occasions: 'The tempter going up to him, says, "If you are the Son of God, tell these stones to turn into bread"; "Throw yourself down from here"; "All

---

³As in the main text [134], the Hidden Life precedes the Temple incident, reversing the order of Luke's gospel. While, however, the main text refers to the 'Child Jesus', here the title 'Christ our Lord' is used in connection with the Hidden Life and Jesus' obedience to his parents.

⁴Here, as will frequently be the case in subsequent mysteries, Ignatius' points draw upon Gospel material which is not included in the reference or references given in the title.

that you see, I shall give you if you prostrate yourself on the ground and adore me."'

[4] Third. 'The angels came and served him.'

[275][1] THE CALL OF THE APOSTLES

[2] First. It seems that St Peter and St Andrew were called three times:

    i)   to some knowledge, this is evident from the first chapter of St John;

[3]   ii)   to follow Christ in some way, but with the intention of going back to the possessions they had left, as Luke says in chapter five;

[4]   iii)   to follow Christ our Lord always; St Matthew chapter four and St Mark chapter one.[5]

[5] Second. He called Philip, as the first chapter of St John relates, and Matthew, as St Matthew himself says in chapter nine.

[6] Third. He called the other apostles, the Gospels making no mention of particular vocations.

[7] Three further things are also to be considered: (1) how the apostles were from an uneducated and low station in life, [8] (2) the dignity to which they were so gently called, [9] (3) The gifts and graces by which they were raised above all the fathers of the New and Old Testaments.

[276] [1] THE FIRST MIRACLE PERFORMED AT THE MARRIAGE FEAST OF CANA. JOHN 2: 1–11

[2] First. Christ our Lord was invited along with his disciples to the marriage.

[3] Second. The mother informs the son about the lack of wine, saying: '"They have no wine", and orders the waiters, "Do whatever he tells you."'

[4] Third. 'He changed the water into wine, and showed his glory and his disciples believed in him.'

[277] [1] CHRIST OUR LORD DROVE THE SELLERS OUT OF THE TEMPLE. JOHN 2:13–25

[2] First. He threw all the sellers out of the Temple with a whip made of cords.

[3] Second. He overturned the tables and coins of the rich bankers who were in the Temple.

[4] Third. To the poor who were selling pigeons he gently said: '"Take

---

[5]The vocation of Peter and Andrew is presented as a process (in contrast to the instant call and response in the case of Matthew, cf. [175]). The detail that the brothers had intended to return to their possessions is taken from Ludolph's interpretation of Luke 5:11 ('they brought their boats to land') and has, of course, no exegetical basis.

those things away from here and avoid making my house into a market-place."'

[278] ¹ THE SERMON ON THE MOUNT. MATTHEW 5:1–48
² First. He speaks separately to his beloved disciples about the eight beatitudes:⁶ '"Blessed the poor in spirit, the gentle, the merciful, those who weep, those who undergo hunger and thirst for the sake of justice, the pure of heart, the peacemakers, and those who suffer persecutions."'
³ Second. He exhorts them to make good use of their talents: '"So may your light shine before all people that they may see your good deeds and glorify your Father, who is in the heavens."'
⁴ Third. He shows himself to be not a transgressor of the Law, but the one who brings it to completion, explaining the precepts not to kill, not to commit fornication, not to perjure and to love enemies: '"I tell you that you should love your enemies and do good to those who abhor you."'

[279] ¹ CHRIST OUR LORD STILLED THE TEMPEST AT SEA. MATTHEW 8:23–7
² First. While Christ our Lord was asleep at sea, a great storm arose.
³ Second. His terrified disciples woke him, and he rebukes them for their little faith, saying to them: '"What do you fear, men of little faith?"'
⁴ Third. He ordered the winds and the waves to stop, and with their stopping the sea became calm, so much so that the men were amazed, saying: '"Who is this, that the wind and sea obey him?"'

[280] ¹ CHRIST OUR LORD WALKING ON THE SEA. MATTHEW 14:24–33
² First. While Christ our Lord was on the mountain he made his disciples go to the boat,⁷ and when he had sent the crowd away he began to pray on his own.
³ Second. The small craft was being threatened by the waves. Christ comes to it walking over the water, and the disciples thought it was a ghost.
⁴ Third. As Christ said to them, '"It is I, do not be afraid,"' St Peter at Christ's command came to him, walking over the water: then having doubts he began to splash about, but Christ our Lord saved him, and he rebuked him for his little faith. Then he went aboard the boat and the wind dropped.

⁶The order of the beatitudes here given is that found in Ludolph and does not quite correspond to the gospel of Matthew.
⁷Literally, 'little boat' (*navecilla*). The same word is repeated in Points two and three.

[281] ¹ THE SENDING OF THE APOSTLES TO PREACH. MATTHEW 10:1–42
² First. Christ calls his beloved disciples and gives them power to expel demons from people's bodies and to cure all sicknesses.
³ Second. He teaches them about prudence and patience: '"Look, I am sending you like sheep among wolves; therefore be prudent like serpents and simple like doves."'
⁴ Third. He instructs them how they should go: '"Do not desire to possess gold or silver; whatever you receive free of charge, give out free of charge"'. And he instructs them on what they should preach: '"Go and preach saying, 'The Kingdom of Heaven has drawn near.'"'

[282] ¹ THE CONVERSION OF THE MAGDALEN. LUKE 7:36–50
² First. While he is seated at table in the house of the Pharisee, the Magdalen enters there, carrying an alabaster vase full of ointment.
³ Second. Taking a position behind the Lord, near to his feet, she began to water them with her tears and to wipe them with the hair of her head, and she kissed his feet and anointed them with the ointment.
⁴ Third. As the Pharisee was accusing the Magdalen, Christ speaks in her defence, saying: '"Many sins are forgiven her because she loved much", and he said to the woman, "Your faith has saved you, go in peace."'

[283] ¹ THE FEEDING BY CHRIST OF THE FIVE THOUSAND. MATTHEW 14:13–21
² First. As it was becoming late, the disciples ask Christ to send away the crowd that was with him.
³ Second. Christ our Lord ordered that the loaves should be brought to him, and that all should sit down at table. He blessed and broke and gave the loaves to his disciples, and the disciples gave them to the crowd.
⁴ Third. They ate and had their fill and twelve baskets were left over.

[284] ¹ THE TRANSFIGURATION OF CHRIST. MATTHEW 17:1–9
² First. Taking in his company the beloved disciples, Peter, James and John, Christ our Lord was transfigured, and his face shone like the sun, and his clothing like the snow.
³ Second. He talked with Moses and Elijah.
⁴ Third. When Peter said that they should make three tabernacles, a voice sounded from heaven saying, '"This is my beloved son, listen to him."' On hearing this voice, his disciples fell on their faces out of fear, and Christ our Lord touched them saying, '"Rise up and have no fear; tell no one about this vision until the Son of Man rises from the dead."'

[285] [1] THE RAISING OF LAZARUS. JOHN 11:1–45

[2] First. Martha and Mary inform Christ our Lord about the illness of Lazarus, and when he knew of it, he held back for two days so that the miracle might be more evident.

[3] Second. Before he raises him, he asks both of them to believe, saying: "'I am the resurrection and the life, anyone who believes in me, though dead, will live.'"

[4] Third. After having wept and prayed, he raises him. The way he raised him was by ordering him, "'Lazarus, come out.'"

[286] [1] THE SUPPER AT BETHANY. MATTHEW 26:6–10

[2] First. The Lord takes supper in the house of Simon the leper, together with Lazarus.

[3] Second. Mary pours ointment over the head of Christ.

[4] Third. Judas speaks disparagingly: "'Why all this waste of ointment?'" But Christ defends Magdalen once more, saying: "'Why are you troubling this woman, since she has performed a kindness to me?'"

[287] [1] PALM SUNDAY. MATTHEW 21:1–17

[2] First. The Lord sends for the ass and the colt, saying, "'Untie them and bring them to me; and if anyone says anything to you, say that the Lord needs them, and at once he will allow you.'"

[3] Second. He mounted the ass that was covered with the apostles' garments.

[4] Third. People come out to receive him, spreading their clothes and the branches of the trees on the road, saying: "'Save us, Son of David. Blesssed be he who comes in the name of the Lord. Save us on high.'"

[288] [1] THE PREACHING IN THE TEMPLE. LUKE 19:47–48

[2] First. He was teaching every day in the Temple.

[3] Second. When the preaching was finished, as there was nobody to welcome him in Jerusalem, he would go back to Bethany.

[289] [1] THE SUPPER. MATTHEW 26:20–29; JOHN 13:1–30

[2] First. He ate the Paschal Lamb with his twelve apostles, to whom he foretold his death: "'In truth I tell you that one of you has to sell me.'"

[3] Second. He washed the feet of the disciples, even those of Judas,[8] beginning with St Peter. St Peter was reluctant to consent to this, as he had in mind the majesty of the Lord and his own lowliness, and he said: "'Lord, are you washing my feet?'" But he did not know that Christ was giving an example of humility in this way. Christ therefore

---

[8]The washing of the feet of Judas is a detail taken from Ludolph.

said, '"I have given you an example, so that you should do as I have done."'

4 Third. He instituted the most holy sacrifice of the Eucharist, as the greatest sign of his love, saying: '"Take and eat"'; when the supper was finished, Judas goes out to sell Christ our Lord.

[290] **1** THE MYSTERIES PERFORMED BETWEEN THE SUPPER AND THE GARDEN (INCLUSIVE). MATTHEW 26:30–46; MARK 14:26–42

2 First. When the supper was finished and the hymn had been sung, the Lord went to the Mount of Olives with his disciples, who were full of fear; and he left eight of them in Gethsemane with the words, '"Sit down here while I go over there to pray."'

3 Second. Accompanied by St Peter, St James and St John, he prayed three times to the Lord, saying: '"Father, if it is possible, may this chalice pass from me; nevertheless, not my will but yours be done"'; and being in an agony, he prayed all the more profusely.

4 Third. He began to feel such fear that he said, '"My soul is sad even unto death"', and he sweated blood so abundantly that St Luke says, 'His sweat was like drops of blood that ran to the ground'. which implies that his garments were soaked in blood.[9]

[291] **1** THE MYSTERIES PERFORMED BETWEEN THE GARDEN AND THE HOUSE OF ANNAS (INCLUSIVE). MATTHEW 26:47–58; LUKE 22:47–57; MARK 14:43–54

2 First. The Lord allows himself to be kissed by Judas and arrested like a thief, while saying to them: '"You have come out to arrest me with sticks and arms as if I were a thief, when I was with you teaching every day in the Temple and you did not arrest me"'; and when he said, '"Which person are you looking for?"', the enemies fell to the ground.

3 Second. St Peter wounded the servant of the High Priest; and then the gentle Lord said to him, '"Put your sword back in its place,"' and he cured the servant's wound.

4 Third. Deserted by his disciples, Christ is brought to Annas, where St Peter, who had followed him from a distance, denied him once. Christ was struck a blow in the face, with the words, '"Is that how you reply to the High Priest?"'

[292] **1** THE MYSTERIES PERFORMED BETWEEN THE HOUSE OF ANNAS AND THE HOUSE OF CAIAPHAS (INCLUSIVE). JOHN 18:24; MATTHEW 26:57–58; 69–75; LUKE 22:54–65

2 First. They take him bound from the house of Annas to the house of

---

[9]The garments 'soaked in blood' is another detail taken from Ludolph.

Caiaphas, where St Peter denied him twice and, under the gaze of the Lord, he went outside and wept bitterly.

³ Second. Jesus spent the whole of that night in bonds.

⁴ Third. Besides this, those who were holding him prisoner mocked him, beat him, blindfolded him and struck him blows in the face; and they asked him, '"Prophesy to us who has struck you?"' They did other similar acts of blasphemy against him.

[293] ¹ THE MYSTERIES PERFORMED BETWEEN THE HOUSE OF CAIAPHAS AND THE HOUSE OF PILATE (INCLUSIVE). MATTHEW 27:1-2, 11-26; LUKE 23:1-5, 13-25; MARK 15:1-25

² First. The whole crowd of the Jews take him to Pilate, and they accuse him before Pilate saying, '"We have found that this man was perverting our people, and was forbidding the tribute of payment to Caesar."'

³ Second. After examining him once, and then again, Pilate said: '"I find no fault whatsoever."'

⁴ Third. Barabbas, a thief, was chosen in preference to him: 'They all shouted out saying, "Do not release this man, but Barabbas."'

[294] ¹ THE MYSTERIES PERFORMED BETWEEN THE HOUSE OF PILATE AND THE HOUSE OF HEROD. LUKE 23:7-11

² First. Pilate sent Jesus, the Galilean, to Herod, tetrarch of Galilee.

³ Second. Herod, who was curious, questioned him at length, and he did not reply to anything at all, even though the scribes and priests were constantly accusing him.

⁴ Third. Herod and all his army treated him with contempt by dressing him in a white garment.

[295] ¹ THE MYSTERIES PERFORMED BETWEEN THE HOUSE OF HEROD AND THE HOUSE OF PILATE. MATTHEW 27:26-30; LUKE 23:11-12, 20-23; MARK 15:-20; JOHN 19:1-6

² First. Herod sends him back once more to Pilate; in consequence, the two men became friends after having been enemies.

³ Second. Pilate took Jesus and had him flogged; and the soldiers made a crown of thorns and they put it on his head, and they clothed him in purple and came up to him saying, '"Hail, King of the Jews"', and they struck him blows in the face.

⁴ Third. He brought him before them all: 'Jesus then came out, crowned with thorns and clothed in red; and Pilate said to them, "Here is the man", and as soon as the High Priests saw him, they shouted out saying, "Crucify him, crucify him."'

[296] [1] THE MYSTERIES PERFORMED BETWEEN THE HOUSE OF PILATE AND THE CROSS (INCLUSIVE). JOHN 19:13–22
[2] First. Pilate, seated as a judge, handed Jesus over to them so that they might crucify him, after the Jews had denied him as king, saying, '"We have no king but Caesar."'
[3] Second. He was carrying the Cross on his back, and when he was not able to carry it, they forced Simon of Cyrene to carry it behind Jesus.
[4] Third. They crucified him between two thieves, putting up the notice, '"Jesus of Nazareth, King of the Jews."'

[297] [1] THE MYSTERIES PERFORMED ON THE CROSS. JOHN 19:32–37
[2] First. [3] He spoke seven words on the Cross: he prayed for those who were crucifying him; he pardoned the thief; he commended St John to his mother and his mother to St John; he cried aloud: '"I am thirsty"' and they gave him gall and vinegar; he said that he was forsaken; [4] he said, '"It is finished"', and '"Father, into your hands I commend my spirit."'
[5] Second. The sun was darkened, the rocks split, the tombs opened, the veil of the Temple was torn in two from the top to the bottom.
[6] Third. They blaspheme, saying: '"You are the one about to destroy the Temple of God; come down from the Cross"'; his garments were divided; when his side was pierced by the lance, it poured out water and blood.

[298] [1] THE MYSTERIES PERFORMED FROM THE CROSS TO THE TOMB (INCLUSIVE). JOHN 19:38–42
[2] First. He was taken from the Cross by Joseph and Nicodemus, in the presence of his sorrowful mother.
[3] Second. The body was carried to the tomb and anointed and buried.
[4] Third. Guards were posted.

[299] [1] THE RESURRECTION OF CHRIST OUR LORD. THE FIRST APPEARANCE.
[2] First. He appeared to the Virgin Mary. Although this is not stated in Scripture, it is assumed to have been included in the statement that he appeared to so many others, [3] for Scripture supposes that we are capable of understanding: as it is written '"Are you also without understanding?"'[10]

[300] [1] THE SECOND APPEARANCE. MARK 16:1–11
[2] First. Mary Magdalen, Mary the mother of James, and Salome make

[10]Matt. 15:16.

201

their way very early in the morning to the tomb, saying, '"Who will lift the stone from the entrance of the tomb for us?"'

³ Second. They see the stone removed and the angel who says, '"Jesus of Nazareth, whom you seek, is already risen from the dead; he is not here."'

⁴ Third. He appeared to Mary, who had stayed near the tomb after the other women had gone.

[301] ¹ THE THIRD APPEARANCE. MATTHEW 28:8–10

² First. These Marys come out of the tomb full of fear and great joy, intending to announce to the disciples the Resurrection of the Lord.

³ Second. Christ our Lord appeared to them on the way, saying, '"May God bless you"', and they came close and fell at his feet and adored him.

⁴ Third. Jesus says to them, '"Do not be afraid, go and tell my brothers to make their way to Galilee, because there they will see me."'

[302] ¹ THE FOURTH APPEARANCE. LUKE 24:9–12

² First. As soon as St Peter heard from the women that Christ was risen from the dead, he went with haste to the monument.

³ Second. Entering the monument, he saw only the cloths that had covered the body of Christ our Lord, and nothing else.

⁴ Third. While St Peter was thinking about these things, Christ appeared to him and that is why the apostles were saying, '"Truly the Lord has risen from the dead and has appeared to Simon"'.

[303] ¹ THE FIFTH APPEARANCE. LUKE 24:13–35

² First. He appeared to the disciples who were on their way to Emmaus talking about Christ.

³ Second. He rebuked them, showing from the Scriptures that Christ had to die and rise from the dead: '"You foolish people and slow of heart to believe all that has been talked about by the prophets! Was it not necessary that Christ should suffer, and so enter into his glory?"'

⁴ Third. At their entreaty he stays there, and was with them until, on giving them communion, he disappeared; and then they returned and told the disciples how they had recognised him in the communion.

[304] ¹ THE SIXTH APPEARANCE. JOHN 20:19–23

² First. The disciples were gathered together 'for fear of the Jews', except for St Thomas.

³ Second. Jesus appeared to them, the doors being closed, and while in their midst said, '"Peace be with you."'

⁴ Third. He gives them the Holy Spirit, saying: '"Receive the Holy Spirit; whose sins you forgive, they will be forgiven them."'

[305] ¹ THE SEVENTH APPEARANCE. JOHN 20:24–29
² First. St Thomas says in his unbelief, because he had not been present at the preceding appearance, '"Unless I see it, I will not believe it."'
³ Second. A week later, Jesus appears to them, the doors being closed, and says to St Thomas, '"Put your finger here and see the truth, and do not be unbelieving, but faithful."'
⁴ Third. St Thomas believed, saying, '"My Lord and my God"' and Christ says to him, '"Blessed are those that did not see and believed."'

[306] ¹ THE EIGHTH APPEARANCE. JOHN 21:1–17
² First. Jesus appears to seven of his disciples, who were fishing; they had not caught anything during the whole night, but when they cast out the net at his command, 'they could not pull it in because of the huge catch of fish'.
³ Second. St John recognized him by this miracle and said to St Peter, '"It is the Lord"', and the latter jumped into the sea and came to Christ.
⁴ Third. He gave them some broiled fish and a honeycomb to eat, and after first examining him three times on charity, he entrusted the sheep to St Peter, saying '"Feed my sheep."'

[307] ¹ THE NINTH APPEARANCE. MATTHEW 28:16–20
² First. At the Lord's command the disciples go to Mount Tabor.
³ Second. Christ appears to them and says: '"All power in heaven and on earth has been given to me."'
⁴ Third. He sent them all over the world to preach, saying, '"Go and teach all peoples, baptizing them in the name of the Father and of the Son and of the Holy Spirit."'

[308] ¹ THE TENTH APPEARANCE. 1 CORINTHIANS 15:6
² 'Later he was seen by more than five hundred brothers together.'

[309] ¹ THE ELEVENTH APPEARANCE. 1 CORINTHIANS 15:7
² 'He appeared later to St James.'

[310] ¹ THE TWELFTH APPEARANCE.
² He appeared to Joseph of Arimathea, as is devoutly meditated and is read in the lives of the saints.[11]

---

[11]The words 'the lives of the saints' is a correction in the hand of Ignatius, who had originally referred this tradition to the (apocryphal) gospel of Nicodemus, mentioned in Ludolph.

[311] [1] THE THIRTEENTH APPEARANCE. 1 CORINTHIANS 15:8
[2] He appeared to St Paul after the Ascension ('Finally he appeared to me, as to one born out of due time'). He appeared also, in soul, to the holy fathers in Limbo, [3] and after bringing them out and taking up his body again, he appeared many times to the disciples and spoke with them.

[312] [1] THE ASCENSION OF CHRIST OUR LORD. ACTS 1:1–12
[2] First. After he had been appearing to the apostles over a period of forty days, giving them many proofs and signs, and speaking of the Kingdom of God, he ordered them to wait in Jerusalem for the Holy Spirit that had been promised.
[3] Second. He brought them to the Mount of Olives, and in their presence he was lifted up, and a cloud took him out of their sight.
[4] Third. As they were looking up to heaven, the angels say to them, '"Men of Galilee, what are you looking at up in heaven? This Jesus, who is taken up from your eyes to heaven, will come in the way that you have seen him go to heaven."'

RULES FOR DISCERNMENT

The rules for discernment incorporate a tradition which reaches back through the fathers of the Church to the New Testament, especially the Pauline and Johannine writings.[1] Immediately, they derive from Ignatius' own experience, both the personal experience of his conversion[2] and his experience in directing others. Their importance in the Exercises, as well as the need to apply them appropriately, is established in the Annotations [8, 9]; the two movements they deal with are of central significance in the prayer of the Exercises from the First Day onwards (cf. [62] and especially [176]). As well as contributing to the process of the Exercises themselves, the rules have considerable value in meeting the particular needs of today's world and Church.

Discernment

Discernment is a function of the wisdom of the Spirit. It can be broadly defined as the wisdom which enables a person to distinguish by inner sense (as well as by objective criteria) between the spiritually authentic and its opposite, between what is and is not of the Spirit. Its operation presupposes particular qualities and dispositions, which include psychological balance, self-knowledge, and good judgement. But more fundamentally, discernment as a gift of the Spirit needs specifically spiritual qualities. It needs an attitude of presence to God's word in all its mediations, and hence a sense of the Church and an openness to God's word in Scripture, prophecy, situations, events; and more particularly, discernment needs the growingly interiorized knowledge of Christ that leads to the feel of his 'mind'.[3] Where these latter qualities are to be found, the conditions for discernment are present; and as a person matures in the Spirit, and according to the graces given them, the

[1]Cf. Rom. 12:3; 1 Cor 1:7 – 3:4; Gal. 5:13–26; 1 Thess. 5:19, 1 John 4:2–3. For the patristic background for the discernment rules see Hugo Rahner, *Ignatius the Theologian*, pp. 165–80; Futrell in Cowan and Futrell, *Handbook*, pp. 139–50. For a comprehensive survey of the history and theology of discernment see Guillet et al., *Discernment of Spirits* (Collegeville, 1970, translated by Innocentia Richards from the *Dictionnaire de Spiritualité*).

[2]See *Reminiscences* §§6–10 [trans., *Personal Writings*, pp. 14–16].
[3]Cf. Phil. 2:5.

discerning sense becomes increasingly refined.

But discernment takes many forms, some integral to human life as such, others connected with specific situations or responsibilities. On all these the rules in the Exercises have a bearing, and discernment of every other kind is conditional upon the particular discernment they deal with. It should be remembered however that the rules do not deal with discernment in all its ramifications; they are mainly concerned with the ways in which the good and bad spirit exert an influence on our 'movements of consciousness' (or movements 'of the soul'), producing respectively spiritual consolation and spiritual desolation.

Consolation and desolation

Ignatius' doctrine on consolation and desolation fully emerges only when the rules for discernment are considered singly and in detail, but since there are points on which the doctrine is frequently misunderstood, it will be helpful to make some initial general clarifications.

It must be noted, first, that both consolation and desolation are defined as *spiritual*,[4] the relation to the spiritual being positive in the case of consolation, negative in the case of the 'anti-spiritual' movement of desolation. To recognize these spiritual movements, one needs to be generally sensitive to the whole fluid and elusive realm of one's feelings and reactions; but not every kind of positive or negative mood or stirring recognizable by a self-aware person is to be equated with 'consolation' and 'desolation' as understood in the Exercises. In the last analysis, consolation 'consoles' because whatever its form, whether unambiguous or implicit and discreet, it is a felt experience of God's love building up the Christ-life in us. And what characterizes every form of spiritual desolation is a felt sense of dissonance which is the echo in consciousness of an influence tending of its nature to undermine the Christ-life, and hence in the case of a person who remains fundamentally Christ-oriented to contradict their most deep-seated inclinations.

On the other hand, as applied to consolation and desolation, the concept of 'spiritual' can itself be misinterpreted. It is easy, for instance, to regard the respective 'spiritual' and 'anti-spiritual' character of these movements as indicating the spiritual quality of the person subject to them; and it is essential to realize that someone in consolation is not necessarily more Spirit-filled or more loving towards God and others than a person not in consolation; and that desolation is not necessarily a symptom of declining commitment. The point must also be stressed that to define an experience as 'spiritual' is not to confine it to situations of withdrawal and prayer. Certainly, when we

---

[4]The definitions in Rules Three and Four [316–317] open respectively with the words *On spiritual consolation* and, significantly, *On spiritual desolation*.

separate ourselves from immediate affairs (to pray or make a retreat) both the spiritual or anti-spiritual dynamisms of inner experience are brought more readily into focus (cf. [6] and [13]). But for the most of the time, spiritual consolation and desolation are entwined in the texture of the mundane, secular and everyday. Their distinctive tones run through our moods, whatever their immediate cause, and the feelings and motivations that influence our daily choices, dealings with people, reactions to events and circumstances. Hence the discerning person not only recognizes consolation and desolation in prayer, but learns in prayer to detect across the whole spectrum of our activity and consciousness the movements through which the Holy Spirit leads and enlightens us, and those through which other influences, if given their head, work against that guiding and light.

Other situations of discernment

As mentioned above, the range of discernment extends beyond the particular focus of the rules. The wider range includes discernment of the 'spirits' working in other people,[5] in groups, in society at large, or in the Church; discernment of the note of wisdom or its opposite in our own or others' stances or lines of reasoning;[6] the total process of discerning God's will in an 'election'.[7] In all these cases discernment may entail procedures not covered by the rules in the Exercises and may call for contingent personal qualifications not essential for the discernment of one's own inner movements – qualifications such as special knowledge or competence,[8] or a particular background, or specific endowments of mind or personality.

[5]For example, discernment of other people's claims to possess prophetic gifts. The Ignatian correspondence contains an instructive illustration of this discernment in a document dealing with allegedly inspired revelations concerning the papacy and the Society of Jesus: MHSI, *Epp. Ig.*, vol. XII, pp. 632–52 [trans., *Personal Writings*, pp. 220–50]. On discerning prophecy in general, see Green, *Wheat among the Weeds*, pp. 29–32.

[6]The discernment required particularly of the preacher, teacher or theologian. It is not always fully appreciated that Ignatius himself was not only a 'feeling' but a 'thinking' mystic, who was graced through the Cardoner enlightenment with a 'new understanding' (*Reminiscences*, §30 [trans., *Personal Writings*, pp. 26–27]). On this aspect of Ignatian mysticism, see Egan, *Ignatius Loyola the Mystic*, pp. 163–5.

[7]The distinction between the 'discernment of spirits' and the more complex process of 'discerning God's will' is developed by Toner, *Commentary*, pp. 131–5. See also his 'Discernment in the Spiritual Exercises', in Dister, ed., *A New Introduction*, pp. 63–72.

[8]With regard to the discernment of true from false prophecy, the report mentioned in note 5 above specifies that the grace of such discernment 'is helped by human effort and operates along with it, in particular with prudence and sound theology', *Personal Writings*, p. 211.

Nevertheless, if other kinds of discernment go beyond the limits of the rules, the movements treated in the rules and the discernment of these movements have an essential bearing on every other kind of discernment. This can be so for various reasons. In general the climate of discerned consolation is the best in which to undertake any more specific discernment. Where perceptions are distorted by desolation, there can be no discerning activity, unless the discernment of spirits has identified the desolate influence. And there are the situations highlighted by the Exercises in connection with 'election', in which the discernment of present consolation and desolation is an essential factor in forming a judgement or making a decision. But to appreciate the bearing of these movements on every exercise of discernment we must realize that they are significant not only as present experiences, but for their place in the processes by which the Spirit teaches us through the experiences of the past. Hence the discerning mind that a Christian brings to any situation comes partly at least from past consolation and desolation, identified, reflected upon, learned from, and carried forward in memory, either consciously or at levels beyond conscious recall.[9] The consolations and desolations of life form, in a sense, a school in spiritual wisdom.

The limits of discernment

Discernment must never be considered, or exercised, in isolation from the whole complex of ways in which we seek and find God's word. Listening to the word within ourselves must be related to two other kinds of listening.[10] Discernment requires listening to God's word in all the mediations through which it comes to us as a 'given', providing truths, directives, boundaries, norms, prophetic insight or challenge. And it calls for a listening stance before the reality of circumstances or situations in so far as these bear on our perceptions, judgements and choices, especially the elements of reality we are tempted to screen out of our personal vision.

In connection with this wider listening, another point must be made. The obstacles that impede our listening are not only those of direct personal sin; they also arise, sometimes in a very significant degree, from the convention and culture of our society, and interiorly, from sources deep in the unconscious

---

[9]On memory in the rules, see [318, 321, 322, 324, 332, 333, 334, 336].

[10]In this connection, Futrell distinguishes between three aspects of the word of God: the 'prophetic word', the 'existential word', the 'word of God here and now', see 'Ignatian Discernment', *Studies in the Spirituality of Jesuits*, 2–2 (1970).

[11]Considered from the standpoint of discernment, there are two facile attitudes towards the unconscious which need to be avoided: (1) the psychological naïveté that ignores the degree to which the 'movements of the soul' can be influenced by unconscious elements; (2) an attitude of psychological reductionism that virtually destroys

mind.[11] This is not to suggest that social or cultural blind spots or areas of psychological unfreedom totally preclude any exercise of discernment. Discernment is a growth process, and we discern within our current possibilities. Nevertheless it must be recognized that in degrees which vary with individuals, discernment can be seriously impeded by limitations of vision and inhibitions of freedom, which it is not the function of discernment itself to remove; and that the context within which discernment grows includes all the learning and helps, whether from spirituality or ordinary human disciplines, which promote maturity, self-knowledge and acceptance of reality.[12]

FIRST SET

Summary of contents

The content of these fourteen rules can be summarized as follows:

- Title [313]
- Preliminary principles (Rules 1 and 2)
- Descriptive definitions of consolation and desolation (Rules 3 and 4)
- Ways of dealing with desolation (Rules 5 to 8)
- Why the experience of desolation? (Rule 9)
- Attitudes towards consolation (Rules 10 and 11)
- Some common tactics of the enemy (Rules 12 to 14)

---

the possibility of God communicating through these movements at all. This said however, it must be acknowledged that discernment does not necessarily give access to deeply hidden psychological dynamics, e.g. unconscious compulsions which affect perception, judgement and choice. On the contrary these can eliminate the conditions in which discernment is possible. In this connection it is of interest to note certain qualities required by Ignatius in a candidate for a retreat of election: such a person 'should be in a position to make a decision regarding his own life', while being at the same time 'uneasy in some respect, with a desire to know what he ought to do with himself and an uncertainty about this ...' On these demands Laurence Murphy remarks pertinently that though expressed in the language of a pre-Freudian culture, they 'bring forcibly home to us the importance of what we today recognize as unconscious motivation. For there is no doubt that the autonomy and openness asked for by Ignatius will be wanting in people unconsciously moved in one or other direction', cf. *Directory, de Vitoria* (MHSI 76, pp. 15–16 [trans., Palmer, pp. 15–16]); also Murphy, 'Consolation', pp. 46–7. On discernment and unconscious motivation see also comments on [330] and [335], and Lonsdale, '"The Serpent's tail": Rules for Discernment', in Sheldrake, ed., *The Way of Ignatius Loyola*, pp. 172–4.

[12]Ignatius' own preferred way of helping a person to grow in maturity was spiritual direction through confession. In the Exercises themselves he relied on the examen, and on an extended use of the Foundation: cf. *Directory, de Vitoria* (MHSI 76, pp. 99–100 [trans., Palmer, p. 20]).

[313] [1] RULES BY WHICH TO PERCEIVE AND UNDERSTAND TO SOME EXTENT THE VARIOUS *MOVEMENTS* PRODUCED IN THE SOUL: [2] THE GOOD THAT THEY *MAY BE ACCEPTED*, AND THE BAD, THAT THEY *MAY BE REJECTED*. RULES MORE *SUITABLE FOR THE FIRST WEEK*.

The tone is practical and experiential. The purpose of the rules is to help the exercitant first to be aware of their movements of consciousness, then to come to a certain understanding of them, on the basis of which to distinguish between the movements to be accepted and those to be rejected.

movements By the term *movements of the soul* the Exercises refer to the inter-actions of feelings, thoughts, and impulses of attraction and recoil, which occur spontaneously in consciousness. It should be remembered that these movements consist in thoughts as well as feelings, 'thoughts' in this context being not dispassionate or solely speculative thoughts, but thoughts as it were 'charged' with feeling. In the vocabulary of the Exercises, 'thoughts' also include the activity of the imagination. [13]

may be accepted ... may be rejected. The movements themselves are invol-untary; freedom consists in the choice to accept or not to accept the direction they impart to the will, the thoughts and the general perceptions of reality to which they give rise. To say that one can decline to accept involuntary or spontaneous movements does not imply, however, that one can always imme-diately get rid of them; cf. note on Rule 5 below.

more suitable for the First Week. The typical First Week exercitant is going through a conversion of feeling and outlook in relation to sin, disorder, the world [63], and there is usually a certain instability in this process, newly emerging patterns creating tension with the surviving force of earlier ones [91].

In this position, a person is particularly vulnerable to episodes of deso-lation. For this reason, it may be desirable in the First Week not only to introduce consolation and desolation as general concepts, but to deal espe-cially, as the present rules do, with recognizing and responding to desolation; *more suitable for the First Week* also means that at this stage no mention is made of possible ambiguities within consolation itself, since this belongs to the realm of temptation under the guise of moral and spiritual good charac-teristic of the Second Week.

---

[13]For 'thoughts' in the Discernment Rules, cf. [315, 317, 318, 322, 324, 332–334]. A fuller definition of the term *movement in the soul* will be found in Toner, *Commentary*, p. 37.

Rules 1 and 2: Preliminary principles

In the opening rules we are introduced to the two kinds of *spirit*, in relation to two types of people, those regressing and those making progress.

As used in the Exercises, the term *spirits*, in the plural, refers to positive or negative spiritual influences or dynamisms that we experience within ourselves. In the case of the *good spirit* the immediate cause of this influence might for Ignatius be an angel (whose action, of course, always mediates that of God), but it must be strongly emphasized today that the rules for discernment are essentially concerned with recognizing the action in human consciousness of the Holy Spirit.[14]

The *bad spirit*, whether understood as an actual preternatural agent or as the effect in ourselves of personal and corporate sin, denotes an influence of the kind described by St Paul as against the Spirit,[15] an influence which if left to itself will put in jeopardy the life of the Spirit within us. In the Exercises this influence is commonly personified as *the enemy* (or in the Two Standards, *the enemy of our human nature*) a term which in the Exercises evokes the idea of a wily and malicious tactician.[16]

The kinds of people described in these opening rules represent not so much notable degrees of dissoluteness and earnestness, as consistent general tendencies of will. Thus, the rules establish from the outset a dynamic perspective. What matters is not only where a person 'is' but whether their direction in relation to God and his will is forwards or backwards. This direction is a crucially important key for discerning the spirits, since as a later rule explains [335], the influence of the spirits ordinarily gives feelings of harmony or conflict according to whether the spirit is moving with or against the general set of will of the person affected.[17]

[14]'Now that the dangers and exaggerations of illuminism are scarcely present the exercitant must be explicitly told that the Exercises will evoke, strengthen, and make more explicit the ever-present experience of the Holy Spirit', Egan, *Mystical Horizon*, p. 122.

[15]Gal. 5:7.

[16]For Ignatius, the identity of *the enemy* is clear; it is Lucifer (the fallen angel of light) with the malevolent angels under his command [140, 141]. Today, the question whether the bad spirits of the Exercises must necessarily be taken to refer to actual spirits, is obviously an important one, but it does not have to be resolved before one can make or give the Exercises. See Toner, *Commentary*, pp. 34–7 (on the spirits in relation to making the Exercises) and pp. 260–70 (survey of theological opinions on the existence of Satan and demons as an object of belief). In the matter of identifying within our experience the action of real bad spirits, as distinct from influences coming from within ourselves, the generally traditional position has been to regard this as difficult and practically of little importance. Cf. Coathalem, *Insights*, p. 252.

[17] In fact human situations are not quite as simple as the first two rules taken in isolation might suggest. For example in a manifestly regressing person there may still be enough spiritual sensibility for the influence of the good spirit to be felt in some-

Since the subsequent rules will be largely concerned with identifying the influence of spirits through positive and negative feelings, and since spiritually insensitive or inexperienced people might mistake complacency for consolation, and compunction for desolation, the need for this initial distinction can hardly be over-emphasized.

[314] ¹ First rule. With people who go *from one deadly sin to another*, it is the usual practice of the enemy to hold out apparent pleasures; so that he makes them *imagine sensual delights and satisfactions* ² in order to maintain and reinforce them in their vices and sins. ³ With people of this kind, the good spirit uses the opposite procedure, causing pricks of conscience and feelings of *remorse* by means of the *natural power of rational moral judgement*.[18]

[315] ¹ Second rule. In the case of people who are making serious *progress in the purification of their sins*, and who advance from good to better in the service of God our Lord, the procedure is the contrary to that described in rule one, ² for then it is characteristic of the bad spirit to *harass, sadden and obstruct*, and to disturb with *false reasoning*, so as to *impede progress*, ³ while the *characteristic of the good spirit* is to give *courage and strength, consolations*, tears, inspirations and quiet, making things easy and removing all obstacles so that the person may move forward in doing good.

from one deadly sin to another 'Deadly sin' seems here a preferable translation to 'mortal sin'. In any case, since the rule indicates orientation rather than state, the term should be taken to refer to anyone whose orientation in relation to the call to renounce sin, and to love and serve God, is one of regression, even if subtle and slow. The Vulgate has, 'those who easily sin mortally, and add sin to sin'.

imagine sensual delights and satisfactions By *sensual delights* one is to understand not only (or even primarily) crass hedonism, but the gratification

---

thing of the way described in Rule 2, and in the case of the progressing person, anti-spiritual instincts may still be strong enough for the bad spirit to produce the feelings of attraction described in Rule 1 (cf. Toner, *Commentary*, pp. 74–8). Moreover people do not progress and regress at the same pace over the entire terrain of the moral and spiritual life, so that a person might experience the spirits more according to the Rule 1 mode in relation to some aspects of Christian life and more according to a Rule 2 mode in others. An experienced director will be aware of, and will easily take into account, complexities of this kind, which do not diminish the foundational importance of the boldly drawn distinctions of the first two rules.

[18]In the Autograph and the Latin texts, the term *synderesis*, a technical Thomist term, is used here: it designates the natural capacity of the human mind to know the first principles of the moral order.

of any instinct – e.g. for power, wealth, fame – insofar as the instinct is not integrated into, and ordered by, a true relationship to Christ. *imagine*: the creative faculty of imagination, which plays so positive and central a part in the Exercises, is also a key component of the dynamic of temptation, serving in this case to protect it against disturbance from reason or reality.

remorse The echo in emotion of the rational perception that one is doing, or has done, wrong ought to be distinguished from guilt feelings of an irrational kind. 'Remorse' is a quite different kind of experience from desolation as described implicitly in Rule 2 below and explicitly in Rule 4. While desolation draws a person backward, true *remorse* is a movement forward, and therefore to be 'accepted'.

natural power of rational moral judgement Against the effective criterion of instinctual satisfaction, the good spirit appeals to moral principle.

progress in the purification of their sins As in Rule 1, the characteristic emphasized is movement, here that of conversion in its correlative aspects of 'turning from' and 'turning to'.

harass, sadden and obstruct — effects often caused by the desolate imagination playing on the actual or possible implications of a converted life.

false reasoning Since the maturing Christian is committed to truth, any plausible subversion of progress must now present itself not only as pleasant but as reasonable. The principle will be picked up in the rules of the second set, where its implications are more subtle and oblique. The false reasonings referred to here are those which directly undermine commitment by bringing about distress and anxiety. The Vulgate translates the effect of the evil spirit as 'difficulties, scruples, false reasonings and other such disturbances' (note the inclusion of 'scruples').

impede progress The purpose of the *bad spirit* is eventually to reactivate the backward élan towards a life dominated by the capital sins. But as a preliminary, it must neutralize the emerging appeal and sense of meaning being found in God's service by making that service look unattractive and pointless.[19]

---

[19]The strategy of the *bad spirit* as described in the Rule 2 recalls Ignatius' own spiritual crisis at Manresa, when the dynamics here described had been painful realities of experience. In his account Ignatius recalls in particular two causes of distress: thoughts of the future as an unbearable prospect, and the *false reasonings* of scrupulosity. See *Reminiscences*, §§22–5 [trans., *Personal Writings*, pp. 22–4]. The theme of *false reasonings*, backed by desolate imagination in connection with the future, also appears in the letter of spiritual direction to Teresa Rejadell of 18 June 1536 (MHSI, *Epp. Ig.*, vol. 1, pp. 99–107 [trans., *Personal Writings*, p. 130]).

characteristic of the good spirit It is God's ordinary way to support the beginner with the kind of helps here described.[20] The rule does not say that in the beginning such experiences will predominate; but whether more frequent or less, they promote growth and progress, and when they occur they should be yielded to and followed through.

courage and strength Unlike the other effects here listed, these are always offered us by the Spirit, though according to circumstances they may be felt to a greater or less degree. They are gifts we especially need in times of desolation.

consolations The word is to be understood in the broadest sense, irrespective of the distinctions to be made in the rule following, where tears and quiet are themselves forms of consolation, and in [330, 331]. The plural suggests moments or episodes of consolation.

Rules 3 and 4: Descriptive definitions of consolation and desolation

[316] **[1] Third rule. On spiritual consolation.** *I use the word 'consolation'* **when any interior movement is produced in the soul which leads her to become** *inflamed with the love of her Creator and Lord,* **[2] and when as a consequence, there is no creature on the face of the earth that the person can love in itself, but they love it in the Creator and Lord of all things.**
[3] Similarly, I use the word 'consolation' when a person *sheds tears* **which lead to the love of our Lord, whether these arise from grief over sins, or over the passion of Christ our Lord, or because of other reasons immediately directed towards his service and praise.**
[4] Lastly, I give the name 'consolation' to *every increase* **of hope, faith and charity, to** *all interior happiness* **which calls and attracts to heavenly things and to the salvation of one's soul,** *leaving the soul quiet and at peace in her Creator and Lord.*

I use the word 'consolation' Three experiential situations to which the word 'consolation' can be applied; but the definition does not claim to be exhaustive, and in describing three situations of consolation, does not exclude others The Vulgate gives: 'Spiritual consolation, properly so-called, is known to be present when, etc.'

[20]For Ignatius' experience of this, see *Reminiscences*, §20 [trans., *Personal Writings*, pp. 21–2]. In the letter to Teresa Rejadell referred to in the previous note, Ignatius mentions 'the abundant comforts and consolations normally given by the Lord' to his 'new servants', loc. cit., p. 130.

inflamed with the love of her Creator and Lord The first definition describes
an intensely felt love for God into which the love of creatures is integrated.
Such a love is one of the major keys to Ignatian spirituality. The goal and
high-point of that spirituality is a love defined not only in terms of God
himself, but a love of God in which all other loves are included. The definition recalls a text in the *Constitutions* where a love of this kind is proposed
as an ideal towards which all should aspire and be frequently exhorted.[21]

How should the distinction between loving a creature 'for itself' and
loving a creature 'for God' be understood? The answer hinges on the principle that the perfection of all love consists in its being integrated into God's
own love, so that 'God is loved in the creature and the creature in God'.[22]
Understood in this perspective, what Ignatius calls 'love of the creature for
itself' is a love which disjoins the creature from the Love which is the ground
of its being, and such a love is therefore a defective love. Elsewhere Ignatius
heavily accentuates the purifications and relinquishments which may be
needed in order to love 'in God'; and to bring these out, he sometimes uses
a language, especially the word 'only', which appears to imply that our
immediate loves are diminished by being taken into God's love (Jesuit
novices, for example, should love their relations with 'only' that love which
well-ordered charity requires[23]). But the 'only' which usually appears in the
present text is an exigence of translation and does not occur in the Spanish
(where the text has, '*ninguna cosa ... puede amar ... sino* ['if not'] *en el
Criador*'). As the Latin versions make clear, the point is the wholly positive
one that there is a grace of consolation in which the experience of loving God
takes all other loves into itself. Such consolation, while it lasts, is incompatible with any feeling or attitude that, in the name of love, disconnects
creature from Creator and the Creator's love.[24] The Versio Prima text gives:
'when we can love no created thing in itself, but whatever it may be, we love
it in God the Creator of all'. And the Vulgate: 'one can no longer love any
creature except for his sake'.

sheds tears Tears constitute spiritual consolation only when two conditions

[21]*Constitutions* III, 1, §26 [288], ed. Ganss, p. 165. The attentive reader of the
text of the Exercises will note similarities between the present definition and the First
Time of Election [175] and the consolation identified in [330] below. The relationship
between the three experiences (and indeed between the two latter with one another) is
not absolutely clear, but the present text does not appear to describe an out-of-the-
ordinary phenomenon, as [175] and [330] plainly do, and this impression is supported
by the text from the *Constitutions* just mentioned.

[22]*Constitutions*, loc. cit.

[23]*General Examen of Candidates*, ch. 4, §7 [trans., Ganss, p. 95]. The text
refers to Matt. 19:29; Luke 18:30.

[24]Though the word 'love' can only be properly used in reference to human relationships, the principles of Ignatius' doctrine can be applied to attitudes of desire and
appreciation towards things, or situations (e.g. a benefice, or office).

are fulfilled: that the tears arise from the kind of source here indicated and that they in some way move the person forward to God's greater service and praise. Ignatius considered the response of tears, given these conditions, to be a quite distinctive gift. The distinctiveness becomes lost from view if the concept of *tears* is simply equated with the more general idea of powerful emotion. Nevertheless, in spite of his own gifts, and the clear value he sets on tears in the Exercises, Ignatius held that tears were not 'absolutely good and fitting for everyone' and should not be asked for 'unreservedly'.[25] We have also to remember that culture and personal character have much to do with a person's susceptibility to tears.

every increase, etc. I.e. the intensification of faith, hope and love on the level of feeling, which is an aid to the growth of the essential faith, hope and love, which do not of course consist in feelings.

all interior happiness In this final clause, which contains no mention even of increase, the idea of consolation reaches its widest extension.

leaving the soul quiet and at peace in her Creator and Lord. As with the other forms of consolation, the fruit of the experience here described is still relational, i.e. not any joy with a vaguely religious flavour will meet this account.

[317] [1] **Fourth rule. On spiritual desolation. *'Desolation' is the name I give* to everything contrary to what is described in Rule Three;** [2] **for example, darkness and disturbance in the soul, *attraction to what is low and of the earth*, disquiet arising from various agitations and temptations.** [3] **All this *leads to a lack of confidence* in which one feels oneself to be without hope and without love. One finds oneself thoroughly lazy, lukewarm, sad, and as though cut off from one's Creator and Lord.** [4] **For *just as consolation is contrary to desolation*, in the same way, the *thoughts* that spring from consolation are contrary to the thoughts that spring from desolation.**

'Desolation' is the name I give Whereas in consolation affectivity is under the influence of the Holy Spirit, in desolation it is under the influence of the *bad spirit*. The rule describes this situation by delineating some of its character-

---

[25]Cf. the letter written by Polanco on Ignatius' behalf to Nicholas Gouda, 22 November 1553 (MHSI, *Epp. Ig.*, vol. V, No. 3924, p. 135 [trans., *Inigo: Letters*, p. 214]). The letter develops the point at some length and serves to complement the impression given by the copious allusions to tears in the *Spiritual Diary*, written some nine years previously. Joseph A. Munitiz comments on Ignatius' gift of tears in the introduction to his translation of the *Diary* (*Inigo: Discernment Log-Book*, pp. 17–18).

istic manifestations. On a careful reading of the rule it becomes apparent that each of these manifestations is a particular negative experience in relation to God and his will, the experience of a believer. Spiritual desolation is a faith-experience, yet at the same time an anti-faith experience, and hence an experience characterized by *disturbance in the soul, disquiet, agitation* (even if these are not always instantly recognized).

The purpose of Ignatius' descriptive definition is to convey a sense of the nature of desolation which will help an exercitant recognize it in him or her self. It should be noted, however, that the rule describes desolation mainly in the forms in which it is encountered in prayer, and that a wider account would be required in order to sketch out the typical expressions of desolation in relationships and in various circumstances.

attraction to what is low and of the earth In the situation of spiritual desolation, the 'attraction' (literally, 'motion') is more paradoxical than the attraction of apparent pleasures aroused by the enemy in people cutting loose from the Spirit and spiritual values (Rule 1). Here, Ignatius is describing the experience of a person drawn to things which are at the same time contrary to their own higher values. Such an experience will contain a note of dissonance (at least implicit), making it of a piece with the climate of desolation conveyed by the rule as a whole.

leads to a lack of confidence In the Vulgate: 'leading to a lack of confidence in salvation and banishing hope and charity'.

just as consolation is contrary to desolation The *thoughts* that spring from consolation are contrary to the thoughts that spring from desolation. The Vulgate (more satisfactorily) has: 'as desolation is opposed to consolation, so the thoughts that arise from each are altogether opposed to one another'.

The concluding reference to *thoughts* is evidence of the importance of the implicit or explicit 'thoughts' (in the sense of judgements, opinions, projects, fantasies) which interact with feelings in the total experience of consolation or desolation. The thoughts in question are those which arise directly out of, and are in a sense 'charged' by, consolation and desolation, and do not include everything that suggests itself to the mind in the course of these situations. Otherwise there would be no temptations during consolation, and no thoughts from the good spirit during desolation.

However *thoughts that spring from desolation* are often implicit and unacknowledged thoughts about God and his will.[26] It is important that such thoughts be brought into the open and articulated.

[26]Thoughts, for instance, that God is not good, trustworthy or loving; that life in God's service cannot be happy; that prayer has no meaning, etc.

Rules 5 to 8: Ways of dealing with desolation

It can hardly be overstated, that no reproach should be attached to the experience as such of desolation,[27] nor should one seek to repress or deny the experience. But positively to assent or yield oneself to desolation is to be drawn into a downward momentum deleterious to faith, hope and love. Against this it is necessary to reassert freedom, negatively by admitting no decisions or changes directly inspired by desolation [318], positively by countering the effects of desolation in affirming one's love, faith and hope. Thus against the apathy of will that undermines love, one deliberately initiates systematic acts of love [319], and against discouragement and the sense of meaninglessness one dwells upon considerations or thoughts that build up faith and hope [320, 321].

Such initiatives might or might not bring an episode of desolation to an end. But when we *go against* desolation, even if the experience persists, we change its meaning. Regressive when left to itself, desolation now becomes a situation of progress, in which the enemy is resisted and we trust nakedly in a divine help we do not for the moment feel [320].

As always, however, over-literal interpretations of the principle of *going against* must be avoided. It must be remembered that the object of the principle is to establish a mean, not to canonize stress.[28] Moreover practical expressions of it must correspond to the total situation of the individual exercitant; thus the present rule might not be applied exactly as it stands, if in a particular case the effects of spiritual desolation are compounded by physical or psychological factors, such as fatigue, poor health or depression. Nevertheless it is essential to retain the basic point, that in desolation the prime initiative required of one, and the prime grace offered, is that of affirming freedom against the unfreedom intrinsic to desolation itself.

[318] [1] **Fifth rule. In time of desolation, *one should never make any change* but should stand firm and constant in the resolutions and decision by which one was guided the day before the desolation or during the preceding time of consolation.** [2] **For just as *in consolation it is more the good spirit* who guides and counsels us, so in desolation it is the bad**

---

[27]Cf. Letter to Teresa Rejadell, 11 September 1536 (MHSI, *Epp. Ig.*, vol. 1, no. 8, pp. 107–9 [trans., *Personal Writings*, p. 137: 'Just as I am not due to be saved simply thanks to the good efforts of the good angels, so I am not due to be harmed by the bad thoughts and weaknesses that the wicked angels, the world and the flesh put before me'.])

[28]The principle of *agere contra* ('to go against') is 'dialectical and not systematic. Ignatius is not proposing it as a general rule for spiritual conduct in all circumstances; he is suggesting it as the direction to follow in order to check the action of the enemy and of sin in us', Pousset, *Life in Faith and Freedom*, p. 214.

spirit, and by following his counsels we can never find the right way forward.

one should never make any change Occasionally in times of desolation decisions have to be made, and it is possible when one is *in* desolation to make decisions which do not come *out of* desolation.[29] But desolation is not the state in which to make any, except non-postponable, decisions. It is especially not the moment to make decisions which would change directions already taken on the basis of discernment (cf. [173]). The Vulgate makes explicit the bearing on election: 'In time of desolation, one must not deliberate on anything, or make any change concerning the resolution taken by the soul, or regarding one's state of life, but persevere in what had been established previously, for instance, the day or the hour when one was in consolation.'

in consolation, it is more the good spirit Not in the sense that decisions at this time are necessarily, or even usually, made under the direct inspiration of the Spirit. The implication is rather that when we are in consolation, our decisions, or the steps of our decision-making process, are taken with a will and judgement influenced by the Spirit-given effects of consolation: felt love for God, the felt desire to hear and to do his word, a vision influenced by the Gospel, and a certain clarity of perception. The word *more* introduces an important nuance. As will appear later [331], the bad spirit can also be at work in consolation, and we are not, of course, without the guidance of the good spirit in desolation [320]. The Vulgate has: 'For as, whilst anyone enjoys that consolation of which we have spoken, he or she is led not by their own instinct, but by that of the good spirit; so when desolation presents itself to a person, he or she is urged on by the evil spirit, by whose instigations nothing right is ever effected.'

[319] [1] Sixth rule. Although in desolation we must make no changes in our former decisions, it is nevertheless very profitable to attempt vigorously to *make changes in ourselves* against this desolation; [2] for example, by more insistence on *prayer and meditation*, by much *examination*, and by doing *penance* in some suitable way.

make changes in ourselves The exercitant is not asked to try directly to change the fact of being in desolation, but to make changes in one's spiritu-

---

[29]Such decisions require, however, the ability to discount the influence of desolation even while experiencing it, and to draw on the general spiritual wisdom and specific precedents carried in the memory even under these circumstances. The ability to do this should not be presumed lightly. Moreover, a decision made in a time of desolation cannot have the quality of an election made in any of the Three Times.

al regime enabling one to resist the destructive tendencies of desolation.

prayer and meditation ... examination ... penance Three initiatives each of which meets a specific need of the person in desolation, but which also serve to sustain the overall level of dedication and service which desolation of its nature tends to erode. Thus one prays in whatever ways will directly help one deal with desolation, and one opposes the tendency to curtail *prayer* or even to drop it completely [13]. *Examination* will seek possible reasons for desolation in one's own attitudes or conduct [322.1] or in one's circumstances. *Penance* is both a form of petition and also an act of commitment [87]. The criterion of suitability of any particular form of penance is the spiritual quality of its effects on oneself; hence decisions in the matter of penance are themselves a matter of discernment, often made through experiment [89].

[320] [1] Seventh rule. A person in desolation should *consider* how *our Lord has placed them* in a trial period, so that they are to resist the various disturbances and temptations of the enemy by their own natural powers. [2] For *this they can do* with the divine help which remains with them at all times even though they may not clearly perceive it; [3] although the Lord has withdrawn their fervour, deeply-felt love and intense grace, he has still left them *the grace sufficient for eternal salvation*.

consider The content of the rules gives a faith-meaning to the experience of desolation. The experience itself tends to obscure this meaning, hence to *consider* it is to choose to dwell on thoughts of another kind than those to which desolation spontaneously gives rise.

our Lord has placed them, etc. Part of the meaning of desolation is that in it we learn to carry on in God's service, even when we feel left on our own. Worded in order to bring this out, the rule might at first glance give a misleading impression. What is withdrawn in desolation is only the grace of consoling feelings. It is not implied that we are left entirely to ourselves, a position which would contradict the insistence in the next sentence on the *divine help* which is always with us and on *sufficient grace*.

this they can do i.e. *resist* (cf. [13] above). Ordinarily, one is not empowered in desolation instantly to banish these effects of the bad spirit (the disturbance and clouding of feelings and immediate perceptions); one is empowered only to resist them. But this, far from implying diminished fidelity, may well be a situation of deeper and purer fidelity than might be attained in consolation.

the grace sufficient for eternal salvation The grace *sufficient* for us, if we accept it, is precisely the grace so to resist the *disturbances and temptations* as in this resistance to be completely faithful, and to grow in God's love.

[321] [1] **Eighth rule. A person in desolation should** *work to remain in patience,* **for patience is opposed to the annoyances which come upon them;** [2] **and they should** *keep in mind that consolation will not be long in coming,* **if they make use of all their powers against this desolation, as has been explained in Rule Six.**

work to remain in patience Desolation tends of its nature to destroy patience; hence if patience is to be effective in desolation, it must be *worked at* but, of course, patiently, not frenetically.

keep in mind (lit 'think') that consolation will not be long in coming That is to say, one chooses to think about the future on lines contrary to the thoughts spontaneously engendered by desolation. To the person experiencing it, desolation can seem the normal state of affairs and the future an endless bleak perspective.[30]

Rule 9: Why the experience of desolation?

Rule 9 outlines three 'causes' (or explanations) of the phenomenon of desolation. Of these the first belongs to the realm of our own freedom and responsibility. The second and third have to do with the intentions of God in allowing desolation and acting through it, but without implying that God directly 'causes' desolation. Under the second cause, desolation is presented as a testing situation, under the third as a learning situation. What is tested is our perseverance, and if we accept the test from God's hand and trust to God's concealed presence in it, the quality of our perseverance is enhanced; precisely in being tested, perseverance becomes less dependent on immediate satisfactions, more genuinely a commitment to God for himself. In the third situation, desolation makes us aware of, and helps us to stay rooted in, the fundamental truth about the human person and God. It thus promotes a radical humility of attitude, purifying us of the complacency, misplaced trust in our own powers, even the vainglory which Ignatius sees as the inherent temptations in frequent, prolonged or intense consolation.[31]

---

[30]See *Reminiscences*, §20, and the Letter to Teresa Rejadell referred to in note 6 above (trans., *Personal Writings*, pp. 21, 130).

[31]In connection with the idea of desolation as 'purifying', it may be well to recognize that desolation as understood by Ignatius is not to be equated with every kind of mystical suffering. More specifically, while there are certain correspondences between Ignatius and John of the Cross, considerable difficulties arise if the desolation of Ignatius is equated with the passive night. See Toner, *Commentary*, Appendix Two, 'Spiritual Desolation and the Dark Night', pp. 271–82.

[322] [1] **Ninth rule. There are** *three principal causes* **for our finding ourselves in desolation.**
  The first is that we are lukewarm, lazy or *careless in the practices of the spiritual life*; **so spiritual consolation** *goes away* **because of our faults.**

  [2] **Secondly, spiritual desolation tests our quality and shows how far we will extend ourselves in God's service and praise without the generous** *remuneration* **of consolations and overflowing graces.**

  [3] **Thirdly, spiritual desolation gives us** *true knowledge and understanding, so that we may perceive within ourselves* **that on our part we cannot arouse or sustain overflowing devotion, intense love, tears or any other spiritual consolation, but that all this is a gift and grace from God our Lord.** [4] **So we are not to** *build our nest where we do not belong*, **becoming elated in mind to the point of pride and vainglory, and putting down to our own account devotion or other forms of spiritual consolation.**

three principal causes The rule is not an exhaustive treatment of the causes of desolation. In the Versio Prima: 'We fall into desolation mainly on account of three things' (the word 'cause' is not used).

careless in the practices of the spiritual life (lit. 'in our spiritual exercises') Causes of desolation within ourselves include: our positive sin, our resistances to God's word, decline in fidelity to our life commitments (to name only a few). Here the cause Ignatius singles out is 'neglect of spiritual exercises'. Applied to a person engaged in making a Twentieth Annotation retreat, the sense of this is clear (cf. [6]). Interpreted more generally, the expression 'spiritual exercises' can be taken to refer to the broad practices listed in the First Annotation.

goes away In the Versio Prima, 'Spiritual consolation ordinarily deserts us and distances itself from us'. In the Vulgate: 'We are deservedly deprived of the divine consolation'. The active verbs of the Autograph and the Versio Prima simply state that a decline in fidelity leads to a falling off of consolation, while the passive verb in the Vulgate accentuates the idea of God himself taking consolation away. It should be noted, however, that the rule is proposing a *possible* cause of desolation, one which a person in desolation may need to check on before going on to consider the second and third causes. Nor does the rule claim a necessary connection between indolence and desolation; God is free in the use of his gifts.

remuneration (literally, in the Autograph and both Latin versions, 'stipend') suggests the normal and regular, as well as the gratuitous. Yet it is precisely when consolation seems a normal state of affairs that we can take it for granted; and when taken for granted, it can endorse an unconscious attitude towards perseverance as conditional on remuneration rather than as an unconditional personal commitment. Intervening episodes of desolation have the effect of challenging this attitude.

true knowledge and understanding, so that we may perceive within ourselves
Note the movement from knowledge and understanding to an 'inner' perception, which is other than 'head-knowledge' and affects a person's outlook and self-understanding.

build our nest where we do not belong I.e. settle down in, and regard as our own, what is God's property, not ours.[32]

Rules 10 and 11: Attitudes towards consolation

Rules 10 and 11 deal with *consolation* in relation to desolation, and include in Rule 11 an additional point about desolation. In both rules, consolation and desolation are regarded not as isolated present experiences but as part of a time-sequence, and hence as involving memory and anticipation. Thus, during consolation memory of the weakness and poverty of past desolation is considered as a corrective to present complacency, and as a realistic preparation for further times of desolation. When strength is felt in consolation, one recognizes that consolation is given not only for the present but as a resource for the future, while in desolation, helped by the memory of consolation, one adverts in faith to the reality of a graced strength one might not for the moment feel.

A key-word in these rules is *think*. One is not asked either to relive a desolate incident of the past, or to anticipate the experience of desolation to come, in such a way as actually to be made desolate here-and-now.

[323] Tenth rule. A person in consolation should *think how they shall bear themselves* in the desolation which will follow later, and gather renewed strength for that moment.

---

[32] In a slightly different way, the nest image is used in the *Imitation of Christ*, Book 3, ch. 6: 'These souls who aspired to build their nests in heaven, became needy and wretched outcasts, in order that, through humiliation and poverty, they might learn not to fly with their own wings but to trust themselves under my wings' (trans. L. Sherley-Price, Penguin Classics, 1952).

[324] **¹ Eleventh rule. Persons in consolation should try to *humble and lower themselves* as much as possible by *thinking how little they are worth* in time of desolation without this grace of consolation. ² On the other hand, *the person in desolation should keep in mind* that they *can do much* if they draw strength from their Creator and Lord, *having the grace sufficient* to resist every enemy.**

think how they shall bear themselves Consolation is a time of clarity, desolation a time of confusion, when we need to remember (and follow) the direction already perceived (cf. [318]). Both the Versio Prima and the Vulgate amplify the idea of *forearming*: Versio Prima: 'Let the person in consolation consider the desolation which is imminent, and be fortified against it with the arms of constancy, fortitude and patience'. Vulgate: 'He who is enjoying consolation must consider for the future how he will be able to bear himself when desolation afterwards occurs; in order that even for that time he may gain spirit and strength of mind to repel its attack.'

humble and lower themselves With a view not to self-belittlement, but to authenticity (cf. comment on *lowliness* in [258] above).

thinking how little they are worth Again, one is not asked to go into desolation, but without reliving the experience to reflect on the weakness and poverty revealed in it.

the person in desolation should keep in mind This final sentence reverts to the theme of the previous block, in particular picking up Rules 7 and 8.

can do much I.e. by resistance and the specific measures commended in this and the preceding rules, one can do much to contain and even neutralize the involuntary effects of desolation. In the Vulgate the language is even more positive: 'we can do very much and will easily conquer all our enemies', but 'do much' and even 'very much' imply that one cannot do everything. In desolation, it is not in our power to replace the unfree movements of desolation by those of consolation.

having the grace sufficient The point made in connection with Rule 7 must be repeated: withdrawal of the grace of consoled experiences does not imply withdrawal of the grace needed for total fidelity and commitment.

Rules 12 to 14: Some common tactics of the enemy

The First Week rules conclude by setting out three aspects of temptation of which the progressing person described in Rule 2 may need to be particularly aware.

The comparisons in Rules 12 and 13 are intended to draw on the less pleasing traits of men and women respectively. But each contains an image of women which will not meet with general acceptance today; and as in the case of the Kingdom exercise, obsolete analogies should not be allowed to impede the insights they once served to illustrate. These two rules are not about the behaviour of men and women,[33] but about two guises under which we experience temptation: aggressive on the one side, devious and ingratiating on the other, and about corresponding ways of dealing with these: to hold one's ground, to seek counsel.

In Rule 14 Ignatius suggests no practical conclusions leaving the exercitant to draw his or her own. Since, however, we have to do with an enemy able to use against us every weakness, including our unrecognized ones, the rule suggests self-knowledge as a further indispensable resource for dealing with temptation.

[325] **[1]** **Twelfth rule. The behaviour of the enemy resembles that of a woman in a quarrel with a man,[34] for he is weak when faced with strength but strong when faced with weakness.** **[2]** **It is characteristic of a woman when she quarrels with a man to lose heart and to take flight when the man shows a bold front;** **[3]** **on the other hand, the moment the man gives way and loses courage, then the rage, vengeance and ferocity of the woman overflow and know no bounds.** **[4]** **In the same way, it is characteristic of the enemy to weaken and lose courage and to turn to flight with his temptations,** **[5]** **when the person engaged in the spiritual life shows a bold front against those temptations and acts in a way *diametrically opposed to them*.** **[6]** **If, on the contrary, such a person begins to be afraid and to lose courage in sustaining temptation,** **[7]** **no wild beast on the face of the earth is as ferocious as the enemy of human nature in the surging malice with which he pursues his *wicked purpose*.**

[326] **[1]** **Thirteenth rule. The enemy also behaves as a false lover behaves towards a woman.[35] Such a man wants to remain hidden and not to be discovered.** **[2]** **In using dishonest talk to try to seduce the daughter of a good father, or the wife of a good husband, he wants his words and inducements kept secret.** **[3]** **On the other hand, when the daughter reveals**

---

[33]Nor does the image used in Rule 13 give grounds for thinking of Ignatius as a misogynist, a notion which will be rebutted by even a slight acquaintance with his life and letters.

[34]The words 'in a quarrel with a man' do not occur in the original text. They are inserted in order to bring out the complementarity of the images used in this rule and the following.

[35]'behaves towards a woman'. Words added in translation.

his smooth words and corrupt intentions to her father (or the wife to her husband), he is very much put out, for he then easily recognizes that his plans cannot succeed. [4] In the same way, when the enemy of human nature brings his deceits and inducements to bear on the just soul, he wants them to be received and kept in secret. [5] When they are revealed to a good confessor or some other person who knows his trickery and perversity, he is very displeased, [6] realizing that once his tricks are revealed his malicious purpose cannot succeed.

[327] [1] Fourteenth rule. Likewise, he behaves like a military leader, setting about the conquest and seizure of the object he desires. [2] The commander of an army, after setting up his camp and inspecting the fortifications and defences of a fortress, attacks it at its weakest point. [3] In the same way, the enemy of our human nature makes his rounds to inspect all our virtues, theological, cardinal and moral, [4] and where he finds us weakest and in greatest need as regards our eternal salvation, there he attacks and tries to take us.

diametrically opposed to them The Versio Prima adds: 'This is why James says: "Resist the devil, and he will flee far from you"' (James 4:7).

wicked purpose The Versio Prima adds: 'Therefore Job says rightly of the demon: "There is no power on earth to compare with him"' (Job. 41:25).

SECOND SET

The second set of rules envisage a person living the interiorized love-relationship, known as the 'illuminative way' (cf. [10]), and hence growing in integrity of intention and in spiritual sensitivity. For such a person they propound two distinctions in connection with consolation. To have mentioned these earlier on could have been unproductive and confusing (cf. [9, 10]), but they are crucial aids for the journey into spiritual maturity, and can have particular importance in the Exercises if the Second Week includes the process of discerning God's will in an 'election'. Of these distinctions, the first deals with the curiously named categories of consolation, those *without cause* and those *with cause*. The second distinction, between the consolation from God (or *the good angel*) and that which comes from *the bad angel*, raises the possibility that even consolation might contain deception. Only in 'consolation without preceding cause' is such a possibility precluded, though even here deception can infiltrate the after-affects of consolation [336]. In other kinds of consolation, initial similarities between the authentic and the deceptive can be so close that on their first occurrence the experiences may always contain hidden deceptions which reveal themselves only after further discernment [331, 332]. Hence the rules of the second set establish the principle that we can find God's will through two kinds of consolation, one intrinsically unambiguous, the other requiring the processes of testing (cf. [176] and [184–8]).

Summary of contents

The content of these eight Rules can be summarized as follows:

- Title
- Opening principle (Rule 1)
- Consolation without preceding cause (Rule 2)
- Distinction between 'without cause' and 'with cause' (Rule 3)
- Possible deception in 'consolation with cause' (Rules 4, 5, 6)
- Action of the spirits in relation to the orientation of the person (Rule 7)
- Deception in the afterglow of consolation without cause (Rule 8)

[328] RULES FOR THE SAME PURPOSE, SERVING FOR A MORE ADVANCED DISCERNMENT OF SPIRITS. RULES *MORE APPLICABLE TO THE SECOND WEEK*

more applicable to the Second Week Not on the grounds that the First Week rules are now no longer needed, but because the present rules deal with 'temptation under the appearance of the good' [10]. This is the characteristic temptation of the illuminative way. Only by temptation of this kind is the bad spirit likely to jeopardize the election of a highly motivated exercitant.

Rule 1: Opening principle

[329] [1] *First rule*. **It is characteristic of God and his angels in the movements prompted by them to give** *true gladness and spiritual joy*, **whilst banishing all the sadness and distress brought on by the enemy,** [2] **whose characteristic it is to fight against** *this joy and spiritual consolation* **by bringing forward** *specious arguments, subtleties* **and one fallacy after another.**

The *First Rule* resumes the positions of Rule 2 of the first set in connection with the action of the spirits in those making progress (cf. [315]). The effects of the good spirit in such persons is now epitomized as *true gladness and spiritual joy*. Not all *joy*, however, is *true* as here understood. The words used in the Autograph, *alegria y gozo*, echo the Fourth Week petition [221],

227

in which the exercitant prays for a joy which will be a sharing in the joy of Christ himself.

this joy and spiritual consolation True spiritual joy and spiritual consolation are synonymous.

specious arguments, subtleties On the place of argument in the tactics of the bad spirit against converted people, see comment on [315] above. In the Second Week this tactic can take the form of extremely subtle rationalizations, and it is with these that the present rules are especially concerned.

Rule 2: Consolation without preceding cause

Two main questions are posed by this rule: first, what kind of experience does it describe? and second, does the experience fall within the range of the ordinary or is it of its nature an extraordinary phenomenon?

In answer to the first question, basically the rule refers to a particular spiritual experience, which in the case of a person moving from good to better, Ignatius holds to be an unambiguous sign of God's leading. While its implications reach into the whole of life, the rule envisages immediately the collaborative relationship of the director of the Exercises and the exercitant [22], and its purpose at this stage of the Exercises is to help the exercitant, through the director, to recognize and respond to this experience, should it be given.

The definition contains three characteristics and three only:

- the experience is one of consolation;
- there is no preceding cause;
- the person affected is *drawn entirely into love of the Divine Majesty*

There is nothing about emotional vehemence, and it is not claimed that the experience always communicates a specific conceptual content, a God-given insight, or 'message' or 'call'. There may be such a content or there may not be.[36]

With regard to the second question, neither the present text nor other sources enable us to know Ignatius' own position with certainty.[37] Later atti-

---

[36]In the letter to Teresa Rejadell of 18 June 1536, in connection with an experience which clearly corresponds to 'consolation without cause', Ignatius writes of God as moving a person to 'one action or another' (Cf. MHSI, *Epp. Ig.*, vol. 1, No. 7, pp. 99–107 [trans., *Personal Writings*, p. 133 §15]). Rule 8 below clearly indicates that there are situations when a 'content' is given.

[37]The words 'many times' (*muchas veces*) in the above personal letter is insufficient ground for a general position.

tudes, as might be expected, have ranged across a spectrum. In the past the tendency was to classify the phenomenon as a limit case, virtually without practical relevance.[38] More recently Karl Rahner has interpreted consolation without cause on lines that imply that the experience is an element of ordinary Christian life.[39] On this point Rahner's position is not, however, generally accepted by Ignatian commentators, even if many of them, while not allowing that consolation without cause is an ordinary feature of Christian life,[40] would admit that many sincere and searching Christians may have known it in their lives, usually in quiet and unspectacular ways, but always with profound and lasting effects.[41]

[330] [1] **Second rule. Only God our Lord can give consolation to the soul without preceding cause; for it is the Creator's prerogative** *to enter the soul and leave her,* **and to arouse movements which** *draw her entirely into love of his Divine Majesty.* [2] *When I say 'without cause'* **I mean without any previous perception or understanding of** *some object due to which* **such consolation could come about through the mediation of the person's own acts of understanding and will.**

to enter ... and leave To commence and terminate an action: the verbs are used in the same way of the evil spirit in [332] below. The action thus delimited is precisely that of giving consolation, the action of God in a person's experience.

draw her entirely into love of his Divine Majesty Similar phrases are found in

[38]Coathalem, for example, identifies it with St Theresa's 'prayer of union' or the 'substantial touch' of St John of the Cross. Thus, in connection with Rule 8 below, he writes that 'because the experience < of consolation without cause > is rare, the rule does not seem to have much practical utility', *Ignatian Insights*, pp. 270–1, 276.

[39]In a provocative and complex essay, Karl Rahner sees in this paragraph of the Exercises a foreshadowing of his own theology of grace and the 'first principle of all Ignatian discernment'. The theological concerns behind Rahner's essay (to stress that prayer can actually make a difference to the way we take decisions) are important. But they can be grounded in other Ignatian texts, and the majority of Ignatian specialists do not accept Rahner's exegesis of the present rule. His position is the basis however of Egan's *The Spiritual Exercises and the Ignatian Mystical Horizon*. Rahner's essay is available in English, 'The logic of concrete individual knowledge in Ignatius Loyola', in *The Dynamic Element in the Church*, New York, Herder and Herder (1964), pp. 84–170; for a critique of Rahner, cf. Toner, *Commentary*, pp. 301–13.

[40]For example, 'It seems clear to me that such an experience of God could scarcely be the normal, or even the ideal experience, of us human beings', Green, *Weeds among the Wheat*, p. 130.

[41]A point brought out by Gouvernaire's study of this rule, *Quand Dieu entre à l'improviste*, p. 140. For examples of consolation without cause in ordinary life, see also Green, *Weeds among the Wheat*, pp. 130–32, and Cowan and Futrell, *Handbook*, p. 157.

other texts, which cast light on the consolation that the Exercises denote as 'without cause'. In the letter to Teresa Rejadell already referred to, Ignatius speaks of God as 'raising us entirely to his divine love'; in the *Diary* he writes of 'being drawn wholly to [God's love]' and of 'impulses, sobs and many floods of tears, all drawing me to a love of the Blessed Trinity'.[42] Consolation without cause is not any kind of powerful spiritual experience arising without preliminaries; it is quite specifically an experience of intense and single-intentioned love. Being taken up into God's love is as much a defining characteristic of the experience as is the more abstract-sounding absence of preceding cause.

When I say 'without cause' To discuss in detail the sense of 'without' and 'with' cause would be to enter one of the more debated fields of Ignatian study. But the essential difference between the two experiences is clear. Consolation *with cause* is a proportionate effect of considering, contemplating or reacting to an 'object' (e.g. an idea, a text, an image, a memory, a Gospel incident). It is therefore 'consolation' as the term is ordinarily understood in the Exercises. On the other hand consolation *without cause* does not depend on such an object or activity. It is gratuitous and impossible to induce. Even if it occurs during 'ordinary' prayer with its 'ordinary' consolation, it will be experienced as breaking into this, not as a natural development of it. In relation with anything that might have been already happening, it is discontinuous and disproportionate.[43]

It should be noted that neither the absence of cause nor the characteristic love-quality of this consolation are amenable to precise objective verification. Both are recognized by a spiritually self-aware person in the experience itself; moreover a person unversed in matters of the spirit might easily mistake for such consolation a spiritual experience of a far more ordinary and more ambiguous kind. On the director's side, in order to sense these qualities in an exercitant, a director will draw not only on definitions, but on his or her own experience and discerning sense.

some object due to which In the Versio Prima: 'any object on account of

---

[42] Letter to Teresa Rejadell (MHSI, *Epp. Ig.*, vol. 1, No. 7, pp. 99–107 [trans., *Personal Writings*, p. 133 §15]); *Spiritual Diary* 3 and 7 March 1544); cf. *Personal Writings*, pp. 90, 95.

[43] It is sometimes suggested today that the experience Ignatius describes might have an unrecognized cause in the unconscious. While the unconscious doubtless has its place in some of Ignatius' own experiences (e.g. the serpent visions described in the *Reminiscences* §19, 31 [trans., *Personal Writings*, pp. 21, 27]), with regard to *consolation without preceding cause* two points may be made: first, the possibility of such consolation is not ruled out by the existence of the unconscious; and second, an experience which consists in being wholly drawn to God's love cannot be completely explained by the unconscious mind, since it is incommensurate with such a source.

which the divine consolation might come to us'. In the Vulgate: 'no object which can of itself be the cause of such consolation'.

Rule 3: Distinction between 'without cause' and 'with cause'

[331] [1] Third rule. When there is a *cause*, consolation can be given by the good or the bad angel, but these give consolation for opposite purposes; [2] *the good angel* for the soul's profit, so that the person grows and rises from good to better, [3] *the bad angel* for the contrary purpose, so as eventually to draw the person into his own evil intention and wickedness.

cause Ordinarily God gives consolation through the mediation of a *cause* in the sense explained above. But consolation can be aroused through a *cause* by other agents too, bad as well as good. Consolation *with cause* does not, then, have the transparency of a consolation of the first kind, and the quality of its source may not be instantly clear.

the good angel The assumption that God's ways of communication include the mediation of angels does not imply that normally one can or should recognize whether a movement of consolation is given by an angel or not. But consolation from an angel is a possibility, and Ignatius' insistence on it might be explained, partly at least, by an unwillingness to emphasize too strongly the personal intervention of the Holy Spirit. However this may be, the references to angels in connection with *consolation with cause*, should not lead us to distance the ordinary consolations of life from the Holy Spirit.

the bad angel Consolation can be given by the bad angel, i.e. by playing on a person's love for God, their values and aspirations, their emotional capacity. The same process forms part of the dynamics of rationalization; and through it, too, the manipulative leader, preacher, teacher, or indeed spiritual director arouse consolation for their *own purposes*.

Rules 4 to 6: Possible deception in consolation with cause

The fact that consolation can mask and even endorse a disordered motivation does not justify a generally suspicious attitude towards the experience of consolation. Indeed, such an attitude would work against, rather than promote, the development of habitual discernment. Nevertheless both for his or her overall formation in discernment, and especially for any specific discernment to be made during the Exercises themselves, it is vital that the Second Week exercitant be aware of what the Exercises have to say about deception within consolation and about ways of testing consolation.

[332] **¹ Fourth rule. It is characteristic of the bad angel** *to assume the form of an angel of light,* **in order** *to enter the devoted soul* **by her own way and** *to leave with his own profit.* **² That is to say, he proposes** *good and holy thoughts* **well adapted to such a just soul, and then succeeds little by little in getting his own way, drawing the soul into his hidden snares and his perverted purposes.**

to assume the form of an angel of light An image taken from 2 Corinthians 11:14. It is precisely as consolation – as the desire for, and satisfaction in, God and his service – that the experience induced by the disguised angel of darkness deceives us.

to enter the devoted soul ... to leave with his own profit The effectiveness of this tactic as practised by the enemy led Ignatius to advise apostolic workers to take a leaf from the enemy's book and adopt the same procedure in winning people to God.[44]

good and holy thoughts The Second Week exercitant is a person converted in values and habits of mind, 'Christified' in outlook, yet still subject to disordered motivations. In such a person, these motivations tend to seek concealment under guises that fit the ideals of the converted level of the self. The bad spirit adopts a strategy of rationalization.

[333] **¹** *Fifth rule.* **We must pay close attention to the whole course of our thoughts; if the beginning, middle and end are entirely good and tend towards what is wholly right, this is a sign of the good angel.** **² But if the course of the thoughts suggested to us leads us finally to something bad or distracting, or** *less good* **than what one had previously intended to do, ³ or if in the end the soul is** *weakened, upset or distressed,* **losing the peace, tranquillity and quiet previously experienced – ⁴ all this is a clear sign of the bad spirit, the enemy of our progress and eternal well-being.**

Fifth rule This rule applies to ordinary consolation the principle that a spirit is recognized by its fruits. But the fruits can take time to appear. At first the real quality of an underlying motivation, masked by thoughts in themselves 'good and holy', may be imperceptible.[45] Where deception exists, then, it is identified not in the thoughts we start with; but in a declining process. The

---

[44]Cf. his 'Instructions for the mission to Ireland' entrusted to Salmeron and Broet in 1541, MHSI, *Epp. Ig.*, vol. 1, pp. 179–81 [trans., *Inigo: Letters*, p. 53].

[45]Motivations of the kind that easily go underground in this way include the desire for security, status, or power, or less crudely, for a heroic or saintly self-image. The claim however that these and other 'hidden agendas' are unmasked by

process is described in terms of both thoughts and feelings. Thus the influence of *the bad spirit* can be identified when over a continuous sequence:[46]

(1) *thoughts* seemingly tending *towards what is wholly right*, lead on to other thoughts tending towards the *bad, or distracting or less good*;
(2) what initially gave rise to *feelings* of *peace, tranquillity, and quiet*, now gives rise to being *weakened, upset or distressed*.

less good to be understood as 'less good for me'. In the Vulgate: 'what is of itself evil or diverts from good or impels to a lesser good than the person had previously resolved to do'.

weakened, upset or distressed To avoid misunderstanding this criterion, we must recall again that when Ignatius refers to positive and negative experiences in connection with discernment, the context in which such experiences are to be interpreted is that of the person's overall orientation in regard to God and his will. Since we are dealing here with a positively orientated, 'progressing' person, the 'negative' experience (weakness, disquiet, distress) like the initial positive experience, arises out of the relation between a specific thought or project and such a person's converted desires and values. The thought which was first experienced as being in harmony with these values and desires – and which accordingly gave peace – now in relation to these same desires and values causes loss of peace.

The rule is not dealing with reactions of fear, anxiety or reluctance that might be caused by the difficult or unpleasant personal implications in putting a thought or project into effect. To interpret such reactions may itself require discernment; but the present Rule is not suggesting that reactions of this kind suggest of themselves that the thought or project is not from the good spirit.[47]

---

discernment does not mean that discernment has the same function as psychotherapy. While discernment certainly reveals levels of previously unrecognized motivation already near the surface of consciousness, it does not necessarily open up the deeper realms of unconscious motivation. The prime effect of discernment, then, is to make one aware of a quality and direction in our conscious 'movements' in which we sense the effect of the *bad spirit*. The way in which the bad spirit may be working, through unconscious compulsions or fears, may not be clear from discernment alone, and may emerge only, if at all, through long processes of self-discovery. On these distinctions see Lonsdale, 'The Serpent's tail', Sheldrake, ed., *The Way of Ignatius Loyola*, p. 172.

[46]For examples in Ignatius' own life, see *Reminiscences*, §§26, 54, 55 [trans., *Personal Writings*, pp. 24, 39–40]. Note that continuous sequence should be understood as a series of related events rather than a chronological sequence without gaps. 'There may be minutes, hours, even days between steps in the process', Toner, *Commentary*, p. 233.

[47]There are situations when carrying out a truly discerned decision will lead a person through a Gethsemane-like crisis. However an upsurge of recoil towards something previously desired might sometimes indicate a rashly (as distinct from discerningly) made decision (cf. [14]).

[334] **¹ Sixth rule.** *When* **the enemy of human nature has been detected and recognized by his serpent's tail, and the evil end to which he leads, ² it profits the person who has been tempted by him to retrace immediately the whole sequence of good thoughts he has suggested, looking for their starting-point, ³ and noting how the enemy contrived little by little to make the soul fall away from the state of sweetness and spiritual joy she was in, until he drew her into his own depraved intention. ⁴ By recognizing and taking note of this experience one is put on one's guard for the future against his habitual deceits.**

When the work of the bad spirit has been recognized by its fruits, reflecting back over the whole episode of deception gives insight into the ways of the bad spirit in the dynamics of our motivation. Thus the very experience of being deceived, if reflected upon, contributes to growth in discernment. Again, we are made aware of the value of 'examen', and of the habit of 'reflective living' which the Examen represents.[48]

Rule 7: Action of the spirits in relation to the orientation of the person

Rule 7 reiterates the principle already set out at the beginning of the first series [314, 315], but couches it in language which reflects more a Second Week sensibility of spirit. Possibly the Rule is intended to answer the question that might be prompted by Rules 4 and 5: can it be assumed that if the procedures in these rules are followed, the presence of the deceiving spirit will always be finally detected?[49] Ignatius seems to have held that in the case of a person who is seeking God and becoming growingly sensitive to interior experience – and especially if they have a wise companion in discernment – the answer to that question is 'yes'. To such a person some note of dissonance or unease must in the end betray the deceiver's presence.[50]

[335] **¹ Seventh rule. With those who go from good to better, the good angel touches the soul** *gently, lightly, and sweetly,* **like a drop of water going into a sponge, ² while the bad spirit touches her sharply with**

---

[48]For an example in Ignatius' life: 'And since he now had some experience of the difference in kind of spirits through the lessons God had given him, he began to mull over the means through which the spirit < of scrupulosity > had come', *Reminiscences*, §25 [trans., *Personal Writings*, p. 24].

[49]Cf. Toner, *Commentary*, p. 237 and note.

[50]In some cases, however, this may take considerable time to happen. Moreover the distinction (made in Note 45 above) between the echo of the bad spirit in consciousness and the explicit disclosure of unconscious motivation, must be kept in mind.

noise and disturbance, as when a drop of water falls on a stone. **³ With those who go from bad to worse, these same spirits touch the soul the opposite way. ⁴ The reason for this difference is that the disposition of soul of the person touched is either contrary or similar to these angels: ⁵ when it is contrary, the spirits enter with noise and disturbance, making their presence felt; ⁶ when the disposition is similar, they come in quietly, as one would enter one's own house by an open door.**

gently, lightly, and sweetly Terms used in the Exercises to denote not only pleasant (as opposed to painful) experiences, but the depth and subtlety of spiritual consolation properly so-called. The terms *gently* (*suavemente*) and *sweetly* (*dulce*) recall *suavidad y dulzura*, words with which Ignatius refers to the qualities of the virtuous soul or the sense of the divine [124] in the Prayer of the Senses. Note again the danger of allowing Ignatius' language to distance the Holy Spirit. The effects attributed to the action, under God, of the *good angel*, classically describe the action of the Holy Spirit.[51]

Rule 8: Deception in the 'afterglow' of consolation without cause

Though consolation without preceding cause contains no deception, the experience can leave a kind of 'afterglow', and 'thoughts and plans' which may come to the mind during this time should be distinguished from any content of the consolation itself.

[336] ¹ The eighth rule. When consolation is without cause, even though there is *no deception* in it (since as has been said, it comes solely from God our Lord), ² nevertheless the spiritual person to whom God gives this consolation must scrutinize the experience carefully and attentively, so as to distinguish *the precise time of the actual consolation* from the period following it, ³ during which the soul is still aglow and favoured with the benefits and after-effects of the consolation now passed. ⁴ For during this second period, it often happens that owing either to thinking based on conclusions drawn from the relations between our own concepts and judgements, or to the agency of the good or bad spirits, ⁵ we form various *plans and opinions which are not directly given by God our Lord.* ⁶ These require, therefore, to be *examined with very great care* before being given complete credence and put into practice.

---

[51]For an exposition of the language of this Rule as descriptive of the experience of the Holy Spirit, see Egan, *Mystical Horizon*, p. 123.

no deception That is to say, deception arising from sin, from ambiguity (of intention or of attitude), or from the 'enemy of human nature'. The same word (in Spanish, *engaño*) is used of the works of the latter in [139] (trans. 'deceits'), [326] (trans. 'trickery'), [332] (trans. 'snares'), [334] (trans. 'habitual deceits'). In connection with the deception-free quality of consolation without cause questions come to mind regarding the identification of this consolation that the wording of Rule 2 leaves open: whether, for example, the divine origin of the experience is always explicitly recognized by its recipient, or whether it will sometimes be recognized only with the director's help,[52] or even whether certitude in the matter may sometimes only be that of prudential judgement.[53]

precise time of the actual consolation 'Consolation without cause' terminates with the termination of God's action in giving it.

plans and opinions which are not directly given to us by God our Lord Hence there can also be *plans and opinions* which are given us by God; a *content*, that is to say, so integrally part of the consolation that comes from God that it is known, at least on reflection, to have the same origin.

examined with very great care These developments may arise in various ways: from the person's own trains of thought, from the 'bad spirit', or indeed from the Holy Spirit working in the time immediately following consolation without cause, but not in the same way as during it.

The fact, however, that thoughts arise during the time of the 'after-glow' and are suffused with that glow does not in itself confer special significance on them. The position has returned to that of ordinary discernment. But *very great care* is called for because in this situation it is easy to blur Ignatius' careful distinction between the two phases of experience.[54]

---

[52]In responding to another's account and interpretation of their own experience, the director should be aware that a person can think they have had a self-authenticating experience, and be wrong. Nor should a director be too hasty on his or her side to claim to identify so interior and inadequately describable an experience as 'consolation without cause'. See Green, *Weeds among the Wheat*, p. 134.

[53]In any case the certitudes of religious experience are not of the same kind as those of logic or sense experience. It is interesting to note the blend of conviction and diffidence in which Ignatius tends to express his own certitudes: e.g., 'it was his clear judgement then, and has always been his judgement, that God was dealing with him in this way. On the contrary, were he to doubt this, he would think he was offending his Divine Majesty', *Reminiscences*, §27 [trans., *Personal Writings*, p. 25]. And in one of his Letters, 'If I did not act thus, I would be (and indeed am) quite certain in myself that I would not give a good account of myself before God our Lord' (MHSI, *Epp. Ig.*, vol. IV, No. 2652, pp. 283–5 [trans., *Personal Writings*, p. 245]).

[54]Mention of plans and projects arising in a climate of intense fervour may recall Annotation 14, where the Director is warned of the possibility of an exercitant making hasty or precipitate promises or vows. Though Ignatius is especially concerned there

In this last rule Ignatius is still concerned with the ways in which consolation is undermined by elusive forms of deception. In the ordinary case of 'consolation with cause' deception can be present in the very inception of consolation; but even in the case of a consolation coming directly from God deception can infiltrate the thoughts and feelings subsequent to consolation.[55]

---

with the exercitant of unstable character, the generous impulses, which he sees as calling for careful consideration before being acted on, could be a case of deception within the afterglow of consolation without cause.

[55]The principle embodied in this rule is relevant to other situations than the one immediately envisaged, e.g., to the interpretation of mystical literature. See Coathalem, *Ignatian Insights*, pp. 276-7.

RULES FOR ALMSGIVING

Rules 1 to 6: Almsgiving and rules for election

Composed during Ignatius' Paris years, the Rules for Almsgiving deal with some of the concrete implications of the reform and amendment of life in the sixteenth-century Church and society. Rules 1 to 7 are addressed to clerics charged with the ministry of distributing ecclesiastical revenues (from benefices or foundations) in alms. The use of this ministry to divert the goods of the Church to personal or family advantage was rife in the Middle Ages,[1] and still prevalent in the time of Ignatius. The present rules are concerned, however, with subtle rather than gross abuses; they make the point that almsgiving is a ministry to be exercised at the highest level of love, a ministry which demands sensitive and conscientious discernment and the constant application of the doctrine of the Exercises on election and the reform of life.

The final rule turns to the responsibility of every Christian towards the materially poor, and specifically to the consequences of this responsibility in the matter of choices bearing on one's personal standard of life.[2]

[337] RULES TO BE OBSERVED *IN THE MINISTRY* OF ALMSGIVING

in the ministry The Vulgate translates: 'Some rules to observe in the distribution of alms', omitting the reference to 'ministry', and thus widening the scope of these rules from the outset.

[338] [1] **First rule. If I distribute alms to relations or friends, or to persons to whom I am attached, I should consider *four things* of which some mention has already been made in connection with the election.**

[1]A vehement passage in Ludolph's *Life of Christ* castigates use of the goods of the Church to advance the prosperity of one's relations, and especially to provide dowries. 'These goods are the patrimony of Christ, everything beyond what is necessary for personal maintenance, food and clothing, belongs to the poor, and to take this patrimony from the poor is a sacrilege.'

[2]The rule thus touches on the themes of justice and the preferential option for the poor. Its perspective, however, is that of its age. Ignatius' basic concept is the charitable practice of almsgiving, rather than the more radical concept of a justice that challenges the very structures and the ways of distributing wealth in society.

² **Firstly, the love which moves me and makes me give the alms should descend from above, from the** *love of God our Lord*; ³ **so I must first of all feel within myself that the love, greater or lesser, that I have for these people is for God and that in my motive for loving them more, God must shine forth.**

four things This and the three rules following are a precise application of the Second Way of making an Election in the Third Time. [184–187]

love of God our Lord The norm here given does not exclude the immediate human love we may experience for relatives or those close to us. But our immediate loves can be relied upon to guide us, and not to eclipse other claims, only in so far as they are taken up into, and transformed by, the love which *descends from above* [237]. The integration of the former love into the latter is the main theme of these rules.[3]

[339] ¹ **Second rule. Secondly, I should look at the case of someone whom I have never seen or known,** ² **and for whom I desire full perfection in their ministry and state of life. The norm which I would like such a person to observe in the way of distributing alms, for the greater glory of God our Lord and for their greater perfection of soul,** ³ **I myself shall keep to, acting in the same way, neither more nor less. So I will observe the rule and norm I would want for someone else and which I judge to be appropriate.**

[340] ¹ **Third rule. Thirdly, I should consider, supposing I were at the point of death, what procedure and what norm I would then wish to have followed in the duties of my administration;** ² **taking that as my rule, I should put it into practice in my particular acts of distribution.**

[341] ¹ **Fourth rule. Fourthly, I should look at my situation on the Day of Judgement, and think well how at that moment I would want to have fulfilled my duties and responsibilities in this ministry;** ² **the rule which I would then want to have observed I shall adopt now.**

[342] ¹ **Fifth rule. When one feels a preference and attachment for the persons to whom one wants to give alms,** ² **one should stop and carefully ponder the four rules just given, using them to examine and test one's attachment.** ³ **The alms should not be given until in keeping with these rules one's disordered attachment has been rejected and got rid of.**

---

[3]On this and other points made in the above comments, see Kolvenbach, 'Preferential Love for the Poor'.

[343] **¹ Sixth rule. There is no fault in taking the goods of God our Lord for distribution, when one is called by our God and Lord to such a ministry. The possibility of fault or excess can arise, ² however, in regard to *the amount and proportion that one should appropriate and allot to oneself* out of goods held for donation to others. ³ So it is always possible to *reform one's life and state* by means of *the above rules*.**

the amount and proportion that one should appropriate and allot to oneself In the Vulgate: 'in deciding the just proportion for one's own expenses'.

reform one's life and state Emphasis shifts from the particular decisions about almsgiving to the life-style of the almsgiver.

the above rules I.e. the foregoing resumption of [184–187], together with the principles of the section on the 'reform and amendment of one's personal life and state' in [189].

Rule 7: The 'Golden Rule' and the imitation of Christ

The final rule opens up a wider perspective, in which central themes of the Exercises – conversion of heart, personal poverty, the imitation of Christ, commitment to one's 'state' – are brought to bear on the service of the materially poor. Three sections are easily recognized: (1) the 'Golden Rule' [189], (2) application to bishops, (3) application to all Christians.

[344] **¹ Seventh rule. For the foregoing reasons, as well as many others, in what touches ourselves and our standard of living we will always do better and be more secure ² *the more we cut down and reduce expenses* and *the closer we come to our High Priest, our model and rule, Christ our Lord*. ³ It was in this spirit that *the Third Council of Carthage* (at which St Augustine was present) *decided and decreed that the furniture of a bishop should be ordinary and cheap*.**
⁴ The same consideration applies *to all walks of life*, adapted and with account taken of the circumstances and state of persons. ⁵ Thus, for marriage we have the example of *St Joachim and St Anne*, who divided their means into three parts; the first they gave to the poor, the second to the ministry and service of the Temple, the third they took for the support of themselves and of their household.[4]

[4]A detail derived from the Apocryphal Gospel of Matthew, and incorporated into the *Golden Legend*, trans., William Granger Ryan (Princeton University Press, 1993).

the more we cut down and reduce expenses The rule is concerned with the specific material implications of the universal principle, the 'Golden Rule', enunciated in [189]: progress will be in the measure that one puts off 'self-love, self-will and self-interest'.

the closer we come to our High Priest, our model and rule, Christ our Lord The reference to the imitation of Christ, implicit in [189], is here made explicit.

the Third Council of Carthage The rule is given an ecclesial dimension. The decree of the Council represents the 'mind of the Church' in relation to those who exercise office in the Church.

decided and decreed that the furniture of a bishop should be ordinary and cheap The key to the 'mind' here expressed is found in the significance of Jesus' poverty precisely as his way of exercising his office as High Priest. Imitation of Christ in poverty is therefore particularly apt for those who possess the fullness of the ministerial priesthood. But the imitation of Christ's way by 'reducing expenses' is a matter not only of personal union or of general witness. The context of the rule is almsgiving. Personal life-style is linked with the service of the poor.

all walks of life Irrespective of 'state in life', use of resources must always meet the demands of Christian responsibility to the poor. By extending to everyone – albeit for 'adaptation' – the standard commended to prelates, the rule insists that for every Christian with material or financial resources, responsibility to the poor will have consequences for their own standard of living.

St Joachim and St Anne These are the apocryphal names of the parents of our Lady. For the devout of Ignatius' time these would have been real and familiar people in a way the modern reader might find hard to understand, all the more real and familiar because among the comparatively few exemplars of ordinary married life among the saints.

NOTES ON SCRUPLES

Though one of the last sections to be added to the text, the Notes on Scruples, like the Rules for Discernment, to which they form a complement, have their source in Ignatius' conversion and its sequel. They also reflect his long experience of ministry and direction.

The notes are intended as a practical resource for those who run into the experience of scruples, especially during the Exercises.[1] As modern commentators[2] have pointed out, however, scrupulosity can be more complex than these notes might lead a reader to believe. Nowadays, directors should especially be aware that although scruples do not necessarily have a pathological component, an adequate treatment of the subject would need to recognize this possibility. But the Notes on Scruples provide valuable guidance in a number of respects – in defining the term, in commenting on the hypersensitivity of conscience common in the early stages of conversion, in dealing with different states of conscience on the principle of agendo contra, and in their approach to the particular kind of scruple described in Note 6.

[345] *THE FOLLOWING NOTES* WILL BE HELPFUL IN IDENTIFYING AND UNDERSTANDING SCRUPLES AND THE *INSINUATIONS* OF OUR ENEMY

The following notes The word 'rules' used in [210, 313, 328, 352], is replaced by the less definite term 'notes'. Only two of these Notes (the Fifth and Sixth) are 'rules for conduct'.

insinuations In Spanish, *suasiones*; the same word is used in [326] of the inducements of a false lover.

---

[1]In the Exercises, the need for help with scruples is, of course, especially likely to arise in the First Week. It is noteworthy however that the *Directories* which mention this section insist unanimously that it is to be given to an exercitant only if and when necessary, not as a matter of course (see MHSI 76, pp. 292, 404, 458, 535, 541, 742–3 [trans., Palmer, pp. 127, 180, 215, 266, 270, 346]).

[2]E.g. Coathalem, *Insights*, p. 291, Fleming, *Exercises*, p. 86.

Notes 1 to 3: The nature of a scruple

[346] **¹ First note. People commonly give the name of 'scruple' to something coming from our own judgement and freedom, i.e. a situation when *I freely take something to be sin* which is not a sin, ² as would be the case if a person having accidentally trodden on a cross³ formed by two straws were to make the personal judgement that a sin had been committed. Properly speaking, this is an *error of judgement*, not a scruple in the true sense.**

I freely take something to be a sin I.e. on the basis of information or principles I make a conscious personal judgement that something is a sin.

error of judgement Such an error of judgement would have to be based either on false information, or a mistaken application of a general moral principle. Judgements are not marked by doubt. A judgement, whether mistaken or not, produces conviction, unless or until the judgement itself is challenged by new arguments or data. The scruple, on the other hand, is essentially an experience of doubt.

[347] **¹ Second note. After I have trodden on that cross, or indeed after anything I may have thought, said or done, the idea may come to me *from outside* myself *that I have sinned*, while on the other hand *it seems to me that I have not sinned*. ² However, I feel *disturbed* about the matter, at the same time *doubting and not doubting*. It is this which is a 'scruple' properly so called, and a temptation suggested by the enemy.**

from outside I.e. coming unbidden into the mind, as distinct from arising out of our conscious and free judgement based on evidence or argument. Today, we might prefer to say that such a thought comes from 'somewhere inside ourselves'.[4]

the idea ... that I have sinned I.e. a thought lacking reasonable basis yet invasive and disturbing.

it seems to me that I have not sinned Despite the suggestions to the contrary, there appear to the person tempted no reasonable grounds for thinking they have sinned.

³In sixteenth-century Spain, treading on the cross was a way of declaring apostasy.
[4]See note on [32] above.

disturbed For a sense of the kind of experience that might be denoted by the word 'disturbed', see Ignatius' account of his own searing ordeal of scrupulosity at Manresa.[5]

doubting and not doubting In a real scruple the characteristic disturbance of feeling arises from a conflict within the mind itself, which doubts, but at the same time does not doubt, because it is still able, even though in conflict and deprived of security and peace, to hold to the reasonable opinion that sin has not been committed.[6]

[348] [1] Third note. *The first scruple*, mentioned in the First Note, *is much to be abhorred*, being as it is a total error. But for a soul committed to the spiritual life, the second, mentioned in the Second Note, is of *no small benefit* for a time. [2] Indeed, to a great extent, it cleanses and purifies such a person, separating his or her spirit far from anything with even the appearance of sin. As St Gregory says, 'It is the mark of a good soul to see a fault where none exists.'

The first scruple is much to be abhorred On this Polanco expresses himself strongly. If an exercitant considers some act to be sinful which actually is not, they 'should not only be set right with regard to the particular error but also warned against being so quick to make this kind of judgement in the future. The reason for this (apart from the useless torment of conscience over past actions) is that in acting against such a conscience, even though the action were objectively not sinful, they would be committing sin.'[7]

no small benefit Scrupulosity is often present at times of conversion, or at transition points in spiritual growth, as was the case with Ignatius himself. In these situations, scrupulous doubt can promote a sharpening of moral sensibility, while the characteristic disturbance of scruples can strengthen faith and trust. However an episode of scrupulosity can be of profit only in so far as it is part of a movement towards the eventual mean between the insensitive and the over-sensitive conscience (see Note 5 below).

Notes 4 and 5: The coarse and the sensitive conscience[8]

[349] [1] Fourth note. The enemy observes whether a person is of coarse

[5]*Reminiscences*, §§20–25 [trans., *Personal Writings*, pp. 22–4].
[6]Ignatius is assuming that a person afflicted by scruples is capable, even if with difficulty, of distinguishing these two levels. For a scrupulous person in a pathological anxiety state the distinction itself breaks down.
[7]*Directories*, Polanco (MHSI 76, p. 326 [trans., Palmer, pp. 147–8]).
[8]The doctrine of this section is also to be found in the letter of 18 June 1536 to Teresa Rejadell, written at about the time Ignatius was composing the Notes on Scruples in the form in which they appear in the Exercises; cf. *Personal Writings*, p. 132.

or sensitive conscience. If the conscience is sensitive already, he attempts to sensitize it further, to the point of excess, in order the more easily to cause trouble and confusion. [2] He may see, for instance, that a person consents neither to mortal nor to venial sin, nor to anything that looks like a deliberate sin at all, [3] and in such cases, unable to make such a person fall into anything that seems to be a sin, he endeavours to make them see sin where there is none, as in some word or passing thought.

[4] But if the conscience is coarse, the enemy attempts to coarsen it still further. [5] For example, if up to now someone took no account of venial sins he will try to make that person take little account of mortal sins, and in the case of a person who up to now took some account of them, he will try to diminish the sense of venial sin or eliminate it completely.

[350] [1] Fifth Note. The person who wishes to make progress in the spiritual life must always go in the opposite direction to that of the enemy; [2] that is to say, if the enemy wants to make the conscience coarser, one should seek to become more sensitive; [3] and likewise if the enemy tries to refine the conscience, in order to bring it to excess, one should seek to *establish a position in the just mean* so as to be entirely at peace.

establish a position in the just mean On the principle of 'going against' a temptation or disordered tendency precisely in order to establish a mean see [13, 321, 325] and below [351].

Note 6: A particular case

The final case of scrupulosity consists not in doubt about the moral quality of a past action, but about the quality of one's motivation in wishing to take a course of action perceived as good in itself and approved. The note is especially relevant to apostolic ministry, and illustrates the importance for Ignatius of not allowing any aspect of the service of the Kingdom to be jeopardized by specious self-doubt.

[351] [1] Sixth note. *A good person of this kind* may wish *to say or do something in accord with the Church and with the mind of authorities*, something which *promotes the glory of God*; [2] and in these circumstances a thought, or rather a temptation, may come from without not to say or do that thing, a thought proposing specious arguments about *vainglory* or *something similar*. In that case, one should *raise the understanding to one's Creator and Lord*, [3] and if one sees that the

245

proposed action is for God's due service, or at least not against it, *act in a way diametrically opposed to the temptation – like St Bernard* in his answer to a similar temptation, 'I did not begin because of you, and I am not going to give up because of you'.

A good person of this kind A conscientious and spiritually sensitive person, aware of their own sinfulness and capacity for self-deception.

to say or do something While 'something' admits of extremely wide application, an activity Ignatius had specially in mind was preaching, as the concluding reference to St Bernard makes clear.

in accord with the Church and with the mind of authorities Literally, 'within the Church and within the understanding of our superiors'; the same phrase is used in [170]; *promotes the glory of God*. In deciding whether a project is for the glory of God, one looks not only to personal spiritual benefit, but also to the effects of an action in advancing God's Kingdom in the world. To the extent to which these three overlapping criteria are met, the rightness and appropriateness of the act in itself are clear.

vainglory The temptation that constitutes the scruple is not to vainglory itself, but to the false humility through which fear of vainglory might inhibit a person from doing something good.[9]

something similar E.g. the fear of presuming on God, which on one occasion tempted Ignatius to abandon a project he saw to be good.[10] Other ways in which scrupulous people might decline a good action out of fear of a wrong motive will come easily to mind.

raise the understanding to one's Creator and Lord Hence, turn the mind away from arguments recognized as spurious; one does not further scrutinize or debate with such arguments. Action however is based on a prayer in which the rightness of the action and its consistency with God's service are recognized before God and chosen as motivation.

act in a way diametrically opposed to the temptation Cf. [350] above, and [325].

---

[9]On false humility, see the letter to Teresa Rejadell, *Personal Writings*, pp. 130–32. On the subject of vainglory, Ignatius remembered how on the eve of his departure from Spain, he kept secret his plan to go to Jerusalem 'for fear of vainglory', *Reminiscences*, §36 [trans., *Personal Writings*, p. 30].
[10]*Reminiscences*, §79 [trans., *Personal Writings*, p. 51].

like St Bernard The incident referred to is described in the *Golden Legend*: 'Once when he was preaching to the people and they were paying devout attention to his every word, a tempting thought crept into his mind: "Now you're preaching at your best and people are listening to you willingly, and they all esteem you as a wise man." But the man of God, feeling himself beset by this idea, paused for a moment and thought whether he should go on with his sermon or end it. At once, strengthened by God's help, he silently answered the Tempter: "You had nothing to do with my beginning to preach, and nothing you can do will make me stop", and calmly continued to the end of his sermon.'[11]

---

[11]*The Golden Legend*, pp. 103–4.

TOWARDS A TRUE ATTITUDE OF MIND WITHIN THE CHURCH

Ignatius' writings are undergirded by a sense of the Church of which the significance is not to be measured by the frequency of explicit ecclesial references in the Exercises. These are indeed few, and only in the concluding rules is the subject of the Church treated systematically.[1]

The rules must be read in an awareness of their purpose and essential method. Their purpose is to inculcate in the exercitant, and provide norms for recognizing in others, a *sentido*, or fundamental ecclesial attitude, and Ignatius achieves this mainly by illustrating how such a *sentido* will express itself in relation to certain contentious issues especially alive in the age of the Reformation.[2] In his ways of dealing with these we sense Ignatius responding to, and holding in balance, three dimensions of the Church: the Church as transcendent reality of faith; the Church as an organic institution possessing authority in doctrine and discipline; the Church as a human society subject, like any other human society, to challenge and threat from outside and to inner tensions, ambivalence and sinfulness.

Though carrying the imprint of their historical origins, the rules can nevertheless provide a distinctive, and indeed distinctively Ignatian, resource for people seeking a true attitude in the Church today; but in this they can be hindered by various mistaken uses and interpretations. Thus it is a mistake to think that every time the rules commend a general attitude, they intend to remove personal freedom and discernment from the handling of specific

---

[1]The implicit ecclesiology of the Exercises, and indeed of the whole of Ignatian spirituality, is developed by Hugo Rahner on the basis of the incarnational principle that 'spirit always tends towards flesh, and that the movement of God's spirit means incarnation and building up the body of Christ', *Ignatius the Theologian*, ch. vi, 'The Spirit and the Church', p. 214. Outside the rules the word 'Church' is found in the Eighteenth Annotation (commending prayer on the precepts of the Church) and four times in connection with the objective boundaries of personal choice, cf. [18, 170, 177, 229, 351].

[2]The rules commend particularly 'those things which the heretics of our time, or those showing affinity to their doctrine, are prone to attack or scorn in their books or sermons or conversations', *Directory, Polanco* (MHSI 76, p. 327 [trans., Palmer, p. 148]).

cases.[3] It is also a mistake to regard the rules as opening up the entire scope of Ignatius' ecclesial vision and concern.[4]

More importantly, the rules must be considered today in relation to the interplay between the continuous and the new that constitutes development in the Church. Their potential is therefore particularly subverted by uses or interpretations that disregard subsequent expansions of the Church's own self-understanding, the numerous differences between today's Church and world and those which were the context of the rules. If the rules are to help people today, they must help them find right attitudes in a church whose self-understanding contains the themes of People of God, ecumenism,[5] and dialogue between Church and world. Today theological exploration reaches far beyond Ignatius' horizons, and the climate of thought is affected by exposure to, and dialogue with, cultures other than that of the sixteenth century. In this situation the rules cannot provide a completely adequate guide to the formation of a contemporary ecclesial mind, but make their distinctive contribution to this as one resource among others.

In what might this contribution consist? For a person unevasively seeking a contemporary ecclesial attitude, but at the same time open to tradition, the rules can bring a wide range of insights, challenges or practical norms. In order to find these it seems best to approach the rules on the lines of the Second Annotation, as material in which the discerning individual makes his or her own discoveries. It should be stressed however that the rules derive their value not only from points of detail, but from their witness to an overall cast of mind, and in this connection it should be noticed that while in many respects utterly uncompromising, they are also characterized by a positive and non-condemnatory pervasive tone, by sobriety, by the sense of nuance, and by openness to both sides of an issue. For all their defensiveness of purpose, the rules bear no trace of the acrimony that was a dominant trait of theological controversy at the time of Ignatius, and is seldom far from the controversies of our own.

---

[3]Thus Rule 3 did not inhibit Ignatius from trying to have singing and the organ banned in Jesuit churches. That the proposal was turned down by Paul III does not alter the fact that Ignatius saw nothing contradictory about wanting in the case of the Society of Jesus to diverge substantially from a liturgical style generally commended by his rules (cf. Introduction to Rules 2–9, footnote).

[4]A person with only the present rules to go on would be unaware of ecclesial concerns which appear even in the Exercises (such as ambition for benefices); they would have only a limited grasp of Ignatius' missionary vision. In fact neither in the Exercises nor elsewhere does Ignatius provide a complete formulation of his vision of the Church, nor indeed would he have been capable of doing so. Cf. Philip Endean, 'Ignatius and Church Authority', *The Way, Supplement* 70 (1991), p. 79.

[5]One significant outcome of ecumenism has been the development of an interfaith dimension of the ministry of the Exercises.

Practical questions

While some exercitants might benefit from a totally unaided reading of it, the text of Ignatius' rules ordinarily needs to be presented with some form of guidance or interpretation. There are two ways of doing this: (1) The literal text is offered together with a basic accompanying commentary and explanation; (2) the rules are given in an adapted form, preserving the essentials of the Ignatian text while omitting or altering points of detail.[6]

Which of these approaches is best suited in a particular case will depend on the capacity of the individual concerned. Both should be distinguished however from another procedure, which consists in constructing completely new rules, inspired by those of Ignatius, yet quite different from them and designed expressly to meet current circumstances.[7] Difficult as it is today to draw up a set of universally applicable rules,[8] contemporary rules can obviously be of considerable worth, both in their own right and as a complement to the rules of Ignatius. But only in his own rules does Ignatius speak for himself, and they are significant precisely for this reason.[9]

It may be asked whether the rules should always be proposed in the course of the Exercises themselves. Certainly the Exercises cannot be made authentically except in a consciousness of the Church; but this need not always be the kind of consciousness required by the rules. This indeed is acknowledged in the *Directories*, which insist that the rules should be given not as a matter of course, but only to those who need them,[10] either for their own 'reformation of life',[11] or – and more especially – for dealing with situations of religious contention after the Exercises.[12] While individual need is in the end identified through discerning judgement, it can be said in principle that recourse to the rules within the Exercises is the more appropriate the

[6]As done by Fleming, *The Spiritual Exercises*, pp. 231–37.

[7]For an example of rules expressly composed for the twentieth century, see Örsy, 'On being one with the Church today'.

[8]Avery Dulles suggests that given the diversity of situations in which the Church now exists across the world, it would hardly be possible today 'to draw up a single set of rules that would guard against the many threats to the integrity of Catholic Christianity': see 'The Ignatian *sentire cum ecclesia* today', pp. 32–3.

[9]It might eventually be helpful for a person to articulate his or her own ecclesial *sentido* in the form of a personal equivalent of Ignatius' rules, but such an exercise presupposes some kind of dialogue with sources, and it is with these that we are concerned here.

[10]*Directories, Polanco* (MHSI 76, p. 292 [trans., Palmer, p. 127]), *Miró* (ibid., p. 404 [p. 180]), *1599* (ibid., pp. 712–3 [p. 346]).

[11]When made with a view to reformation of life the Rules were given at the appropriate place in the Second Week: cf. *Directories* (MHSI 76, pp. 436, 458 [trans., Palmer, pp. 201, 215]).

[12]*Directories, Mercurian* (MHSI 76, p. 248 [trans., Palmer, p. 104]), *Polanco* (ibid., p. 327 [148]), *Dávila* (ibid., p. 529 [p. 264]).

more the exercitant's relationship with the Church emerges in the Exercises as an issue integral to the processes of conversion or election. If brought into the Exercises, the rules should serve as matter for a discerning reflection, which in turn becomes matter for the dialogue between exercitant and director. And the director should recognize that this dialogue calls for discernment of the quality of his or her own *sentido* in relation to the Church, in so far as this might influence them precisely as director. [13]

But if the rules may not always figure in the Exercises themselves, they are also a resource for life outside the Exercises, for study, teaching, discussion, reflection on the interactions within a faith-community, and other modes of ecclesial formation which have no place in the Twentieth Annotation retreat. In all these situations the underlying principles of the rules and their overall outlook, if blended with other aids and resources, have a distinctive contribution to make to the sometimes complex and difficult processes through which the Spirit works in forming attitudes in and towards the Church in our own time.

Summary of contents

The rules fall into two distinct categories:

(1) pivotal rules, dealing with the nature of the Church, its authority and the response called forth by this authority (Rules 1, 9b, 11);
(2) Rules commending practical attitudes in relation to specific institutions, usages, situations, points of doctrine.

The contents may thus be outlined as follows:

– Title
– Nature of the Church: Spouse, Mother, Hierarchical
    Basic disposition of the member (Rule 1)
– Elements of traditional piety,
    the sacraments,
    the life of the counsels,
    liturgy, devotions (Rules 2 to 8)
    The basic attitude restated (Rule 9)
– Kinds of authority (Rules 10 to 12)

[13]Since exercitants from both ends of the radical-conservative spectrum can experience problematic personal relationships with the institutional Church, and since the same is true of directors, the director must be capable of being present to strong feelings in another person that might be deeply at variance with his or her own.

- Re-statement of basic attitude, and a test case (Rule 13)
- The Mind of the Church in Three Issues: predestination, faith, grace
  Positions to be adopted in preaching and catechesis (Rules 14 to 17)
- Love and Fear: Note on motivation (Rule 18)

< RULES FOR THINKING WITH THE CHURCH > [14]
[352] RULES TO FOLLOW IN VIEW OF THE TRUE *ATTITUDE OF MIND* THAT
WE OUGHT TO MAINTAIN *IN THE CHURCH MILITANT*

attitude of mind translates the Spanish *sentido*. In the vocabulary of Ignatius the word carries multiple connotations, which include intellectual perception and insight, but go beyond the domain of the intellectual into that of intuition, feeling, inclination. Here it refers to the basic attitude that affects the ways one habitually thinks, feels and behaves in relation to the Church.

in the Church militant The word *in*, suggestive more of a relationship of participation, is replaced in the Vulgate by 'with', which suggests more an external relationship of conformity.[15] *Church militant* in its broadest sense designates the Church on earth, hence the Church as visible and more specifically as existing in conflict, both as a body and in its individual members, with the 'enemy of human nature'. In the context of the spirituality of Ignatius, the term evokes especially the missionary Church, engaging her members actively in the struggle for the salvation of the world.[16] While the rules themselves convey little of the missionary vision as it appears in the Kingdom exercise or in the foundational documents of the Society of Jesus, they are addressed primarily to people in apostolic ministries: preaching, teaching, conversation. In the Vulgate, *Church militant* becomes 'the orthodox Church'.

Rule 1: Nature of the Church: the basic attitude of the member

[353] *First rule.* **Laying aside all judgement of our own, we should keep our minds *disposed and ready* to obey in *everything the true bride of Christ our Lord, which is our holy mother the hierarchical Church.***

[14]The familiar English form of the title, 'Rules for Thinking with the Church' is inspired by, but does not exactly correspond to, the Vulgate translation. It has the merit of providing a conveniently concise way of designating the text, but can be misleading unless interpreted in relation to Ignatius' own more prolix title.

[15]Of the two versions, the Vulgate is slightly more authoritarian and defensive in tone throughout.

[16]Buckley, 'Ecclesial Mysticism', p. 443.

First rule The opening rule has been described as a kind of 'Principle and Foundation' for all that follows.[17] Its implications will be clarified in Rules 9 and 13.

disposed and ready describe attitude.

everything, namely Church teaching as well as matters of practice and discipline.

the true bride of Christ our Lord ... our holy mother the hierarchical Church
The two images of spouse[18] and mother, standing respectively for the Church's relationship to Christ and to ourselves, express the 'mystery' of the Church. For Ignatius they were powerful images with strong affective overtones, and together they establish the characteristic 'filial' quality of his ecclesial spirituality. *Hierarchical*, like *militant*, denotes the visible church, but now in its inner structure. To understand Ignatius' attitude towards the Church as hierarchical it is important to realize that for him all created reality (the angels, human society, the cosmos itself) is hierarchical.[19] While he recognizes that the Church, precisely as hierarchical, is always in need of reform and authority always liable to abuse, for him the hierarchical character of the Church is in itself the particular way in which the Church is endowed with a structure written by God into all creation.[20] The words 'bride', 'mother' and 'hierarchical' come together again in Rule 13 [365]. The Versio Prima adds to *hierarchical Church* the clause 'which is the Roman Church', an addition to be understood not as distinguishing the 'Roman' from 'non-Roman' Churches, but as further accentuating the material and visible dimension of the Church.

Rules 2 to 9: Elements of traditional piety

The wide-ranging contents of this section cover matters in varying degrees

---

[17]Coathelem, *Ignatian Insights*, p. 350.

[18]For the sponsal image of the Church, cf. especially Eph. 5:21–23, Rev. 21:2.

[19]See his expositions of obedience in his letters, e.g. *Personal Writings*, pp. 20, 31 (Letters 20, 31).

[20]It should also be noted that in the present rules the word 'hierarchical' refers to a quality of the Church as a whole, not exclusively to particular holders of authority within the Church (cf. Corella, *Sentir la Iglesia*, Bilbao [1995], p. 91). Indeed it is claimed by Yves Congar that the term 'hierarchical Church', as distinct from 'hierarchy of the Church', may actually originate with Ignatius: see *L'Eglise de S. Augustin à l'Epoque Moderne*, Paris (1970), p. 369. A contemporary reading of Ignatius' Rules must of course place his emphasis on the hierarchical Church in relation to the wider portrayal of the Church set out by the Constitution *Lumen Gentium*, and especially in relation to the images of the Body and the People of God.

integral to the tradition of Catholic Christianity, together with a number of adventitious institutions and usages, many of which have since disappeared. Though at first sight a somewhat random selection, they have three things in common: each institution or usage mentioned (i) enjoys the sanction of the hierarchical Church, (ii) is a point of contention in the religious climate of the time, and (iii) forms or formed part of the *de facto* symbol-structure of Catholic Christianity.

Since faith is and must be incarnated in concrete symbols, Ignatius can assume that a person with a true ecclesial attitude will tend to act and feel positively towards the approved symbols which at a particular time embody and promote the faith and devotion of the ordinary believer.[21]

Positive acting and feeling are epitomized in the concept of 'praise', one of the key-words of the rules (cf. [355, 356, 357, 358, 359, 360, 361, 362, 363, 370]). As a form of action, praise consists in 'speaking well of'; as a way of feeling it consists in a preference for approval against censure. It is the antithesis of habitual cynicism. In its highest form, it is the integration of our attitude towards a creature into the praise given to God himself (cf. [22]). The emphasis placed by the rules on praise does not mean, of course, that praise may in any degree extend to the realm of the corrupt and sinful (see Rule 10 below). Nor does it mean that one might not in particular cases depart from a general and normative practice while continuing to praise it.[22]

[354] Second rule. We should praise confession made to a priest. We should also praise the reception of the blessed sacrament once a year, much more its reception once a month, and very much more its reception once a week, given the duly required dispositions.

[355][1] Third rule. We should praise frequent attendance at Mass; also hymns, psalms, and long prayers, whether in or out of church;[2] and likewise, the appointment of fixed times for all divine services, prayers and the canonical hours.

[21]Ignatius is concerned to defend religious culture as a stable heritage, rather than to acknowledge the need of a living group not only to remain in continuity with its past but also to part with obsolete symbols while developing new ones. To expect him to have taken any other position in the present rules would be to misunderstand the situation in which the rules were composed. Today, needless to say, a right ecclesial sentiment includes a positive attitude to both tradition and change.

[22]Thus, while abandoning for themselves the monastic habit and penances of rule, the first Jesuits insist that they 'praise and admire these greatly in those who observe them'. Similarly they insist that the chant, singing, and the use of the organ, from which they sought dispensation for themselves 'laudably enhance the divine service of other clerics and religious'. For the text of the *Prima Instituti Summa*, where these details are to be found, see MHSI, *Monumenta Constitutionum Praevia*, pp. 1–7. An English translation is available in Futrell, *Making an Apostolic Community of Love*, pp. 188–94.

[356] Fourth rule. We should praise greatly religious life, virginity and continence, and we should not praise marriage to the same extent as these.

[357] [1] **Fifth rule.** We should praise the vows of religion – obedience, poverty and chastity – and other vows of perfection made voluntarily.
[2] It should be noted, however, that since a vow has to do with things which lead to *evangelical perfection*, one ought not to make a vow in matters which withdraw from it, for instance to go into business or to marry.

evangelical perfection For the sense of this concept, see commentary on [135] above.

[358] Sixth rule. We should praise the relics of the saints, venerating the relics, and praying to the saints themselves, and we should also praise the stations, pilgrimages, indulgences, jubilees, *crusade bulls* and the lighting of candles in churches.

crusade bulls Such a 'bull' was a dispensation from fasting and abstinence in return for alms; originally this was a dispensation granted to those taking part in crusades. It is of interest to compare this with [42], where the practice is included among usages which it might be morally wrong to fail to observe oneself, or encourage others to neglect. Two reasons were there advanced for this position: the intrinsic piety of the practices themselves but also the fact that they are commended by authority. While Ignatius will certainly have considered the practices 'pious', we also see in his stress on this particular detail a more general concern to defend where possible an approved element of existing culture. However in both the Versio Prima and the Vulgate the references to *crusade bulls* are omitted. The Vulgate concludes with the addition: 'and all the other things of this kind which help piety and devotion'.

[359] Seventh rule. We should praise the decrees concerning fasts and abstinences, such as those of Lent, the *ember days*, vigils, Fridays and Saturdays; and similarly penances, not only interior but *exterior*.

ember days These were the fast days (Wednesday, Friday and Saturday) marking the beginning of each of the four seasons.

exterior penance Cf. note on [82] above.

[360] Eighth rule. We should praise church buildings and their decorations[23] and also images, which should be venerated for what they represent.

[361] Ninth rule. *Finally*, **we should** *praise* **all the precepts of the Church, keeping the mind ready to** *seek arguments in their defence* **and never in any way to attack them.**

Finally The preceding rules form a section of their own which Rule 9 brings to a conclusion.

praise ... seek arguments in their defence The principle of Rule 1 is here resumed, but the slant is now pastoral and apologetic. In the climate of the times, the desire to obey (the focus of Rule 1) will engender the desire to defend and will exclude any public criticism or dissent.[24] In the Vulgate the rule is placed explicitly in the context of the Reformation and its contentions: 'to uphold in the fullest degree all the precepts of the Church and not to attack them in any way, but to defend them promptly against those who do attack them seeking reasons from every source'.

Rules 10 to 12: Kinds of authority

The following three rules deal with attitudes towards various kinds of authority – the authority of office, of theological sources, of personal holiness or charism – and in each case attention is drawn to pitfalls which a right ecclesial attitude will avoid. The theme of praise is continued, explicitly in Rules 10 and 11, implicitly in Rule 12; but the point is made now that a true and Spirit-guided praise will avoid naïveté, and does not necessarily reflect current enthusiasms.

[362] [1] *Tenth rule.* **We should be** *more ready* **to approve and praise the** *decrees* **and regulations of those in authority, and their conduct as well;** [2] **for although some of these things are not, or were not, such as to merit approval, to speak against them either in** *public sermons* **or in conversations in the presence of** *simple people* **would give rise more to grumbling and scandal than to benefit.** [3] **In that way people would become hostile towards authority, either temporal or spiritual.** [4] **But just as harm can be done by speaking ill to simple people about those in authority in their absence, it can do good to speak of their unworthy behaviour to the actual people who can bring about a remedy.**

---

[23]The Vulgate gives, 'church buildings and their decoration', while the Autograph and the Versio Prima have, 'church decorations and buildings'.
[24]On this see Rule 10 below.

Tenth Rule On the eve of the Council of Trent, the Church was in need of far-reaching reform in the realms of both custom and legislation, and clerical behaviour and life-style. In these circumstances, to be faithful to the Church was to crave its reform. But there were various ways of promoting reform. One way, especially associated in the time of Ignatius with the name of Girolamo Savonarola,[25] was that of public denunciation. A quite different approach was that of the present rule, with its emphasis on the dangers of public censure and its insistence that criticism be made behind closed doors. In addition to the reason given in the rule itself (the need to save simple people from disaffection), numerous other considerations help to explain the reticent tone of the rule: Ignatius' personal diplomatic instincts, his aware-ness of living in dangerous times [369], his instinctive respect for any legitimate authority, even if corruptly exercised. Moreover, the rule is addressed to people prone to ill-considered zeal, rather than to those tempted to meet abuse with self-interested inertia. And it must also be remembered that in Ignatius' view, reform was primarily achieved by the positive witness of a *de facto* reformed manner of life, built on a visible repudiation of what he saw as the main roots of corruption, namely avarice and ambition.

more ready The general stance that would always prefer if possible to praise and approve rather than to blame has already been commended in the Presupposition of the Exercises [22], of which the present rule is in many respects a particular application.[26] It is not, however, a stance that produces blinkered attitudes in regard to actual situations.

decrees, etc. Both the Autograph and the Versio Prima recognize that these can in fact be open to question. Indeed, at the time of the composition of the rules, abuses of many kinds were officially connived at and even ratified canonically: such, for example, in Ignatius' eyes, was the official sanctioning of relaxations in the poverty regime of mendicant orders.[27] The Vulgate, on the other hand,

---

[25]A Dominican reformer executed in 1498 in consequence of denunciatory preaching against the curia of Alexander VI. Though critical, Ignatius was also surprisingly positive in his attitude towards Savonarola, whose writings were prohib-ited in the Society of Jesus not because of any fault in them but only because there was disagreement as to whether the author was a saint or was 'justly executed'. See O'Malley, *The First Jesuits*, p. 262. For a sympathetic estimate of Savonarola's char-acter see Ignatius' *Letter on Prophecies and Revelations* (MHSI, *Epp. Ig.*, vol. 12, pp. 632–52 [trans., *Personal Writings*, p. 213]).

[26]It is impossible for a late twentieth-century person to read this rule without being made aware of the questions that arise in our own time concerning the public and private forum, accountability, access to information, and comment and debate within the People of God. The rule provides no easy answer to these questions but has much to say about the attitudes with which we approach them.

[27]Cf. *Constitutions of the Society of Jesus*, ed. Ganss, §553 and p. 252 note 2.

while accepting that 'the personal conduct of those in authority may be wanting in moral integrity', takes a more inflexible line on decrees, commandments, traditions, and rites, all of which, it insists, must be firmly approved. Commentators have generally recognized, however, that the rule is primarily concerned with scandalous personal conduct or life-style.

public sermons A similar insistence on restraint in public sermons appears in Rules 14 to 17.[28]

simple people The people referred to are mentioned twice in the present rule and again in Rules 15, 16, 17 [367–369]. In the Autograph they are described here and in [367] as 'little'; in the Versio Prima they appear here as 'ignorant' and in [367.8] as 'untaught'. They would correspond to the simple and unlettered persons (*rudes*), whose need for basic catechesis is given special emphasis in the Jesuit *Constitutions*.[29] The Vulgate refers to the 'people', without diminutives, thus widening the need for prudence and reticence.

[363] [1] *Eleventh rule*. **We should praise both positive theology and scholastic theology. For as it is more characteristic of the positive doctors, such as St Jerome, St Augustine and St Gregory, to move the heart to love and serve God our Lord in all things,** [2] **so it is more characteristic of the scholastics like St Thomas, St Bonaventure, the Master of the Sentences,[30] etc.,** [3] **to define or** *explain for our times* **what is necessary for eternal salvation, and for the more effective refutation and exposure of every error and fallacy.** [4] **This is because the scholastic doctors,** *being more modern*, **not only benefit from the true understanding of Sacred Scripture and from the holy positive doctors,** [5] **but also while being themselves enlightened and illuminated by divine grace, they avail themselves of the councils, canons, and decrees of our holy Mother Church.**

[28]In the late Middle Ages the kind of preaching to which Ignatius refers was highly popular: 'As soon as a homilist broaches this subject < on the moral defects of the clergy >, his hearers forget all the rest; there is no more effective means of reviving attention when the congregation is dropping off to sleep, or suffering from heat or cold. Everybody instantly becomes attentive and cheerful.' Thus the Franciscan St. Bernardino of Siena (1380–1444). See J. Huizinga, *The Waning of the Middle Ages*, Edward Arnold (1924), p. 161.

[29]Cf. on the teaching of Christian doctrine to *rudes*, cf. *Formula of the Institute*, 2, 3, *Constitutions*, §§410, ed. Ganss, pp. 64, 66, 203 with note 7.

[30]Peter Lombard (c. 1095–1160), author of the *Sententiarum libri IV*, a standard theological textbook in use throughout the Middle Ages. Ignatius' first encountered it at the beginning of his studies at Alcalá: cf. *Reminiscences*, §57 [trans., *Personal Writings*, p. 40].

Eleventh rule. This turns to two movements of the time, each with its inherent tendency to one-sidedness: evangelical humanism, characterized by zeal for the Church fathers and a dismissive view of scholasticism; and a conservative tendency, in which the scholastics continued to hold pride of place. The present rule is addressed to this state of affairs. It is non-partisan, not only advocating the 'praise' of both authorities, but explaining how the two are mutually complementary. The appeal to the heart that he ascribes to the fathers is for Ignatius a quality of the highest importance. Appreciation of this quality should not, however, diminish respect for the clarity and the particular authority of the scholastics.

explain for our times an addition in the hand of Ignatius.

being more modern Though Ignatius has no explicit and worked-out theology of the development of doctrine, the concept is implicit in this sentence.

[364] [1] ***Twelfth rule*. We should beware of making comparisons between those of our own day and the blessed of former times. For there is no small error,** [2] **in saying of someone, for example, 'He knows more than St Augustine', 'He is another St Francis or greater', or 'He is another St Paul for virtue, sanctity, etc.'.**

Twelfth rule This rule concerns a type of authority particularly to the fore in times of change, the authority grounded in personal holiness or charisma, the authority which gives credibility to prophecy, for instance, or spiritual leadership. Ignatius recognized the existence of such authority in the Church, though the present rule hardly shows enthusiasm for it. The warning, however, is not so much against the charismatic individuals themselves as against the exalted status often conferred on these figures by their followers. The rule warns especially against tendencies to confer on people a status which no living individual can appropriately be given, and which virtually places the person above criticism.[31]

---

[31]In the circumstances of the time, the point was not merely hypothetical. Erasmus was reputed to have been spoken of by his followers as another St Jerome or St Augustine. In one of Erasmus' own propositions, objected to by the Sorbonne, a German humanist is described as a saint comparable to Jerome. Ignatius may also have heard that Luther at the Diet of Worms had been publicly eulogized as holier than St Augustine. See Arzubialde, *Ejercicios Espirituales de S. Ignacio*, p. 825 note 63.

Rule 13: The basic attitude re-stated, with a further consideration, and a test case

[365] **¹** *Thirteenth rule. To find the right way* **in everything, we must always hold the following:** *the white I see* **I shall** *believe to be black*, **if the hierarchical Church so** *decides* **the matter; ² for we believe that between Christ our Lord the bridegroom, and the Church, his bride, there is the same Spirit who governs and directs us for the good of our souls, ³ because our holy Mother Church is directed and governed by that same Spirit and Lord of us all who gave the Ten Commandments.**

Thirteenth rule Perhaps the most famous of the rules. Indeed, for many people the very mention of the 'Rules for thinking with the Church' will bring immediately to mind this challenging assertion of the primacy of belief in the teaching of the Church over personal opinion.

The essential point can be briefly summarized. If one holds the Church capable, under the guidance of the Spirit, of declaring her belief on a specific point, it follows that assent to such a declaration might require the abandonment of a contrary personal opinion, which otherwise there might appear to be no reason to question. In the formulation of the rule, the terms *bride* and *mother* and the reference to the Spirit, establish the faith-context within which the rule is to be understood. The black/white antithesis is likely to have been a direct riposte to a statement of Erasmus;[32] but the analogy of sense experience figures in classical arguments about the criterion of truth which had been revived in the Catholic/Protestant polemic of the sixteenth century.[33]

In the case posed by the rule, a final declaration of the Church stands in diametrical opposition to the way a matter appears to a member who is, by implication, faithful, committed, and open to the Spirit. To regard such a situation as frequent or normal would have difficult implications for the relationship between the teaching Church and the 'sense of the faithful', and in general for the way in which judgements are reached by the People of God. It seems best regarded, then, as a limit case, but the limit case is also a test case.

---

[32]The statement, to the effect that black would not be white even if the Pope declared it so, appears in a pamphlet written by Erasmus in defence of propositions censured by the Paris theological faculty. On the general question of Ignatius' attitude towards Erasmus, it should be noted, however, that while objecting to the tone of many of his polemical writings, Ignatius was in more sympathy with the reforming ideas of Erasmus than commentators on the Exercises have recognized. See O'Malley, *The First Jesuits*, pp. 260–64. For more extended treatment, see O'Reilly, 'Erasmus, Ignatius Loyola and Orthodoxy', and 'The Spiritual Exercises and the Crisis of Mediaeval Piety'.

[33]See Boyle, 'Angels Black and White'.

To find the right way The same phrase (*para acertar*) is used in the Rules for Discernment ('by following his counsels we can never find the right way' [318]). In the Vulgate: 'that we might be altogether of one mind with the same Catholic church and in conformity with her'.

the white I see, etc. The Vulgate: 'If anything which appears to our eyes to be white'.

believe to be black The Vulgate (putting the emphasis on external conformity): 'pronounce to be black'.

decides In the Latin versions, 'defines'. Both words suggest deliberations and a formal engagement of the teaching authority, and a finality often reached only through complex processes and the tensions, inherent in the Church's life, between tradition and development.

Rules 14 to 17: The mind of the Church in three issues: predestination, faith, grace

The next four rules deal with aspects of the relationship between divine freedom and our own real, free, and necessary collaboration. They form together a distinct section, with its own unity;[34] Rule 14 introducing three themes, predestination, faith, and grace, which are then treated in Rules 15, 16, and 17 respectively. Ignatius is not concerned with the often difficult theology of these issues. His interest is practical: to affirm the importance of these themes while cautioning strongly against deviant approaches to freedom and responsibility, which he considered to be easily engendered by careless preaching and conversation.

Though the concerns they express might seem to be those of another age, the Rules make a number of points which bear on our own situation. But more fundamentally, their significance for ourselves lies not so much in literal parallels as in the general attitude they exemplify. In many areas of belief, a right attitude consists in a balance between complementary truths. This balance is destroyed when one truth is so highlighted as to eclipse the other, a situation which frequently occurs when attitudes are dominated by prevailing trends or reactions. Against the influence of these, it is necessary

---

[34]The rules in this section, together with the final rule, date either from Ignatius' stay in Venice 1536–7, or from his and the companions' first years in Rome. On the latter supposition, their context would have been the conflict that arose between the companions with influential Roman preachers in whose sermons they detected Lutheran positions. For the history of the rules, see Dulles 'The Ignatian *sentire cum ecclesia* today', p. 29, and the references given there.

to reaffirm the neglected truth, but without producing a new over-reaction and imbalance. The basic Christian instinct is to affirm, not to deny. Again the principles of the 'Presupposition' are pertinent: a good Christian seeks to put good interpretation on another's statement, but does not evade the difficulties it might nevertheless raise.

[366] [1] Fourteenth rule. *Granted that it is very true* **that** *no one can be saved without being predestined,* **and without having faith and grace, [2] much care is needed in the way in which we speak about and communicate these matters.**

[367] [1] Fifteenth rule. We must not make a habit of talking too much about predestination. But if in some way, the subject is occasionally mentioned, our language should be such that *simple people* **do not fall into any error, as sometimes happens with them saying, [2] 'Whether I am to be saved or condemned, is already decided, and whether I do good or evil can change nothing now'; [3] paralysed by this notion, they neglect the works which lead to the salvation and the spiritual progress of their souls.**

[368] [1] Sixteenth rule. In the same way we should be careful lest by *speaking about faith* **at great length and with much emphasis, without distinctions or explanations, [2] we give people occasion to become indolent and lazy in works, either before they have a faith informed by charity or afterwards.**

[369] [1] Seventeenth rule. Similarly, *we should not talk of grace* **at such length and with such insistence as to** *poison people's attitude to free will.* **[2] Thus we should speak about faith and grace, as far as is possible with God's help, in a way that results in the greater praise of his Divine Majesty, [3] but not in such a way and with such expressions (especially in times as dangerous as ours) that good works and free will come to be undermined or held for nothing.**

Granted that it is very true While the rules warn against misrepresenting these truths, they should not be read as in any way playing them down.

no one can be saved without being predestined The truth embodied in the term *predestination* is that we are saved not by our own performance but by God's initiative, cf. Romans 8:28–30, a key text for understanding the doctrine. Predestination is to be understood in connection with God's universal salvific will, but God's purposes require our free collaboration, and it is this, with its seriousness and responsibility, that Ignatius is insisting on in the rule. The human being can freely refuse this collaboration in an ultimate sense, but this does not imply that the concept of predestination applies also to the damned. Both the Versio Prima and the Vulgate add to Rule 14 an explanatory clause: 'lest in attributing too much to predestination and grace, we infringe the powers and endeavours of free will; or while extolling excessively the powers of free will, we derogate from the grace of Christ' (Versio Prima), 'lest perhaps extending too far the grace or the predestination of God, we should seem to wish to play down the strength of free will and the merits of good works, or on the other hand, attributing to these latter more than belongs to them, we derogate meanwhile from grace and predestination' (Vulgate).

simple people The rules show the regard for the 'ordinary people'[35] which marks the series as a whole.

speaking about faith Even more than predestination, *faith* was a central issue of the Reformation. How to understand the relationship of faith and works to one another and to salvation, are questions of theology into which, again, Ignatius does not enter; he simply insists that tendentious preaching on faith can have the practical consequence of leading ordinary people to neglect the *works* of Christian life.

we should not talk of grace Note that *grace* here is 'actual' grace, namely the graces through which God concurs in our particular acts, not the 'sanctifying' grace which transforms our nature and makes it possible to live a new life in the Spirit.

poison people's attitude to free will The reconciliation of *grace* and *free will* was for many years to be a major subject of theological debate. Again, Ignatius' preoccupation is practical. In whatever manner one preaches about grace, care must be taken not to seem to make light of free will, and hence of the human person's co-operation with grace.[36] (19)

Rule 18: Love and fear

[370] 1 Eighteenth rule. Given that the motive of *pure love in the constant service of God our Lord* is to be valued above all, nevertheless we ought also greatly to praise the *fear* of the Divine Majesty. 2 For

[35]See comments on Rule 10 above.

[36]For Ignatius' approach to the balance between grace and initiative see Hugo Rahner's commentary on a famous maxim of Ignatius on prayer and work, *Ignatius the Theologian*, pp. 25–9.

not only is filial fear a good and holy thing, but where a person can attain nothing better or more useful, even servile fear can be a great *help in rising from mortal sin*, ³ and once having risen, one comes easily to filial fear, which is wholly acceptable and pleasing to God our Lord as it is all one with *divine love*.

pure love in the constant service of God our Lord A phrase which epitomizes the 'service spirituality' of the Exercises. For Ignatius, *love* of its nature realizes itself in the actions of service. But the love that fully motivates service is a love which consists in the complete gift of self [234], transcending self-love, self-will and self-interest [189].

fear Servile fear is defended (against Luther) as appropriate to a stage in the conversion process but at the end of the process *pure love* takes over, and in this love the only fear that has a place is the reverential or *filial fear* that is inseparable from love itself.³⁷ Pure love, nevertheless, is not lightly to be presumed, and in the course of growth and conversion *servile fear*, not as a permanent situation but as a step on the way, has real though limited value.

help in rising from mortal sin Servile fear *helps* by putting a restraint upon the will and thus bringing about the affective space for the motivation of love to grow. But while it curbs the expression of our unconverted desires, servile fear does little of itself to change them.

divine love The place and legitimacy of fear, the subject of the concluding rule, is dealt with in such a way that the final phrase of the entire Exercises is *divine love*, a term which the Autograph has not previously used, and which describes a love which is at once the self-giving initiative of God and the creature's self-giving response.

³⁷1 John 4:18.

INDEX